S0-BLA-256

PRINCIPLES OF POST-SECONDARY VOCATIONAL EDUCATION

THE MERRILL SERIES IN CAREER PROGRAMS

PRINCIPLES OF POST-SECONDARY VOCATIONAL EDUCATION

ANGELO C. GILLIE, SR.
The Pennsylvania State University

CHARLES E. MERRILL PUBLISHING COMPANY
A Bell & Howell Company
Columbus, Ohio

Published by
Charles E. Merrill Publishing Company
A Bell & Howell Company
Columbus, Ohio 43216

International Standard Book Number: 0-675-08866-6

Library of Congress Catalog Card Number: 73-87883

1 2 3 4 5 6—79 78 77 76 75 74

Printed in the United States of America

THE MERRILL SERIES IN CAREER PROGRAMS

In recent years our nation has literally rediscovered education. Concurrently, many nations are considering educational programs in revolutionary terms. They now realize that education is the responsible link between social needs and social improvement. While traditionally Americans have been committed to the ideal of the optimal development of each individual, there is increased public appreciation and support of the values and benefits of education in general, and vocational and technical education in particular. With occupational education's demonstrated capacity to contribute to economic growth and national well being, it is only natural that it has been given increased prominence and importance in this educational climate.

With the increased recognition that the true resources of a nation are its human resources, occupational education programs are considered a form of investment in human capital—an investment which provides comparatively high returns to both the individual and society.

The Merrill Series in Career Programs is designed to provide a broad range of educational materials to assist members of the profession in providing effective and efficient programs of occupational education which contribute to an individual's becoming both a contributing economic producer and a responsible member of society.

The series and its sub-series do not have a singular position of philosophy concerning the problems and alternatives in providing the broad range of offerings needed to prepare the nation's work force. Rather, authors are encouraged to develop and support independent positions and alternative strategies. A wide range of educational and occupational experiences and perspectives has been brought to bear through the Merrill Series in Career Programs National Editorial Board. These experiences, coupled with those of the authors, assure useful publications. I believe that this title, along with others in the series, will provide major assistance in further developing and extending viable educational programs to assist youth and adults in preparing for and furthering their careers.

Robert E. Taylor
Editorial Director
Series in Career Programs

PREFACE

This work is one of several texts in the Merrill series in career programs and deals with a subject that falls within the rubric of career education.The overall conceptual structure of career education evolves out of career develpment theory, and is coupled with facets of vocational and general education. For greater understanding of the nature of career education as a totality, the reader is urged to peruse another book in this series: *Career Education: Perspective and Promise*, by Goldhammer and Taylor.

The material contained in this book deals with post-secondary vocational education, and the training of the middle level worker and his occupational role in our society. The author believes this is a critical aspect of American education which has not received the public attention and financial support it deserves.

This is a sixteen-chapter treatment of educational matters relating to middle level workers; it deals specifically with the manner in which they are educated and trained for their activities and their roles in the world of work. The author has written this book with several kinds of audiences in mind. First are the graduate students engaged in a study of post-secondary institutions that offer vocational programs. For them, this work draws upon some of the significant studies relating to middle level worker preparation, thereby placing vocational education within the proper context of the American career education movement. A second audience, which overlaps the first to some extent, is comprised of faculty members and administrators, and members of educational governance boards in institutions concerned with post-secondary occupational education. For this group, the author seeks to illuminate the potential difficulties which may be encountered when conducting viable occupational programs for middle level occupations. A considerable portion of this manuscript deals with approaches and techniques for establishing, conducting, and evaluating occupational programs for the preparation of people for middle level occupations. Considerable attention is given to the fact that the largest portion of future post-secondary vocational school enrollment is likely to consist of adults who return to these institutions to be updated or upgraded in their work skills, or to be completely retrained for new jobs. This book urges that the two-year colleges more aggressively seek to serve in this capacity, to the extent that the overwhelming majority of two-year college students will be enrolled in occupation-oriented programs.

The third kind of audience which can profit from the contents of this book are nonvocational educators and laymen who are interested in two-year colleges, occupational education, and the confluence of these two very significant movements in American education. For these readers, the book provides an inventory of the kinds of institutions in which occupational education is offered, with detail as to their characteristics and the part they play in American post-secondary occupational education. These institutions include public community colleges, area vocational schools, private vocational schools and other institutions of higher education which are involved with preparing people for middle level occupations.

The first part of this book attempts to provide a comprehensive description of vocational education and its overall role in education. It also includes an analysis of the role of the middle level worker in American society. This is followed by a description of the paraprofessional, who is the kind of worker found in the upper regions of the middle level occupations.

The second portion of *Principles of Post-Secondary Vocational Education* delves into the important aspects of educating and training the middle level worker. This section includes a description of present sources of education and training. A review of the major characteristics of students who prepare for middle level jobs is given. The final chapter in this section deals with designing new programs.

In the third section, the book shifts from present concerns to considerations for the future. The first concern relates to planning curriculum, assessing the need for new programs, and modernizing existing programs. A chapter emphasizing ways to select faculty and administrators for occupational programs follows. The importance of institutional research and ways by which new ideas can be inaugurated into curricula are given special treatment in two chapters. Suggestions for the wise utilization of the 7,100 private vocational schools 1,900 area vocational schools, and 1,100 public community colleges are made in Chapter 13. Another chapter considers the continued low status of occupational education, and the reasons for this dilemma; suggestions for doing something about this problem are offered. A discussion and analysis of statewide articulation in occupational education, and its relationship with state master planning is the topic for Chapter 15. The book concludes with a plea for the two-year colleges to become more occupation oriented and less concerned with the academic-type student who can be served by the senior colleges and universities.

A major underlying theme throughout this work is that community colleges and area vocational schools must come together in some kind of new institutional configuration if their maximum benefits are to be realized. The universal college, which would incorporate both these kinds of schools as well as the last two years of high school, thereby creating a 6-4-4 public education plan, is proposed. The possible benefits and drawbacks of this approach are described and analyzed.

Another major theme in this book is the overall format of vocational programs. An occupational core approach is suggested which would encompass broad preparation for a family of jobs. This core, the depth of which would be determined for each student according to his abilities and interests, would serve as the basis for obtaining specific jobs. After the student acquired a specific job, skill development would take place in a specifically designed environment called a skill center. The skill center would be a completely task-oriented mechanism for developing specific skills needed by specific people for specific jobs. The skill center would not replace on-the-job training, but would be a very necessary supplement to it. Jobs and their characteristics change too rapidly for us to be able to offer the necessary training in the basic occupational programs, as has been done in traditional occupational education in the past. The skill center is a viable answer to this dilemma; its service-station-like approach can be an effective topping-off process for most occupational programs.

The title uses the term "post-secondary vocational education" because the proposals offered in this book (some of which have yet to be tried) deal with that topic. Vocational education, besides being a positive factor in the two-year college movement, will be the heart of the community college movement for the remainder of the twentieth century. This work represents an effort that has been of major interest to this author for a number of years. The author is indebted to many individuals who have contributed to this work. Space does not permit listing them all. Studies and works drawn upon are cited in the chapters. The author extends a word of appreciation to Mrs. Rosann Moore for her patience in typing the manuscript. Conclusions and judgments made herein are those of the author.

Angelo C. Gillie, Sr.
The University of Pennsylvania

CONTENTS

Part I OVERVIEW

Chapter 1 OCCUPATIONAL EDUCATION: DESCRIPTION AND PURPOSE

The terms occupational education and vocational education are used synonymously in this book. Occupational education has two major people-oriented objectives. It seeks to provide: (1) a sequence of educational and training experiences designed to prepare certain people for initial entry into the world of work; and (2) education and training that will enable other people to continue their employability and to further increase their usefulness in the work society. Occupational education is concerned with new workers and also with the large group of people who are already in the work force. This position is stated in the major federal legislation which supports vocational education (PL 90-576).

Federal support of vocational education really began in 1862 with "an act donating public lands to the several states and territories which may provide colleges for the benefit of agriculture and the mechanical arts" (PL 12-503) and an act of Congress passed in 1884, which provided for the conduct of agricultural extension work in cooperation with the United States Department of Labor (PL 24-440). In 1914 the Smith-Lever Act (PL 63-95) aimed at providing aid in the diffusion of useful and practical information on subjects relating to agriculture and home economics. This act aided the land grant colleges established with the help of the 1862 act. The Smith-Hughes Vocational Act of 1917 (PL 64-

347) was designed "to meet the demands of an economy first reaching industrial maturity" (Fact Sheet: Vocational Education Amendments of 1968. PL 90-576). Thirty-nine years later, in 1946, the George-Barden Act (PL 79-586) was enacted to meet the changes in labor force requirements since the passage of the Smith-Hughes Act. The next adjustment in vocational education via federal legislation was the Vocational Education Act of 1963 (PL 88-210). which provided a significant impetus to post-secondary vocational education. An enrollment increase of over 900,000 is attributed to this act (Fact Sheet: Vocational Education Amendments of 1968. Pl 90-576). In a continuing attempt to keep up with the changing needs of society, the Vocational Education Amendments of 1968 (PL 90-576) were passed. They were designed to reach twenty-five million people annually (Fact Sheet: Vocational Education Amendments of 1968. PL 90-576), and have been catalysts in expanding vocational education. The role of vocational education is as follows (PL 90-576):

> The job of our nation's schools is particularly critical in view of these new and emerging occupations and the resultant demands to be faced by the labor force. Broader training must be offered to high school students in vocational education; students must be encouraged to stay in school and to undertake technical training or other occupational work at post-secondary level. Adults must be retrained to assume the duties of the three to four new careers predicted for the future's of most of them.
>
> Educational programs need to be more relevant. Emphasis should be on how students perform, not just on their mastery of subject matter. Achieving this objective may require a new purpose for the new public schools. Program development must become more closely attuned to individual interest, aptitudes, needs, and subsequent occupational as well as educational requirements for every boy and girl. We can no longer teach some and not others.
>
> The Vocational Education Amendments of 1968 provide a way to bring about the required changes. This act is designed to help the "hard to reach" and the "hard to teach." The program and operation would affect over twenty-five million people a year. This new legislation places resources and program flexibility primarily at the discretion of state and local schools agencies and is designed to focus on major deficiencies of the past.

Several treatments of the history of vocational education point to the importance of federal legislation in the support of vocational education and also in fostering changes in it over the years (Barlow 1967; Bennett 1926a and 1926b; Venn 1964).

Considerable attention is focused on attempts to decide what type of institution should provide what kinds and levels of occupational curricula. What programs should be considered appropriate only for the secondary schools? Should there be any vocational education in the secondary schools? Should the development of special purpose schools be encouraged (such as vocational-technical institutes)? A popular position is to reserve most post-secondary occupational programs for the two-year colleges (Kerr 1970). On the other hand, legislation provides authority to spend federal funds for occupational education in area vocational schools, which are defined as follows (PL 90-576):

> The term area vocational education schools mean—A) a specialized high school used exclusively or principally for the provision of vocational education to persons who are available for study in preparation for entering the labor market, or B) the department of a high school exclusively or principally used for providing vocational education in no less than five different occupational fields to persons who are available for study in preparation for entering the labor market, or C) a technical or vocational school used exclusively or principally for the provision of vocational education to persons who have completed or left high school and who are available for study in preparation for entering the labor market, or D) the department or division of a junior college or community college or university which provides vocational education in no less than five different occupational fields, under the supervision of the state board leading to immediate employment but not necessarily leading to a bacculaureate degree. If it is available to all residents of the state or an area of the state designated and approved by the state board, and if in the case of a school, department, or division described in C or D, it admits as regular students both persons who have completed high school and persons who have left high school.

There is confusion about the terms used in occupational education. The debate about the definition of technical education is typical. Some view a technician in terms of an educational level and describe him as an individual whose education and experience qualify him to work in a liaison capacity between the professional person and the craftsman (Dobrovolny 1969). Others see technical education in terms of occupational areas which include industrial occupations and products, medical and health services, dental laboratories, medical technicians, optical technicians, merchandising, insurance, real estate, banking, office operations, and others (Silver 1970). A third view is that technical education is a subject area, as evidenced by its divisional status in the American Vocational Association.

Tangentially related to the terminology question is the concern for identifying vocational curricula by level. Three levels have been identified by some vocational educators (Harris 1969). The higher level includes the semiprofessional or paraprofessional programs. These are associate degree level programs and have a substantial cognitive and general education content. In chapter 8, they are referred to as "broad-based" programs. Examples of such curricula are associate degree nursing, electronics technology, and legal secretary. The second level contains the high-skilled programs. These programs are described as "narrow-based" programs in chapter 8, and prepare people for specific jobs. Some educators feel these kinds of curricula should not lead to the associate degree unless additional general education requirements are met. Example programs in this category are practical nursing, auto mechanics, office practice, and cosmetology. The third level of curricula encompasses the gamut of job-training programs. These are usually short in duration, very specialized in nature, and the customary certificates or degrees are not awarded upon completion. Example curricula are machine operation, heavy equipment operation, and hotel-maid training.

It should be pointed out that considerable overlapping occurs. For example, some curricula which lead to an associate degree in one institution may be considered only a certificate program in another school. Because of the lack of standardization in these matters, decisions relative to whether a program is "college level" or not are basically subjective in nature.

Even the term occupational education has found several meanings in the literature. One description, common with industrial arts educators, is that occupational education programs are those which require only a minimum of knowledge or skills permitting early entry into available jobs (Bohn 1970). On the other hand, the same term is used to describe all vocational and technical education as expressed in literature on the two-year college (Skaggs 1966; Gillie 1970; Medsker 1971). The latter position is taken here. The three occupational curriculum levels described in the previous paragraph are appropriate concerns for vocational educators only for logistic reasons. The important issue is whether all the people described in the legislation (PL 90-576) are being served.

Occupational Curricula by Subject Areas

Occupational curricula have been identified in terms of subject areas. This is the more traditional approach and was given impetus by some of the earlier federal vocational education legislation. The subject areas of agriculture and home economics appear in the Smith-Lever Act of 1914 (PL 63-95). The Smith-Hughes Act of 1917 dealt with the same areas in addition to trade and industrial subjects. The Vocational Act of 1946 also known as the George-Barden Act (PL 79-586) provided fundings for programs in the same subject areas plus the addition of distributive education (Udell 1971). Inasmuch as funding for vocational programs was tied to their definitions via the Acts, federal legislation has been a major force behind the movement to identifying occupational curricula by subject areas. This type of categorization spread to all of the states, and served as a model for state vocational planning and funding. The American Vocational Association, formed in 1926, also established divisions along the subject area basis (Bartel 1959). These subject matter divisions have proliferated to many more than the four specified in the George-Barden Act. Such areas as agriculture, business and office, distributive, guidance, health occupations, home economics, industrial arts, new and related services, technical education, trade and industrial were commonly identified within the overall rubric of vocational education.

Dividing vocational curricula according to subject areas over a period of years has created a number of difficulties. Of particular note is the tendency to further fragment occupational education into subject areas that do not realistically relate to the world of work. Furthermore, the primary emphasis on people came to the forefront in recent federal legislation. The first important movement away from classifying vocational curricula by subject areas was the Vocational Education Act of 1963 (PL 88-210). This legislation clearly urged a discarding of the subject area categorization, as indicated by the definition of vocational education in its succeeding act (PL 90-576).

> The term vocational education means vocational or technical training or retraining which is given in schools or classes (including field or laboratory work and remedial or related academic and technical instruction incident thereto) under public supervision and a control or under contract with a state board or local educational agency and is conducted as part of a program designed to prepare individuals for gainful employment as semi-skilled or skilled worker or technicians or subprofessionals in recognized occupations and a new and emerging occupation or to prepare individuals for enrollment in advanced technical education programs, but excluding any program to prepare individuals for employment in occupations which the commissioner determines, and specifies by regulation, to be generally considered professional or which requires a baccalaureate or higher degree; and such term includes vocational guidance and counseling (individually or through group instruction) in connection with such training or for the purpose of facilitating occupational choices; instruction related to the occupation or occupations for which the students are in training or instruction necessary for students to benefit from such training; job placement; the

> training of persons engaged as, or preparing to become, teachers in a vocational program or preparing such teachers to meet special education needs of handicapped students; teachers, supervisors, or directors of such teachers while in such a training program; travel of students in vocational education personnel while engaged in the training programs; and the acquisition, maintenance, and repair of instructional supplies, teaching aids, and equipment, but such term does not include the construction, acquisition, or initial equipment of buildings or the acquisitiion or rental of land.

This broadened definition of vocational education resulted in a reorganization of vocational education in the states, with increased emphasis on human needs. The Vocational Education Amendments of 1968 reaffirmed the direction initiated by the 1963 Act, with continued emphasis on *who* is eligible (high school students, those who have completed or left high school, those who have entered the labor market and are in need of retraining, updating, and/or upgrading) rather than *what subject areas* qualify for support. Therefore the identification of vocational curricula by subject area appears to be a discontinued trend and will be less commonly found as the states continue to adjust their state vocational education plans to be in greater harmony with this philosophy (Perkins 1971).

After World War II, with the increased tempo of technological change, there was greater concern about the person being prepared for work. This was manifested by attempts to build core curricula that would serve as the basis for a group or cluster of related jobs (Gillie 1966; Harris 1963). The original job cluster approach prepared potential workers by a two-step process. First, students in a given cluster were provided with the common element associated with all (or most) of the jobs that existed in that particular occupational group. At a later time in the program, each student selected a more narrow area within that cluster and received specific training for the job(s) within it. This was considered an attractive alternative to early job specialization. One of the practical difficulties was determining how far to go with the broad-based portion of the program. Some pressed hard for a minimization of the broad kind of vocational education so that greater emphasis could be placed on the preparation of the student for specific kinds of jobs. They rationalized that industry wanted people who were ready for first job entry. They were certainly right in that industry and business did in many cases prefer people who were prepared for first job entry. But it is difficult to predict what specific job the graduate will take upon graduation. The core curriculum approach, which is an improvement over the older idea of early specialization, still demanded a commitment to a specialized curriculum and job preparation before the student left the institution. Even this is becoming less acceptable, and another approach is needed.

BEYOND THE CORE CURRICULUM APPROACH

The trend toward more frequent job changes is well recognized (PL 90-576) and the need for a more acceptable kind of vocational education is also recognized (PL 90-576). A new approach is proposed in which the original core concept is retained but final specialization takes place *after* the individual is committed to a specific job. This approach first counsels the student into an occupational core area (or cluster). The amount of broad treatment provided would be based on how much he can absorb. Upon reaching his cognitive limits, the student would then be placed in a specific job, at which time the employer would itemize the specific skills needed by the new employee. The student would then enter a skill center for the development of the specific skills needed and report to work upon achieving them. (See chapter 7 for a more complete description.)

People Who Need Occupational Education

Occupational education can also be described in terms of people. The Vocational Education Amendments of 1968 are meant to affect over twenty-five million people annually (Fact Sheet: Vocational Education Amendments of 1968). Further, it intends to affect both hard to teach and hard to reach individuals.

We can be more specific in our description of who would benefit from occupational education. Not more than twenty percent of our population can reasonably expect to eventually enter a profession, if past experiences are indicative of the future (Lerner 1970). Therefore, about eighty percent of the working population are likely candidates for some form of occupational education. Much of this can take place in secondary schools as has been the case up to now (HEW News, November 1970), but enrollments in post-secondary vocational programs grow each year (HEW OE-54003-68). Furthermore, the retraining, upgrading, and updating of persons presently in the work force are important components of vocational education, particularly with recent federal encouragement in this direction (PL 90-576).

Curricula Formats in Occupational Education

Curricula formats can be described in terms of the distribution of courses within the program. Considerable variation is found. One extreme, frequently seen in very short low academic level programs are combinations where the entire curriculum consists of an array of specific skill development courses with no provision for broad occupational education or general education courses. The opposite extreme is a very high academic level two-year program in which general education occupies up to half of the entire curriculum, with the bulk of the remaining course time allocated to the broad occupational courses and very little time given for specific skill development. A relationship between specialization and academic level has been pointed out (Gillie and Pratt 1971). If we consider the elements of specialization and academic rigor in combination, four possible models emerge. These are displayed in table 1-1.

TABLE 1-1

ACADEMIC RIGOR—SPECIALIZATION COMBINATIONS

Academic Rigor	Degree of Specialization	In Practice
Low	Low	Not Common
High	Low	Common
High	High	Not Common
Low	High	Common

The high academic rigor/low degree of specialization and low rigor/high degree of specialization are the two most common models. The more academically inclined students are directed into broad-based programs, and those less interested in academic matters are guided into more specialized curriculums. Not all is satisfactory with these two kinds of arrangements. There should be experimentation to determine if a good broad-based occupational program can be designed for low accademic students and if a good specialized occupational program can be designed for high academic level students. The first is of particular importance because the jobs at the lower skill level are those that most rapidly appear, disappear, and change.

The U. S. Office of Education (Hooper 1969) offers another way of describing occupational programs. The first demarcation occurs along two groupings, (1) science or engineering-related programs, and (2) non-science-and nonengineering-related programs. Some of the curriculum types frequently found in various college publications within these two broad categories (such as catalogues, and so on) are:

1. Science- or Engineering-Related

   Aeronautical technology, architectural or building technology, chemical technology, civil technology, electrical or electronics technology, industrial technology, instrumentation technology, mechanical technology, metallurgical technology, nuclear technology, other engineering related curricula, agriculture, horticulture, forestry, other science-related, dental assistant, dental hygiene, dental laboratory assistant, medical or biological laboratory technician, medical x-ray technician, practical nursing, occupational therapy assistant, surgical technician, other health service occupations, scientific data processing.

2. Nonscience and Nonengineering-Related
   General business, business administration, accounting, business data processing, marketing, distributive education, secretarial studies, other business and commerce related curricula, Bible study and other religious work, education, fine, applied, or graphic arts, home economics, library assistant, technical aide, police technology, other law enforcement curricula.

Equalitarianism Via Post-Secondary Occupational Education

Up to rather recent times, post-secondary education has been primarily limited to those persons who demonstrated the potential for going on to the professions. This kept almost eighty percent of the entire population from ever enjoying the benefits of post-secondary education in any direct sense. Since the end of World War II, the expansion of two-year colleges and occupational education into the post-secondary levels has opened up college-type education of a different kind to a larger percentage of the population. Therefore, people are being prepared for some of the newer and higher level occupations by way of formal programs in such institutions as community colleges. In previous generations much of this was done informally by such methods as on-the-job training. Formal preparation for an occupation in a post-secondary institution affects both the individual and the occupation into which he enters. Since the person receives more complete formalized training for the occupation, his views would be more macro while those who received on-the-job training only incorporate a micro view of their work. The accessibility of the institutions and programs presents more chances to prepare people for jobs than would have been the case if on-the-job training was the only source of job preparation. Therefore the two-year college offers a prospect of upward mobility for many persons (Cross 1968). This prospect is further enhanced by the provision of programs for retraining, upgrading, and updating of persons already in the work force. Equality of opportunity is therefore enhanced for both the young potential worker and the older worker.

Summary

The accepted definition of occupational education is as stated in the Vocational Education Amendments of 1968. A brief review of how vocational education has developed, with the impetus provided by federal funding, is given. Of particular interest is the role of occupational education in providing vocational assistance to as many as twenty-five million people annually. Occupational education is now a people-oriented activity with considerable federal funding support.

REFERENCES

Barlow, M. *History of Industrial Education in the United States.* Peoria, Ill.: Charles A. Bennett, 1967.

Bartel, C. R. "Origin, Development, and Work of the American Vocational Association." Unpublished doctorial dissertation. Columbia, Mo.: University of Missouri 1959.

Bennet, C. A. *History of Manual and Industrial Education Up To 1870.* Peoria, Ill.: Manual Arts Press, 1926a.

______. *History of Manual and Industrial Education from 1870 to 1917.* Peoria, Il: Manual Arts Press, 1926a.

Bohn, R. C. "A New Direction: Occupational Education, Industrial Arts, Vocational Education." *Theory into Practice: Industrial Arts and/or Vocational Education.* Columbus, Ohio: College of Education, Ohio State University, 1970.

Dobrovolny, J. S. "What is Technical Education?" *Industrial Arts and Vocational Education, September 1969.* Greenwich, Conn.: CCM Professional Magazines, 1969.

Gillie, A. C. "Planning Future Content of Electronics Curriculum." *Technical Education News* 26, No. 2. New York: McGraw-Hill, 1966.

______. *Essays: Occupational Education in the Two-Year College.* University Park, Pa.: Department of Vocational Education, Pennsylvania State University, 1970.

Gillie, A.C. and Pratt, A.L. *Marine Technology Programs: Where We Are and Where We're Going.* Washington, D.C.: American Association of Junior Colleges, 1971.

Harper, W.A., ed. *1970 Junior College Directory.* Washington, D.C.: American Association of Junior Colleges, 1970.

Harris, N. C. "A Suggested Core Curriculum for Junior and Community College Technical Education." *Technical Education News* 22, No. 4. New York: McGraw-Hill, 1963.

______. "Identifying New and Emerging Occupations." A paper for the Occupational Education Program Development Institutes. Sponsored by the American Association of Junior Colleges and the Ohio State University. Columbus, Ohio: Center for Vocational and Technical Education, Ohio State University, 1969. Mimeograph.

HEW News. November 1970. Washington, D. C.: U. S. Department of Health, Education, and Welfare.

Hooper, M. E. *Associate Degree and Other Formal Awards Below the Baccalaureate 1967-68.* Washington, D.C.: National Study for Educational Statistics, U.S. Department of Health, Education, and Welfare. Office of Education (OE-54056-68). 1969.

Kerr, C. *The Open Door Colleges: Policies for Community Colleges.* A special report and recommendations by the Carnegie Commission on Higher Education. New York: McGraw-Hill, 1970.

Medsker, L.L. "Strategies for Evaluation of Post Secondary Occupational Programs." *The Second Annual Pennsylvania Conference on Post-Secondary Occupational Education.* Edited by A.C. Gillie, University Park, Pa.: Center for the Study of Higher Education, Pennsylvania State University, 1971.

Opening Fall Enrollments in Higher Education, 1968: Part A—Summary Data. OE-54003-68. Washington, D. C.: U. S. Department of Health, Education, and Welfare, 1969.

Perkins, C.D., Chairman. *Reports on the Implementation of the Vocational Education Amendments of 1968.* Washington, D.C.: U.S. Government Printing Office, 1971.

Public Law No. 95, 63rd Congress (Smith-Lever Act).

Public Law No. 347, 64th Congress (Smith-Hughes Act).

Public Law No. 586, 79th Congress (George-Barden Act).

Public Law No. 210, 88th Congress (Vocational Education Act of 1963).

Public Law No. 576, 90th Congress (Vocational Education Amendments of 1968).

Silver, G. A. "Technical Education and the Junior College." *Industrial Arts and Vocational Education May/June 1970.* Greenwich, Conn.: CCM Professional Magazines, 1970.

Skaggs, K., Project Editor. *Emphasis: Occupational Education in the Two-Year College.* Washington, D. C.: American Association of Junior Colleges, 1966.

Thorton, J. W. *The Community Junior College. Second Edition.* New York: John Wiley, 1966.

Udell, G.G., comp. *Laws Relating to Vocational Education and Agricultural Extension Work.* Washington, D.C.: U.S. Government Printing Office, 1971.

Lerner, W. *Statistical Abstract of the United States: 1970.* Washington, D. C.: U. S. Bureau of the Census, 1970.

U. S. Office of Education. Bureau of Adult, Vocational, and Library Programs. "Fact Sheet: Vocational Education Amendments of 1968— Public Law 90-576." Washington, D. C.: 1969.

Venn, G. *Man, Education and Work.* Washington, D. C.: American Council on Education, 1964.

Chapter 2 THE MIDDLE LEVEL WORKER IN SOCIETY

Although workers with vocational abilities in the broad region between skilled labor and professional jobs, called middle level workers in this book, have been in existence for a long time, their importance to the overall occupational spectrum has increased during the past several decades (Lerner 1970). White collar workers (which includes professional and technical, managers, officials, proprietors, clerical, and sales) increased from 37.5 percent of the total work force of 59.6 million in 1950 to 48.6 percent of the 78.4 million total work force in 1970 (current population reports series P-50; Lerner 1970; and employment and earnings, 1960). Concern with this newer aspect of the American occupational structure has been reflected throughout the nation, and is manifested by the recent upsurge in the number of post-secondary educational institutions that prepare people for middle level jobs—particularly the area vocational-technical schools and the community junior colleges.

The area vocational-technical schools, which have grown in numbers to about two thousand during the past few years (Fact Sheet: Vocational Education Amendments of 1968, 1969), aim primarily at preparing persons for jobs at the lower-skilled levels, but are becoming increasingly more involved with training middle level workers. The community junior colleges, whose numbers increased from about 700 in 1962 to about

1,100 in 1971 (Harper 1972) are multipurpose institutions. One of their objectives is to prepare persons for middle level jobs. The vocational preparation offered by the community junior colleges tends to be reversed to that of the area vocational-technical schools in that their vocational offerings are more concerned with the paraprofessions while the lower skilled preparation programs are the major thrust of the area vocational-technical schools (Harris 1969; Thornton 1966). But these distinctions are disappearing. Sources of education and training for the middle level workers are examined in Chapter 7.

This chapter deals with the role of middle level workers in the American occupational structure. The societal need for individuals at this level of training and educational preparation and how future needs are forecast are considered first. The various generic types of middle level workers in society indicates that classifying them into anything other than the broadest groups is difficult. For the purpose of this work, the middle level worker is an individual whose occupational functions demand: (1) some cognitive skills in addition to the manual type proficiencies, and (2) preparation for both the cognitive and manual aspects of the job by specially designed programs offered by area vocational-technical schools, various types of proprietary schools, and community junior colleges. Although some of these programs are conducted at the secondary school level, the majority are post-secondary curricula with prerequisite high school graduation.

The Need for Middle Level Workers

The traditional approach to determining the need for various kinds of workers in our society has been the job survey. There are two broad survey approaches used in ascertaining the need for middle level workers: (1) the national manpower survey, and (2) the local-state manpower survey. These approaches, individually and collectively, have marked deficiencies. The local job assessment approach provides the details of job availability at the local-state level and is really a small part of the national picture. The prediction of future employment by various industries is a usual ingredient in such surveys. Determining the level of future employment based on the predictions of industrial and governmental decision makers is one of the primary bases of manpower surveys. Those engaged in the conduct of such surveys strive to develop those predictions for each type of activity in the public service and business-industrial spectrum (McNamara and Franchak

1970; BLS Bulletin 1606, 1969). These combined estimates are the basic ingredients for developing the overall future employment profile, although some manpower studies have been based on other factors as well (Manpower Research Inventory for fiscal year 1969; Hodgson 1971; Manpower Report of the President, 1971).

By comparing local employment with national employment in the same kind of industry for the same period of time, data are used to identify trends and changes in the relationships between local and national employment for certain kinds of jobs. This method has most merit for those jobs whose market is national in scope (BLS Bulletin 1606, 1969.

IDENTIFICATION OF CHANGES IN EMPLOYMENT DISTRIBUTION BY OCCUPATIONAL GROUPS

This can provide a crude basis for predicting future employment trends (BLS Bulletin, 1606, 1969). For example, it is common knowledge that agriculture-based occupations continue to decrease (Lerner 1970), and therefore educational programs geared toward preparing people for such jobs should be reduced. The distribution of employment is affected by a number of factors, including the following (Manpower Report of the President, 1971): (1) the introudction and expansion of new technologies; (2) development of industrial-business conglomerates; (3) changes in national priorities, consumer demands etc.; and (4) changes in the national economy. The net effect is generally dichotomous: (1) an increase in the demand for certain kinds of occupations, and simultaneously, (2) a reduction (or elimination) of other kinds of jobs.

These kinds of job changes can be partially predicted by careful observation of employment distribution trends. Overriding these internal changes is the continued increase in the size of the labor force. For example, the work force grew from 59.6 million in 1950, to 78.4 million in 1970 (Lerner 1970), to more than 82 million in 1973. Manpower projections rely heavily on past and present information, from which predictions of job needs for the future are extrapolated. This is largely a "rear-view mirror" approach since the predictions are made on the premise that the four factors listed above will change in the manner predicted. A simultaneous examination of the past and present is a vital initial component in job projection. Combining this with reliable information dealing with an array of factors relating to the future employment market could improve the predictive value of such an approach. Suggestions as to some ways to implement this approach have been proposed (BLS Bulletin 1606, 1969). Occupational projections at the state level using the same approach have been attempted (Manpower

Research Inventory for fiscal year 1969, 1969), including Pennsylvania (McNamara and Franchak 1970, Senier and Slick 1972). In determining the overall growth in employment, the methods described in the preceding paragraphs are essentially only a first step in arriving at a final estimate. There are employment vacancies not reflected directly by the number of jobs to be filled at the time the survey is conducted. These are primarily due to replacement needs created by deaths, retirements, and transfer of experienced workers to other occupations (BLS Bulletin 1606, 1969).

A bench mark study in ascertaining technical manpower at the state level was conducted in five major steps by the New York State Department of Labor (Pearce, et al 1964). First, the number of persons in the labor force were identified by age and sex, followed by establishment of the number of nonfarm wage and salary jobs by each type of industry. The total numbers of jobs in all areas was then established, after which discrepancies were reconciled. Finally, a matrix showing the total number of jobs and occupations by type of industry was constructed.

Predicting future manpower requirements is made very difficult by the great number of factors that impinge on employment needs. Several of the most critical variables whose effects are greatly indeterminable are: (1) the changes in technologies not perceived at the time of the prediction, and (2) changes in the overall national economy (which is quickly reflected in employment demands). Prediction equations have been devised (BLS Bulletin 1606, 1969; McNamara and Franchak 1970) and others will be developed in the future, but they are complex and of undetermined reliability. At this point in time, manpower projections seem to be most accurate for large regions and increasingly less reliable for specific industries and smaller geographic regions (BLS Bulletin 1606, 1969).

TOTAL ASSESSMENT OF FUTURE MANPOWER NEEDS

The most accurate assessment of future jobs in various occupations (BLS Bulletin 1606, 1969) is based first on the change in the distribution of jobs. This is a most difficult variable to determine because of several futuristic factors embedded within it (particularly national economy changes and technology breakthroughs not perceived at prediction time). Death and retirement replacements in the various types of occupations is a second variable. A third factor to contend with is transfer replacements, which are substantial in certain occupations. Also of interest is that this phenomenon is associated with occupational mobility (Blau and Duncan 1967). State and regional gains or losses due to worker migration comprise a fourth significant factor in assessing future manpower needs. This is sometimes caused by formation of large industrial conglomerates, decline of certain industries, movement of certain industries into and out of the region, and emergence of certain new industries.

Worker Losses through Death and Retirement. The prediction element associated with the worker losses resulting through deaths and retirements is the most workable factor in estimating future job vacancies, although it too has considerable variability. The loss by death for each age group can be predicted by the use of actuarial computations. Tables of working life have been developed for this purpose (BLS Bulletin 1606, 1969). Predictions of worker losses due to retirement can also be estimated by use of the tables of working life. In addition, estimated annual death and retirement rates for selected occupations have been developed. These are based on labor force and age distribution, and include the middle level occupations.

Several factors are at work that tend to complicate worker losses due to death and retirement (BLS Bulletin 1606, 1969). Mortality rates and retirement patterns differ from one occupation to another due to unique characteristics of each occupation. The rate of women participation and their pattern of losses due to death and retirement differ by occupation and these in turn are dissimilar from those found for their male cohorts. A final factor is the variation in the distribution of workers by age from one occupation to another, which further affects the mortality rates and retirement pattern.

Worker Losses through Job Transfers. A third element associated with job attrition is the phenomenon of leaving a job for reasons other than death or retirement. In some middle level occupations, a significant proportion of the work force consists of women (Lerner 1970). The presence of women confounds the worker losses factor because many of them leave their jobs to bear children. The more highly educated females are most likely to return to the labor force at a later time (BLS Bulletin 1606, 1969). This in-and-out employment pattern many be repeated several times by some middle level women workers. To accommodate for this pattern in predicting job vacanies is very difficult at best.

Workers are expected to leave one job to take another at least three or four times in their life (PL 90-576). Quite often, these changes result in some upward job mobility (Blau and Duncan 1967). Generally, job mobility tends to be from less skilled to more highly skilled occupations and results after the person acquires experience that is frequently supplemented by additional training and/or education, such as acquiring a certificate or degree not previously held (BLS Bulletin 1606, 1969).

Relationships Between Job Vacancies and Worker Mobility. One of the differences found among workers in an occupation is that some seek additional training in education while others do not (Gillie 1971c). One may speculate that those who do are more highly task-oriented and are most likely to move up the occupational ladder. Such motivated individuals need the opportunity to qualify for the jobs to which they aspire; these opportunities must be available so they can pursue their goals either on a part-time or full-time basis. Many two-year colleges already serve these persons in many places via regular and special course offerings, and can do so to an even greater extent in the future.

Ironically, job mobility is greatest during times of chronic worker shortages. When the need for workers in an occupation is more nearly met, the likelihood that an individual working at a lower job level can transfer into that "better" occupation is reduced. The irony is that if job vacancies are too efficiently filled by educational and training programs, then the chances for workers at lower occupational levels to move upward is reduced. Therefore a discrepancy between the number of worker applicants and available jobs (with more jobs than applicants) is desirable, at least from the upward job mobility point of view. History has shown that industry does not seriously suffer under these conditions. The business-industrial community has managed to make up their shortages by a number of strategies (BLS Bulletin 1606, 1969). In many cases, inplant education and training are provided. Sometimes jobs are redesigned to better fit the available manpower. A third method of accommodation is to introduce new special job assistants. Other times, persons within the organizations are provided with special job upgrading and the work pattern within the institution is reorganized to accommodate certain worker shortages. Another approach used involves hiring selected individuals from outside the geographic area for certain highly specialized jobs. Increased cooperation between post-secondary institutions and the business-industrial community could help in adjusting to worker shortages by providing at least some updating, upgrading, and retraining of present workers and also by carefully preparing new workers for initial job entry.

Forecasting the Number of Middle Level Workers Needed

Several of the important components for predicting the size of the labor force in the years ahead on a statewide basis are (McNamara and Franchak 1970): (1) development of a working age population projection for the time period being considered; (2) ascertainment of the magnitude and composition of worker migration into and out of the state; (3) identification of the specific economic and social events within that state or region which are expected to alter the manpower picture; and (4) determination of changes in the labor force participation rate.

Many states, utilizing increased federal data, are providing meaningful information and data for the planning of vocational programs at both the high school and post-secondary levels. The efforts of New York (Pearce et al 1964) and Pennsylvania (McNamara and Franchak 1970; Slick 1973) are notable examples where federal data were utilized in the initial step in state level planning for occupational programs. Such strategies attempt to ascertain the total annual supply of labor, including predicted vocational program graduates, the total annual manpower demand, and the difference between these two (thereby determing whether there is a shortage or a surplus). Having determined this fact, the projectors are then in a position to point to program needs on a statewide basis.

A Model for Determining the Number of Middle Level Workers to be Trained Annually

In the final analysis, the number of middle level workers to be trained annually for a period of five to ten years can be based on several variable components (BLS Bulletin 1606, 1969; McNamara and Franchak 1970). At the risk of being overly simplistic, an equation or model which displays the variables and the interrelationships is:

$N_{pa\ total} = A - (B + C + D) + E + F$

where

$N_{pa\ total}$ = number of middle level workers to be trained annually for a given period of five to ten years

A = existing number of middle level workers in that field

B = losses due to deaths and retirements

C = losses due to job transfers

D = losses due to predicted technology and economic changes

E = gains due to predicted technology and economic changes

F = gains or losses due to unknown fortuitous elements.

By knowing the number of middle level workers being trained annually, the increase or decrease in the number needed can be ascertained ($N_{pa\ new} = N_{pa\ total} - N_{pa\ present}$). A major shortcoming is that the present means for determining the influence of these variables are relatively primitive, resulting in limited means for predicting future demands for middle level workers. The most intelligent way to compensate for these limitations is to prepare middle level workers in core curricula and to provide specific skill development only after the individual has accepted a particular job.

Two general forecasting methods have been commonly used in the past. The first approach gathers past and present data on variable A in our prediction equation. A series of assumptions are then added (primarily associated with variables D and E in the preceding equation). After examination of compiled data and assumptions, the trend line of future employment in that field is drawn. A second method of forecasting employment demands is to use predictions made by employers.

Both forecasting methods are overly dependent upon the use of *past data* and *future guesses* and miss some of the elements displayed in the prediction equation. Predictions made on such a basis are accurate only when the state of the technology and the national economy undergo no unpredicted changes. The likelihood that the national economy will remain static or even change at a linear rate seems remote, as evidenced by the variation in the rates of economic growth in the past twenty years (Lerner 1970). Therefore a method for combining the suggested approach to job forecasting with curriculum development is in order.

First, the number of positions presently existing for that middle level occupation must be accurately determined. Furthermore, an accurate and somewhat detailed analysis of the work performed by the workers and where they go to work must be made. For example, it has been found that electronics paraprofessionals work in several types of industries (Gillie 1971a), and there is considerable variation in their job characteristics (Gillie 1970b). The distribution of a number of each type of worker by kind of industry and also by job characteristics within each is helpful. Related to this is a determination of the ratio of middle level workers to each professional. The third step is a determination of the annual output of each type of middle level worker. In terms of educational institutions, we need to know which ones are preparing middle level workers, what types they are training, their annual output of graduates, and where their graduates have been going to work. Fourth, an accurate assessment of changes going on in the kinds of knowledge and use of skills needed within each middle level occupation needs to be made. Breakthroughs in these areas within an occupational area can be utilized in curriculum improvements. Frequently when the need for one particular cluster of middle level skills is reduced, the need for a new group of skills simultaneously emerges. If such changes are pronounced and extensive, ambitious programs for updating and in-service training are in order. Follow-up studies can be helpful in identifying these changes. A coordinated effort at the state level, which could serve as an early warning system for translating the observed needs into suggested program changes, is worthy of consideration. Providing for the changing skills and knowledge required of middle level workers is a vital responsibility of schools preparing these persons for job entry. A fifth step would be the determination of new technology breakthroughs that impinge on the demands made of occupational preparation over and above the more gradual changes discussed above. Such breakthroughs often occur quickly with little prior notice. They sometimes create changes in the number of workers needed in several occuaptional areas almost immediately after the technological breakthrough. An example of this is the advent of solid state circuitry in the electronics field. The result was a major curriculum change (with emphasis upon transistors and other solid state devices and deemphasis of vacuum tubes and their associated circuitry). Changes of this magnitude pose difficulties for the schools. It even reaches down to imposing new and often more demanding requirements upon the faculty and their modes of instruction. Incorporating such changes in the curriculum generally lags the actual change in the business-industrial community by several years. For example, there was a lag of several years between the common usage of solid state circuitry in industry and its major inclusion in electronic technology curricula (Gillie 1971b). Step six is the acquisition of knowledge of major social and political decisions. Some changes in the demands for middle level workers relate directly or indirectly to social and political movements. An example of this is the great concern with ecology and environmental control. Continued emphasis in this direction results in the generation of several new types of middle level workers. At the same time, social and political pressures against military ventures brought about a sharp decrease in the demand for several kinds of middle level workers related to the military and aerospace industry (Vetter 1971). Accurate awareness of these changes at the time they are beginning, and a reasonable knowledge of the speed in which they are moving, will better enable educational institutions to prepare for the resulting emerging needs. The final step is to determine expected worker losses through deaths, retirements, and job transfers.

The Manufacturing-Related Middle Level Worker

Turning now from manpower predictions to kinds of middle level workers in the labor force, we first consider those that are associated with manufacturing. There are a large number of post-secondary programs dealing with the preparation of manufacturing-related middle level workers (Hopper 1971). A proliferation of post-secondary programs has occured, particularly during the past twenty years, in response to the great variety of manufacturing-related middle level workers needed. New types of manufacturing-related middle level workers will evolve and respond to continued advances in technology, although the total number needed in the future may not increase sharply, if at all (Vetter 1971).

In recent years, a trend toward continued education beyond the associate degree for certain middle level workers in this category has been observed, resulting in fewer of them going directly into industry. In some programs, fifty percent or more of the associate degree graduates go on to study for a bachelor's degree. Typical of the manufacturing industries are aerospace, ceramic products, chemicals, electrical equipment, electronics equipment, fabricated metal products, household equipment, instruments, machinery, metals, paper, petroleum products, and ship building. Furthermore, many graduates find jobs in such non-manufacturing industries as: construction, public utilities, engineering and architectural consulting firms, engineering services, mining, railroads, and research development. A third major source of employment for this type of middle level worker includes governmental agencies at the federal, state, and local levels (Grinter 1970; Gillie 1971b; Alden 1970). These findings point to the difficulty in determining ahead of time where students will go upon completion of their occupational programs.

There is an interesting ratio of middle level to professional workers in the manufacturing-related occupational areas. In 1970, there were 1,116,000 engineers and 713,000 natural science and engineering technicians (middle level workers), a ratio of 0.64 to 1 (Grinter 1970: Larken and Teeple 1969).

Conceivably an enchanced pattern of technological and economic growth could result if heavy commitments toward pollution control, urban development, future space exploration, and other mass projects are made at the national level. Large-scale spending in the areas of environmental control and social services appears likely (Manpower Report of the President, 1971). If such predictions materialize, the need for manufacturing-related middle level workers may hold at the present level. Otherwise, the annual output of these middle level workers may need to be decreased. But the total number of all types of middle level workers will increase because of the simultaneously large increase in the demand for social-health service-related middle level workers.

The Middle Level Worker in Social-Health Service-Related Occupations

The newest addition to the ranks of the middle level occupations are those concerned with social and health-related services. An examination of the associate degrees awarded for completion of occupational programs and the kinds of programs for which they were recieved indicates the prevalence of social and health-related middle level programs in two-year colleges (seventy-three percent in a recent year). The willingness of community junior colleges to offer such programs as a part of their curriculum is well illustrated by the spectrum of occupational programs offered by Pennsylvania community colleges.

The occupational programs are divided into five categories, four of which fall within our classification of social-health service-related middle level curricula and the fifth coincides with the manufacturing-related programs described in the preceding section. The following is a list of the specific programs under each of the five categories (Sheppard 1970):

1. Public service (falls within the social health related categories): programs in this category include education, community service, fire and emergency protection, instructional assistant, insurance, journalism, law enforcement, library, public services, real estate, social work, and urban affairs.
2. Health (falls within the social health related category): programs within this category include dental, health and physical therapy, and surgical.
3. Business (falls within the social health related category): the following programs are included in this category—accounting, business, clerk-typist, data processing, economics and finance, management, market and retailing, secretarial.
4. Trade and technology (falls within the manufacturing related category): the following programs are included here—architectural, automobile, aviation, banking, broadcasting, carpentry, chemical, civil, commercial art, computer science, diesel, drafting and design, electrical, electrical-mechanical, engineering, forestry, graphic arts, heavy construction equipment, industrial, laboratory, sheet metal, park management, printing, sign painting, small engine and appliance repair, structural, technical illustration, pretechnology, tile setting, toolmaking and design.

Nationally, a total of 206,753 associate degrees were reported for 1969-70 in both academic and occupational programs (Hooper 1971). Eight states reported having more than 5,000 such awards. In descending order, they are: California (51,300); New York (27,200); Florida (17,100); Massachusetts (9,100); Michigan (8,100); Illinois (8,400); Pennsylvania (7,800); and Texas (6,200) (Hooper 1971).

Of these, 108,000 occupational program associate degrees were granted (about 52 percent of all associate degrees offered that year). The leading states in the granting of associate degrees for completion of occupational programs are: California (23,400); New York (16,400); Massachusetts (6,600); Pennsylvania (5,700); Michigan (4,700); Illinois (4,200); Ohio (3,400); Florida (3,000); North Carolina (3,000); Texas (3,000); Wisconsin (2,900); Washington (2,100); Indiana (2,100); Indiana (2,000) (Hooper 1971).

There also are curricula for the training of middle level workers that are less than two years in length. These programs produced just over 27,000 graduates during that same year (Hooper 1971).

Curriculum Emphasis Patterns

Middle level programs have been identified as falling within four rather definitive patterns of curriculum emphasis. These were also identified in a study of social-health related curricula (Kiffer and Burns) and classified as: (1) general education, (2) general specialized education, (3) specialized education, (4) laboratory-practicum.

The following are some details about each one of these patterns, which are also illustrated in figure 2-1.

General Education Emphasis: Kiffer and Burns (1971) found that this sequence is characteristic of human service occupational programs in junior colleges as well as those found in two-year colleges that traditionally emphasize academic programs. A typical program has seventy to ninety percent of its curriculum allocated to general academic subjects and ten to thirty percent to skill theory and techniques, laboratory experience, and practical experience courses.

General-Specialized Emphasis: This is found most often in human service programs in which occupational skills are relatively undelineated either because of the scope of programs offered or because of the newness of a given paraprofession of programs of training for entrance into a new paraprofession. A program usually consists of between fifty to seventy percent general academic and related academic courses, and thirty to fifty percent skill theory and techniques, laboratory, and practicum courses.

Specialized Education Emphasis: Most of the programs in child care, education, health services, hotel-motel-food services, and social work

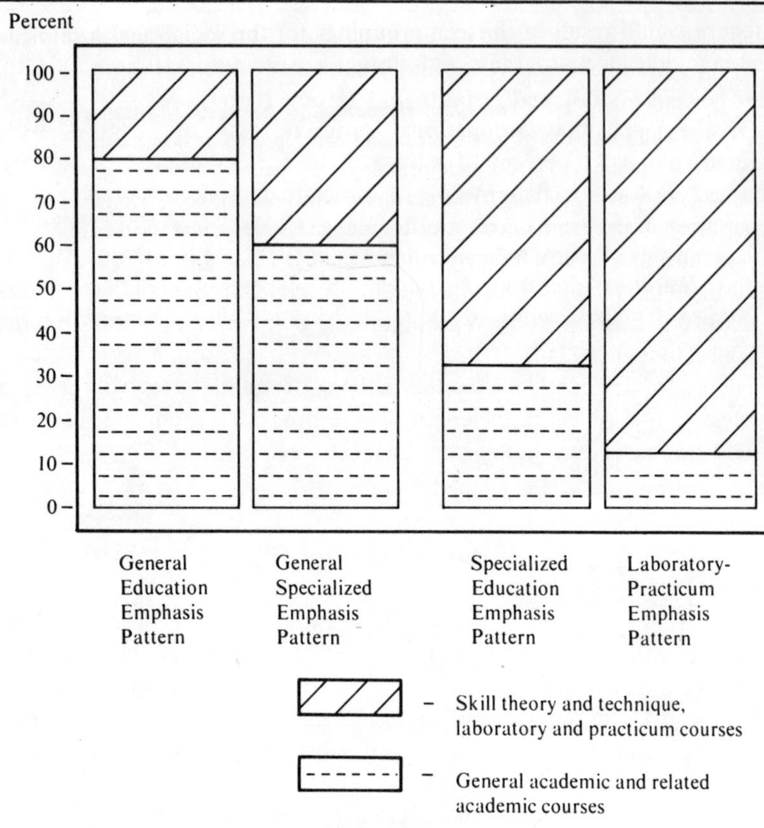

FIGURE 2-1

SOCIAL-HEALTH SERVICE-RELATED PROGRAMS—
CURRICULAR EMPHASIS PATTERN (KIFFER AND BURNS 1971)

fall within this type. Programs with this emphasis usually consist of twenty-five to fifty percent general academic and related academic courses with fifty to seventy-five percent devoted to skill theory and techniques, laboratory, and practicum courses.

Laboratory-Practicum Emphasis: This is characteristic of medical occupational programs as well as social service programs in two-year colleges where emphasis is placed on the practical-experimental aspects of learning occupational skills. Programs of this type generally consist of seventy-five to one hundred percent skill theory and techniques, laboratory, and practicum courses, while twenty-five percent or less of the curriculum is devoted to general academic and related academic subjects.

The Kiffer and Burns study identified twelve major groupings from the 381 occupational titles submitted by the colleges surveyed. It should be noted that all business-related programs were excluded. Adding this category would result in thirteen groupings for the social-health service-related middle level programs, as follows:

1. *Child Day Care Center and Homemaking Services*—awareness of children as they learn, grow and develop, and of home situations in times of stress and normalcy.
2. *Communication and Transportation*—focuses on the dissemination of ideas and information through mass media and the transmission of people from place to place.
3. *Education*—consideration for the varied preprofessional services utilized in the educational process including classroom, library, and audio-visual assistants.
4. *Environmental Services*—concern for the environment of individuals and communities in terms of planning and controlling various housing needs, park lands, and natural resources.
5. *Fire Prevention and Safety*—concern with efficient and effective fire prevention, control, and safety.
6. *Government Service*—regard for the public domain with emphasis on executive aspects of its maintenance and the legal system.
7. *Hotel, Motel, and Food Services*—concern for availability of well-managed hotels and motels, and the provision of commercial and institutional food services.
8. *Institutional Services*—provision of vital services within institutions both public and private such as prisons, hospitals, and orphanages.
9. *Law Enforcement and Corrections*—primary considerations are maintenance of public order, protection of persons and property, and administration of emergency assistance.
10. *Medicine*—consideration is given to the mental and physical health of individuals and the provision of well-run facilities for medical care.
11. *Recreation and Parks*—focuses on adequate recreational facilities and safe and constructive activities of people of all ages.
12. *Social Work*—concern for the physical, social, and economic well-being of individuals as they function within the social settings of their families, neighborhoods, and communities.
13. *Business*—provision of services associated with the conduct of commerce other than those indicated in the earlier categories.

Summary

A general definition of the middle level worker in terms of his occupational functions is given in the introductory section. This is followed by a description of several techniques for the assessment of future manpower needs. Included among these are comparing local with national employment trends and the identification of changes in employment by occupations rather than specific jobs. Many of the factors upon which a total assessment of future manpower needs depend are examined, including changes in the distribution of jobs, replacements needed because of deaths, retirements, transfers, and overall worker migration for a particular state or region. Chronic shortages of workers in an occupational area enhance upward job mobility.

Industry and business have several mechanisms by which they accommodate themselves to worker shortages. Increased cooperative planning between post-secondary vocational schools and the business-industrial community can reduce the chronic shortage of workers in some occupations to manageable proportions. A simplified model for determining the number of middle level workers needed is offered. Previous forcasting methods were heavily dependent upon *past data* and *future guesses*, and lacked access to some of the six elements needed for reliable forecasting.

The second section of the chapter deals with the manufacturing-related middle level workers. The need for middle level workers of this type seems to have reached a plateau. Information on the distribution of these workers by occupations and the ratio of middle level workers to professionals are provided. A surprising finding is that the ratio of technicians/engineers is only 0.64 to 1.

Middle level workers in the social-health service-related occupations are examined in the third section, followed by descriptions of how occupational programs are categorized by some two-year colleges.

The last section examines the curriculum emphasis patterns found in two-year college occupational programs. A logical classification describes them in terms of what occupies the bulk of the academic credits in the program. Using this as a basis, four categories are listed and described: general education emphasis, general-specialized education emphasis, specialized education emphasis, and laboratory practicum. A grouping of occupational curricula is offered.

REFERENCES

Alden, J. D. *Prospects of Engineering and Technology Graduates*. New York: Engineering Manpower Commission of Engineers Joint Council, 1970.

Belitsky, A. H. *Private Vocational Schools: Their Emerging Role in Post-Secondary Education*. Kalamazoo, Mich.: W.E. Upjohn Institute for Employment Research, 1970.

Blau, P. and Duncan, O. D. *The American Occupational Structure*. New York: John Wiley, 1967.

Bureau of Labor Statistics, U. S. Department of Labor. *Technician Manpower, 1966-80.* Bulletin #1639. Washington, D.C.: U.S. Government Printing Office, 1970.

Burns, M. A. and Kiffer, T. E. *New Careers in Human Services: A Challenge to the Two-Year College.* University Park, Pa.: Center for the Study of Higher Education, Report Number 8, Pennsylvania State University, 1971.

Current Population Reports, Series P-50. Washington, D.C.: Department of Commerce, Bureau of the Census, 1950.

Department of Labor and Industry, Commonwealth of Pennsylvania. *1960 Census and 1970, 1975 Projected Total Employment.* Harrisburg, Pa.: Bureau of Employment Security, 1969.

Employment and Earnings. Washington, D.C.: Department of Labor, Bureau of Labor Statistics, 1970.

Fact Sheet: Vocational Amendments of 1968-PL 90-576. Washington, D.C.: Bureau of Adult, Vocational and Library Programs, U.S. Office of Education, 1969.

Gillie, A.C. *Post-Secondary Occupational Education: An Overview and Strategies.* University Park, Pa.: Center for the Study of Higher Education, Pennsylvania State University, 1970a.

______. *Georgraphic-Job Mobility of The Pennsylvania State University Two-Year Technician Graduates.* University Park, Pa.: Department of Vocational Education, Pennsylvania State University, 1070b.

______. *Employment Characteristics of the Pennsylvania State University Associate Degree Graduates.* University Park, Pa.: Department of Vocational Education, Pennsylvania State University, 1971a.

______. *Associate Degree Technicians' Judgments on Quality of Instruction and Course Relevancy.* University Park, Pa.: Department of Vocational Education, Pennsylvania State University, 1971b.

______. *Pennsylvania State University Associate Degree Technician Graduates: Some Demographic Variables.* University Park, Pa.: Department of Vocational Education, Pennsylvania State University, 1971c.

Grinter, L. E. and Defore, J. *Engineering Technology Education Study: Preliminary Report.* Washington, D.C.: American Society for Engineering Education, 1970.

Harper, W. A. *1972 Junior College Directory.* Published by the American Association of Junior Colleges and the ERIC Clearinghouse for Junior Colleges with assistance from the Research Division, National Education Association. Washington, D. C.: AAJC, 1971.

Harris, N. C. "Identifying New and Emerging Occupations," A paper for the Occupational Education Program Development Institutes. Sponsored by the American Association of Junior Colleges and the Ohio State University, Columbus, Ohio: Center for Vocational and Technical Education, Ohio State University, 1969. Mimeograph.

Hooper, M. E. *Associate Degree and Other Formal Awards Below the Baccalaureate: 1969-70.* Washington, D.C.: National Study of Educational Statistics, U.S. Department of HEW. OE-54056-68.1969.

———. *Associate Degree and Other Formal Awards Below the Baccalaureate: 1969-70.* Washington, D. C.: National Study of Educational Statistics, U. S. Department of HEW. OE-54045-70.

Hudgson, J.T. *Manpower Research and Development Practices.* Washington, D.C.: U.S. Department of Labor, 1970.

Larkin, P. and Teeple, J. "National Employment Goals in Higher Education." *College and University Business,* October, November, December 1969.

Lerner, W. *Statistical Abstract of the United States: 1970.* Washington, D.C.: U. S. Bureau of the Census, 1970.

Manpower Report of the President. Washington, D.C.: U.S. Department of Labor, 1971.

Manpower Research Inventory for Fiscal Year 1969. Washington, D.C.: U.S. Department of Health, Education, and Welfare, 1970.

McNamara, J. F. and Franchak, S. J. *Planning Vocational Education Programs in Pennsylvania: Guidelines for the Use of Labor Market Information.* Harrisburg, Pa.: Pennsylvania Department of Education, 1970

Pearce, A.C.: Berman, A.J.; Loeb, H; and Maeier, D. *Technical Manpower in New York State.* (Volumes I and II). Albany, N.Y.: New York State Department of Labor, Division of Research and Statistics, 1964.

Senier, J. and Slick, J. *A Supply/Demand Model for Vocational-Education Planners.* Report Number 1. University Park, Pa.: Department of Vocational Education, Pennsylvania State University, 1972

Sheppard, R. L. *Directory Listing Curriculums Offered in the Community Colleges of Pennsylvania.* Harrisburg, Pa.: Department of Education, 1970.

Slick, J. *A Supply/Demand Model for Vocational-Education Planners.* Report Number 2. University Park, Pa.: Department of Vocational Education, Pennsylvania State University, 1973.

Thornton, J.W. *The Community Junior College. Second Edition.* New York: John Wiley, 1966.

U. S. Department of Labor (Bureau of Labor Statistics). *Tomorrow's Manpower Needs.* Volume I: *Developing Area Manpower Projections, 1971.*

Vetter, B., ed. *Manpower Comments.* Volume 8, No.4. Washington, D.C.: Scientific Manpower Commission, 1971.

Chapter 3 CHARACTERISTICS OF THE PARAPROFESSIONAL

In this chapter we develop a description of the paraprofessional who can be broadly identified as being in the upper part of the middle level worker group. Our treatment of the subject is limited to characteristics extracted from a large follow-up study of fifteen annual graduation groups of two types of manufacturing-related paraprofessionals (Gillie 1970b, 1971a, 1971b, 1971c) and several other research endeavors (Grinter 1970; Alden 1970). The major characteristics dealt with here are: (1) salaries; (2) number of years between graduation and the beginning of their salary plateau; (3) characteristics of present job activities; (4) changes in job characteristics as a function of the length of time the graduate has been out of school; (5) overall trends in continuing their education beyond the associate degree; (6) worker perceptions of certain aspects of their formal program in terms of (a) quality of instruction, (b) need for certain course types after graduation, (c) need for the same topics at the present time, (d) expected need for these topics in the future; (7) job and geographic mobility; (8) relationships between job mobility and job characteristics; (9) the occupational ladder. The follow-up study dealt with graduates of fifteen consecutive classes of electronics engineering technology (EET) and drafting design technology (DDT).

Salaries

The lowest starting salaries were received by the earliest graduation classes. This trend toward increasingly larger beginning salaries leveled off for the last five graduation groups examined. The greatest difference in present salaries were found among the most recent graduation classes, which indicates the graduates are experiencing increases in salary each year after graduation.

Salary plateaus set in about ten years after graduation. This compares favorably with many other paraprofessional and professional occupations (for example, public school teachers traditionally reach the maximum levels of their salary in about that time. Continued salary increases beyond the ten-year period after gradution come to those who advance to higher positions (either to a higher paraprofessional level or into a professional level).

Geographic Mobility

Two aspects of geographic mobility dealt with were: (1) distance between home town high school and first job; (2) distance between home town high school and present job. There is a recognizable trend toward shorter distances between first job and home town high school for the most recent graduation classes. It is interesting to conjecture about this. Back in the early and middle fifties, manufacturing-related middle level workers were not widely utilized. They are more widely accepted today, as evidenced by the present middle level-professional worker ratio of 0.64 to 1 (Larkin and Teeple 1969). Furthermore, they are being employed in a greater diversity of industries, which results in the increased ease of obtaining a first position closer to home town.

A slightly smaller number of graduates are presently employed in places where they must live outside commuting range of their home town high school communities, as compared to their initial employment. This indicates many middle level workers leave their home town communities for their first jobs and continue to live away from their home town. Thirty-four percent of all the graduates sampled reside out of state. Of interest is that nearly seven out of ten of those who did move out of state now live in one of the states contiguous to their home state. One can conclude that although the graduates are geographically mobile, most of them did not move very far from their original homes.

Job Mobility

The average number of job-company changes, differentiating between those that require a change in residence and those that do not, was examined. The kind of job change which requires a change in residence is more purely the job-mobility parameter. The average number of job changes tapers off for older graduates, which implies that the greatest amount of job changing takes place during the first ten years after graduation. The job-resident change statistic is a different parameter from job-company changes, in that several kinds of job changes are included within it: (1) job-company change *and* change of residence, (2) job change, *but* with the same company *and* change of residence. This parameter combines the elements of job changing and residence changing in one package. It can be interpreted as a more pronounced kind of mobility as it requires the worker to do two rather significant things—relocate his family as well as move into a new job. The average number of job-residence changes is consistently lower than the number of job-company changes. The implication is that when considering a job change, paraprofessionals are likely to select new positions that would enable them to remain at their present residences.

Job Characteristics

The study sought to identify the levels at which the paraprofessional's job requires him to deal with data, people, and things. A hierarchy has been established in each of these three areas (*Dictionary of Occupational Titles,* 1965). These heirarchies, in descending order, are as follows. *Data-related tasks:* synthesizing, coordinating, analyzing, compiling, computing, copying, and comparing. *People-related tasks:* mentoring, negotiating, instructing, supervising, persuading, speaking-signaling, and serving. *Thing-related tasks:* setting up, precision working, operating-controlling, driving, operating, manipulating, tending, and handling.

Following are the items selected as being important by more than half of the graduates by curriculum. First, the electronics engineering technology workers. *Data-Related:* coordinating and analyzing. *People-Related:* Instructing and supervising. *Thing-Related:* No item for more than one graduation group. Second are the items selected by the drafting design technology workers. *Data-Related:* Coordinating, analyzing, compiling, computing. *People-Relat-*

ed: Instructing and supervising. *Thing-Related:* No item for any graduation group.

When asked to rank order the three lists so as to indicate which of the hierarchies was of the greatest importance to them in their present job, the more recent graduates assigned a middle ranking for *people-related tasks*, while the older classes indicated this to be the most important of the three categories. The *data-related* category was the most important list for the more recent graduates but was rated second to *people-related tasks* by the older graduation groups. All classes ranked the *thing-related* hierarchy of tasks lowest.

A clearly discernible trend was observed: the longer the time the middle level worker is out of school, the more important the *people-related tasks* are to his present job and the less important the *data-related* items become, with a consistent low rating assigned to the *thing-related* items. Having knowledge of the type of activities the graduate engages in when he is on the job could serve as a major guide in selecting in-school activities for the students.

USING JOB CHARACTERISTICS IN CURRICULUM DEVELOPMENT

How can this be done? Following are several illustrative possibilities for the electronics technology curriculum. This program has three courses dealing with the electrical circuits and two courses concerned with electronic circuitry. Since it has found that the majority of the graduates' most important *data-related* job tasks related to "coordinating" and "analyzing," the program should provide opportunities for the students to strengthen their skills in them. Consider "coordinating": the student can be made more adept at this task by being required to perform via a series of assignments and laboratory projects that would make it necessary for him to: (a) assemble and analyze the data relevant to the project; (b) plan out a sequence of actions designed to achieve the objectives of the project, based on a thorough analysis of the data; and (c) after determining the most appropriate sequence, he must then make judgements as to when and where the assigned project should be conducted. Example A: the student is to develop an approach to trouble-shooting an electronics circuit. He would be called upon to: (a) assemble and analyze the available data related to the particular circuit in question; (b) based on knowledge of the circuit characteristics and how it functions normally, he would establish a sequence of actions and strategies; (c) he would then implement his strategy, thereby testing (and revising if necessary) his original strategy; (d) in some cases the student would assume the role of the "doer" (he would be the trouble-shooter), but in other cases his responsibility would be to mesh the efforts of several other people performing that function and to see that the objectives of the project are met. To first be a "doer" helps the student to better understand some of the complexities associated with coordinating the activities. Role playing can be an effective way to develop coordinating skills.

The same approach can be used in developing "analyzing" skills. Let us consider a way in which the student is called upon to examine and evaluate data for the purpose of finding alternative actions. Example B (again using electronics technology): The student is required to propose two circuits which can be used as signal generators between prescribed frequency limits. In responding to this assignment, the student must (a) select the data to be examined, and examine it with an eye toward solving the problem; (b) evaluate the data; and (c) propose at least two alternative circuits that could be used for the stated purposes, and indicate the comparative advantages and limitations of each. This illustrates how role playing can be used in the development of skills associated with analyzing. The same approach can be used extensively in any curriculum, beginning as early as the second quarter (or semester) of the program. Skills associated with coordinating and analyzing can be developed with carefully planned role playing exercises in realistic situations.

Projects based on the development of skills in "instructing" and "supervising" should also be an integral part of manufacturing-related middle level worker programs, since they are rated very highly by the graduates from all the classes. In the preceding example, the students were asked to select signal generators to meet a predetermined set of specifications. The skill of instructing could be developed in the same activity by having an advanced student assume the role of instructor by teaching the required circuitry subject matter to the other students who are to select the signal generators. The individual playing the role of instructor would be called upon to resort to demonstrations, supervise the performance of the students in the project, and to make recommendations toward its successful completion. Such an assignment has one set of objectives for the students who are the "doers" (those who are to arrive at an intelligent selection of the signal generators) and a second set of objectives for the students who are practicing as instructors.

Projects for developing skills in supervising can be devised in the same manner with a duel set of objectives. Again using the preceding laboratory assignment, the advanced student could be assigned a task of serving as supervisor of the project, in which he would determine and interpret laboratory and work procedures for those students who are assigned to be the "doers" in the project. He would assign specific duties to them, seek out the most expeditious way to achieve the objectives of the project, and seek to maintain harmonious interrelationships.

It is suggested that role playing be the major mechanism for developing skills in the four job tasks of coordinating, analyzing, instructing, and supervising. The adoption of this approach does not necessarily alter the type or the amount of specific subject matter covered in the curriculum.

RELATIONSHIPS BETWEEN JOB MOBILITY AND JOB CHARACTERISTICS

Fifteen significant relationships between the mobility factors and job characteristics were found (these were identified by the linear multiple regression technique, see Gillie, 1970b). They are:

The electronics engineering technology graduates. On the average, those graduates who selected the higher levels of *data-related tasks* are among those who have: (1) shorter distances between home-town school and their first job; (2) lower initial salaries; (3) higher present salaries. Those graduates who selected higher levels of *people-related tasks* are among those who have: (4) graduated from an earlier class; (5) a greater number of dependents; (6) lower initial salaries; (7) smaller distances between home town high school and their first job; and (8) higher present salaries.

The drafting design technology graduates. On the average, those graduates who selected higher levels of *data-related tasks* are among those who have: (9) higher initial salaries; (10) higher present salaries. Those graduates who selected higher levels of *people-related tasks* are among those who have: (11) graduated from an earlier class; (12) higher initial salaries; (13) higher present salaries. Those graduates who selected higher levels of *thing-related tasks* are among those who have: (14) higher initial salaries; and (15) further distances between their home town high schools and their present job.

GRADUATES' REACTIONS TO THEIR PROGRAMS

Information relating to their formal programs was obtained from the graduates. They were asked for opinions about four aspects of the respective curriculums: (1) quality of instruction; (2) need for the course work immediately after graduation; (3) need for the course work at the time they were responding to the questionnaire; (4) the anticipated need for the course work in future jobs. They rated their basic courses in mathematics, science, English, social sciences, and twelve specialized topics unique to their particular curriculums (drafting design had twelve special topics and electronics had a different set of twelve topics).

Quality of Instruction. The older drafting design graduates tended to rate the quality of instruction higher for English and their special topic of report writing, while giving lower ratings for six of their special topics (layout, kinematics, static analysis, dynamic analysis, analysis of structures, product design). The older electronics paraprofessionals rated the quality of instruction higher for English, vacuum tube theory, communications circuits, and assigned lower ratings for five topics (social science, transistor circuit theory, integrated circuits, logic circuits, and binary arithmetic).

Need for Course Work Immediately After Graduation. The older drafting design graduates rated the need for course work immediately after graduation higher for eight topics (science, English, social science, layout, strength of materials, static analysis, dynamic analysis, product design) and assigned a lower rating for only one of their specialized topics. The older electronics graduates rated the need for course work immediately after graduation higher for seven topics (mathematics, science, English, social science, vacuum tube theory, test equipment, and industrial circuits) and lower for five of their topics (transistor circuit theory, integrated circuits, pulse circuits, logic circuits, binary arithmetic).

Need for Course Work Now. The older drafting design graduates assigned higher ratings for eight topics (science, English, social science, sketching, strength of materials, static analysis, manufacturing processes, and report writing). The older electronics graduates rated the need for course work now higher for five of their topics (English, social science, integrated circuits, binary arithmetic, and boolean algebra) and lower for five of their topics (test equipment, communication circuits, industrial circuits, microwave theory, and trouble-shooting).

Anticipated Need for Future Jobs. The older drafting design group assigned higher ratings for social science and English, as did the older electronics graduates. The interrelationships among the ratings (using zero order correlations as a basis, Gillie, 1970b) show that the strongest relationships exists between most of the "need immediately after graduation" and the "need now" ratings.

Continued Education of Paraprofessionals After Graduation

The study found that 12.26 percent of electronics graduates and 10.3 percent of drafting design graduates for a period of fifteen years have earned advanced degrees (most with baccalaureates, a few masters, and one doctorate).

The percentage of graduation classes whose members gained degrees higher than those of the previous class increased slightly. Beyond this, there is a plateau of the next several succeeding older groups and there is a reduction in the proportion of higher degree holders in the oldest groups. If all external factors for earning an advanced degree were equal, it would be expected that a larger proportion of graduates from the progressively older graduation classes would have acquired advanced degrees. The fact that this trend did not continue on to the oldest graduation group leads one to suspect that several constraining factors were at work. We can conjecture about them. From the middle fifties to the middle sixties (the time when the graduates of the first five or six classes in this study would be most likely to have given serious thought to working toward another degree), there were no educational institutions in Pennsylvania (and very few in the nation) that would accept the associate degree graduates of programs of this type as a junior in full standing. In those days, with the absence of the now popular "bachelor of technology" programs, an associate degree technician had to "switch programs" if he wanted to go on to earn a bachelor's degree. Such an ambitious individual would most often seek entrance into a four year engineering program. In such circumstances, he found that none or very little of his previous college work was creditable to the engineering bachelor's degree. The lack of transferability served to block most of the early paraprofessionals from embarking on engineering baccalaureate programs. A major criticism of their program—made by a number of earlier graduates—was that it didn't lead to a four year program during that decade.

During the mid-sixties, when the graduates since 1962 were thinking about going on to an advanced degree, a number of institutions initiated baccalaureate programs in which an associate degree graduate could be admitted as a junior in full standing. At the present time there are over one hundred such programs around the country (Gillie 1970a). The move toward offering baccalaureate programs for associate degree level paraprofessionals continues to grow, and a greater proportion of the associate degree graduates in the future will go on to a four year degree either immediately after acquiring the two year degree on a full time basis, or in later years. Some recent figures bear this out (Alden 1970). Thirty percent of the associate degree technology graduates of 1968 went into full-time study, twenty-six percent of them in 1969, and twenty-eight percent of the 1970 graduates did the same. The percentage of graduates immediately going on to further study is considerably higher for certain specialized paraprofessional groups (see Table 1).

The percentage of associate degree graduates going into advanced studies for other occupational programs is likely to be just as high. Associate degree graduates of occupational programs who do well academically are finding it easy to go on another two years for the bachelor's degree, which leads to a position at the highest paraprofessional or lower professional level.

TABLE 3-1

PERCENT OF SELECTED TYPES
OF MANUFACTURING-RELATED PARAPROFESSIONALS
WHO IMMEDIATELY GO INTO BACCALAUREATE PROGRAMS
(1970 GRADUATES). (ALDEN 1970)

Paraprofessional Specialty	Percent into Baccalaureate Programs
All Engineering Technology Related	28
Aeronautics	42
Chemical	39
Civil	33
Industrial	55
Mechanical	35
Metallurgical	45

THE OCCUPATIONAL LADDER

One of the phrases frequently used in vocational education is "occupational ladder." The term implies that every job occupies a position in a vertical spectrum that extends from the lowest to the highest level. To some, the spectrum deals with levels of skills required on the job, while others view it primarily in terms of status. In actuality, it is probably a blend of skills and status levels that most accurately describes the concept behind the term. Theoretically the idea is an excellent one for a number of reasons. It suggests that an individual can move up occupationally if he acquires the appropriate experiences and/or required education.

Unfortunately, reality has demonstrated that the ladder may have a number of missing rungs—particularly in the higher paraprofessional to lower professional range. An example is the rather consistent difficulty that has persisted with manufacturing-related paraprofessionals and engineers. When the manufacturing-related worker came upon the scene shortly after World War II, there was considerable consternation displayed about him. It took almost a generation for the engineering profession to recognize the paraprofessional component in their occupational spectrum. There still is very little likelihood for a paraprofessional to rise into the professional ranks because of the declared non-applicability of paraprofessional course work in engineering curriculums. But many of these paraprofessionals have the abilities to perform at the professional level, as indicated by the characteristics of the jobs they hold (Gillie, 1970b). This produces considerable pressure for a modification of the ladder so that entry into the professional level can be achieved without becoming an engineer. Bachelor of technology programs emerged and since have proliferated throughout the country, partially as a result of this demand. The attractiveness of these programs is made obvious by the great number of associate degree graduates who immediately seek the additional degree before entering the world of work (Alden 1970). Also, there are indications that many of those who go directly into the work world progress toward a bachelor's degree on a part-time basis (Gillie 1971c). As pointed out earlier, there are well over one hundred such programs, thereby providing easy accessibility to many practicing middle level workers (Gillie 1970a). The bachelor degree programs are creating several kinds of technologists, which can be broadly described as (1) the highly skilled technologists. Some programs continue with advancement of the student in the development of specialized cognitive based skills. They tend to approach the skill levels of the traditional professionals in their respective occupations. (2) The broad based technologists. Other programs do not offer specialized courses in the occupational area beyond the associate degree. Instead, they are given an array of courses that are meant to broaden them and to better prepare them to enter supervisory-leader type positions in the paraprofessional segment of that occupational area, from which they may later enter the full professional levels.

The implication of the emergence of these new types of bachelor degrees is that a *parallel ladder* has been developed in response to obstructions in advancement to the professional levels presented by some traditional professionals via the formalized traditional professional curriculums. Four year bachelor degree programs that draw upon associate degree graduates as their third-year input have also expanded into the social and health-related areas. It is basically an equalitarian movement in that a second path is opened to the professions. One of the most immediate advantages of such programs is the hope offered to the middle level workers by demonstrating that it is possible to move all the way up the occupational ladder. This claim was made before, but the "way up" was to "go back to the bottom" and start up another ladder. The middle level workers' price for such advancement was extremely high, both in time and money. Now, the statement that one "can get ahead" rings more true and these occupations are less likely to be considered "dead end."

The emergence of a new baccalaureate level person raises several questions. Is this individual a paraprofessional or a professional? Where is the point of entry into the professions via education? Some say the bachelor degree should be the entry badge of a professional; others would have the traditional professional programs be the only way to qualify as a professional, implying that the acquisition of a bachelor's degree based upon a middle level worker background elevates the individual to the higher reaches of the paraprofessional hierarchy only. There are those who feel that the minimum academic credential for a professional is the master's degree (witness the requirement of many two year colleges for professional faculty). A second basic question has to do with the role those individuals with bachelor degrees via occupational associate degrees are to assume in the world of work. There are some limited signs that they are not viewed as highly as the traditional professional baccalaureate graduates (Grinter 1970). Perhaps this can be overcome in the same way earlier associate degree graduates had to prove that they were more valuable than the person who received vocational preparation at the high school level. The third question is: What does the emergence of this new kind of individual in the occupational hierarchy do to the traditional professional level? Will it eventually do away with all the bachelor degrees in the professional areas? It would seem that the answer lies within an empirical determination over a period of several years on how the new baccalaureate graduates compare with the traditional ones. One thing of which we can be certain is that this trend has opened a real avenue for the various middle level workers for advancement on to the professional levels.

Summary

Several aspects of paraprofessional characteristics are considered. The findings of several empirical studies of associate degree graduates are used as the basis for much of this chapter. The items considered include salaries, geographic mobility, job characteristics in terms of the data-people-things spectrum, relationships between job mobility and job characteristics, reactions to their associate degree programs in terms of quality of instruction, need for course work immediately after graduation, need for course work now, and anticipated need for future jobs, and continued education after earning the associate degree.

The occupational ladder idea is examined, along with some of the myths associated with the concept. It is pointed out that many middle level workers will advance to the professional rungs of the occupational ladder by the new baccalaureate degrees which accept occupational associate degrees as the basis for full junior standing.

REFERENCES

Alden, J. D. *Prospects of Engineering and Technology Graduates: 1970.* New York: Engineering Manpower Commission of Engineers Council, 1970.

Gillie, A. C. "Technical Education Division." *AVA Convention Proceedings Digest: 1969 Boston, MA.* Washington, D.C.: American Vocational Association, 1970a.

———. *Geographic-Job Mobility of The Pennsylvania State University Two-Year Technician Graduates.* University Park, Pa.: Department of Vocational Education, Pennsylvania State University, 1970b.

———. *Employment Characteristics of The Pennsylvania State University Associate Degree Graduates.* University Park, Pa.: Department of Vocational Education, Pennsylvania State University, 1971a.

———. *Associate Degree Technicians' Judgments on Quality of Instruction and Course Relevancy.* University Park, Pa.: Department of Vocational Education, Pennsylvania State University, 1971b.

———. *Pennsylvania State University Associate Degree Technician Graduates: Some Demographic Variables.* University Park, Pa.: Department of Vocational Education, Pennsylvania State University, 1971c.

Grinter, L.E., et al. *Engineering Technology Education Study: Preliminary Report.* Washington, D.C.: American Society of Engineering Education, 1970.

Harper, A., ed. *1971 Junior College Directory.* Washington, D.C.: American Association of Junior Colleges, 1972.

"Job Mobility in 1971." *Monthly Labor Review.* Volume 86. Washington, D.C.: U.S. Bureau of Labor Statistics, 1963.

Larkin, P. and Teeple, J. "National Employment Goals in Higher Education." *College and University Business.* October, November, December, 1969.

Manpower Report of the President and a Report on Manpower Requirements, Resources, Utilization, and Training. Washington, D.C. : U. S. Department of Labor, 1963.

Manpower Report of the President. Washington, D.C.: U.S. Government Printing Office, 1971.

Occupational Classification. Volume 2 of the Dictionary of Occupational Titles. 3rd Edition, Washington, D.C.: U.S. Department of Labor, 1965.

Public Law 571, 89th Congress (Allied Health Professions Personnel Training Act).

The Economic Report of the President, January 1970 (Bureau of Labor Statistics). Washington, D.C.: U.S. Government Pringting Office, 1970.

Udell, G. G. *Laws Relating to Vocational Education and Agricultural Extension Work.* Washington, D.C. : U.S. Government Printing Office, 1971.

Vetter, B., ed. *Manpower Comments.* Volume 8, No. 4. Washington, D.C.: Scientific Manpower Commission, 1971.

Part II EDUCATION AND TRAINING OF THE MIDDLE LEVEL WORKER

Chapter 4 CURRICULUM PLANNING: GENERAL CONSIDERATIONS

Six general aspects of curriculum planning are considered here: (1) levels of curriculum planning; (2) reasons for national controls; (3) reasons for local controls; (4) decision making in curriculum planning; (5) utilization of educational research; and (6) consideration of student characteristics in curriculum planning. Although each is examined separately for the purpose of discussion and focusing appropriate attention to each, they are intertwined and inseparable entities in the overall curriculum planning process.

Levels of Curriculum Planning

Some aspects of curriculum planning in occupational education takes place at each governmental level (federal, state, and local). None of these three types is completely utilized to the exclusion of others. On the other hand. many aspects of curriculum planning in occupational education do involve controls from each. A good example of this is how the establishment of a new occupational program in a community college might come about in some instances. Sometimes it is possible to obtain federal funding (such as PL 87-415; PL 89-751; PL 90-575; PL 91-516). In order to qualify for these fed-

TABLE 4-1

TOTAL EXPENDITURES FOR VOCATIONAL-TECHNICAL EDUCATION FROM FEDERAL AND MATCHING FUNDS FISCAL YEAR 1969

State	Grand * Total	Federal[1]	% of total expen-diture	State and Local			
				State*	% of total expen-diture	Local*	% of total expen-diture
Alabama	24.9	5.9	23.7	8.1	32.5	10.9	43.8
Alaska	2.6	0.5	20.5	2.3	8.9	1.8	70.6
Arizona	8.6	2.2	25.3	2.2	25.5	4.2	49.2
Arkansas	10.1	3.4	33.5	3.1	30.4	3.7	36.1
California	80.8	18.0	22.2	0.8	1.0	62.1	76.8
Colorado	9.9	2.5	25.4	1.2	12.1	6.2	62.5
Connecticut	23.3	2.7	11.7	15.2	65.4	5.3	22.9
Delaware	4.0	0.6	15.4	3.0	74.3	0.4	10.3
Florida	44.7	7.3	16.4	30.0	67.2	7.3	16.4
Georgia	29.0	7.2	24.7	11.0	37.9	10.8	37.4
Hawaii	3.1	1.0	32.8	2.1	67.2	0.0	0.0
Idaho	4.3	1.2	29.2	1.7	39.0	1.3	31.8
Illinois	39.4	10.7	27.0	8.7	22.0	20.1	51.0
Indiana	23.8	6.4	26.8	1.4	5.8	16.0	67.4
Iowa	27.4	4.2	15.4	11.7	42.7	11.5	41.9
Kansas	11.7	3.1	26.8	2.1	18.1	6.5	55.1
Kentucky	22.3	5.6	25.1	14.8	66.3	1.9	8.6
Louisiana	16.1	5.5	34.1	.8	5.1	9.8	60.8
Maine	6.2	1.5	24.9	2.4	39.0	2.2	36.1
Maryland	23.7	4.1	17.2	8.1	34.3	11.5	48.5
Massachusetts	42.4	5.5	12.9	0.5	1.0	36.4	85.9
Michigan	44.6	9.6	21.5	2.1	4.7	32.9	73.8
Minnesota	28.4	5.1	17.9	10.5	37.0	12.8	45.1
Mississippi	13.5	4.4	32.7	4.0	29.8	5.0	37.5
Missouri	29.9	6.1	20.3	5.5	18.2	18.4	61.5
Montana	4.0	1.1	28.3	0.6	16.3	2.2	55.4
Nebraska	6.5	2.2	34.0	0.8	12.9	3.4	53.1
Nevada	2.8	0.6	21.3	0.6	21.4	1.6	57.3
New Hampshire	6.3	1.0	15.4	3.7	58.7	1.6	25.9
New Jersey	32.3	6.5	19.9	13.5	41.7	12.4	38.4

TABLE 4-1—Continued

State	Grand* Total	Federal[1]	% of total expenditure	State and Local			
				State*	% of total expenditure	Local*	% of total expenditure
New Mexico	4.9	1.6	32.7	0.3	5.5	3.0	61.8
New York	234.0	17.0	7.3	109.5	46.8	107.5	45.9
North Carolina	50.1	9.0	17.9	28.9	57.7	12.2	24.4
North Dakota	4.6	1.3	28.4	1.8	39.2	1.5	32.4
Ohio	54.6	12.4	22.7	20.9	38.3	21.3	39.0
Oklahoma	17.0	3.8	22.3	2.7	15.5	10.6	62.2
Oregon	15.8	2.6	16.3	3.8	23.9	9.4	59.8
Pennsylvania	101.6	14.0	13.8	32.2	31.7	55.4	54.5
Rhode Island	3.9	1.1	28.5	1.7	44.0	1.1	27.5
South Carolina	20.7	4.7	22.7	11.3	54.7	4.7	22.6
South Dakota	3.4	*1.3	38.4	0.4	11.3	1.7	50.3
Tennessee	20.3	6.5	32.2	6.3	31.1	7.5	36.7
Texas	63.5	15.3	24.1	36.9	58.1	11.3	17.8
Utah	10.2	1.5	14.5	2.5	24.9	6.2	60.6
Vermont	4.1	.7	18.0	2.1	50.1	1.3	31.9
Virginia	29.7	6.9	23.2	8.3	28.0	14.5	48.8
Washington	25.0	3.7	14.9	5.2	20.8	16.1	64.3
West Virginia	11.2	3.1	27.2	1.0	9.0	7.2	63.8
Wisconsin	45.4	5.6	12.4	7.3	16.2	32.5	71.4
Wyoming	2.8	0.6	26.7	0.2	6.9	1.5	66.4
Dist. of Columbia	2.7	0.8	28.2	2.0	71.8	0.0	
Guam	0.5	0.2	45.3	0.3	54.7	0.0	
Puerto Rico	15.9	5.1	32.1	10.8	67.9	0.0	
Virgin Islands	0.5	0.8	16.1	0.4	83.9	0.0	
Total	$1,192,862,965	$262,383,716	18.6	$400,362,023	34.1	$530,117,226	47.3

1 Vocational Education Act of 1963, Smith Hughes and George-Barden Acts

2 Dollars rounded to nearest 0.1 million, percentages to nearest whole percent.

* Taken from Vocational and Technical Education: Annual Report/Fiscal Year 1969 Washington, D.C.: U. S. Government Printing Office, 1970. HE 5:280:80008-69

eral funds, certain requirements must be met. These specifications are often translated into workable regulations by an overall state plan. The federal state plan for vocational education, in addition to meeting the requirements of obtaining certain federal funds, also provides an opportunity for state level vocational leaders to inject various degrees of control. This is reinforced by the provision of state support for these programs. This simple example illustrates the extent in which federal and state controls are present in curriculum planning in vocational education. State controls very likely carry into requirements for new facilities, schools, and so forth. There is even some element of control as to the format of the program. Most states mandate in some way the number of semester hours of study required for the associate degree. Some states extend their control over program content by requiring that a minimum percentage of the program be devoted to the specialty courses and another minimum percentage for the general education aspects of the curriculum. The local control in curriculum planning can originate from several quarters. In many states, a two-year college can introduce a new curriculum only after its local board of trustees have approved it, which often is contingent upon requirements over and above those imposed from the federal and state levels. It is likely that the board of trustees would exercise its authority only with reference to the general aspects of the curriculum and leave the specifics (actual courses and their content) to the college president (Hartnett 1969), who in turn delegates this responsibility to the college curriculum committee (Cohen and Roueche 1969). The curriculum committee likely rules on the specific courses proposed for inclusion in the overall curriculum (a second aspect of local control). The final element within local control deals with the subject matter specialists within the school, who usually determine the specific content of each course within the programs considered by the curriculum committee.

American education has a long tradition of favoring as much local and as little state and federal control as possible. Actual control of curriculum planning varies from state to state, from very little local control in some states to almost complete local autonomy in others. Furthermore, the more costly and exotic curriculums are apt to be controlled from the most remote sources since they often depend heavily upon state and federal funding. The author knows of no state in which local governmental agencies have the final authority in designating what institutions are to grant the associate degree. There seems to be no clear cut pattern in the governance of curriculum planning for occupational education, probably because there is no central federal control of all of education.

The most direct way to control an education institution is via its financial support. In occupational education this has come from the local, state, and federal sources. If past occurrences are harbingers of the future in this regard, then the tri-level financial support will continue as federal participation and educational funding increase (Pl 90-576; PL 91-516). Table 1 displays the distribution of expenditures for vocational technical education at the three levels. About 1.193 billion dollars were spent for vocational-technical education in fiscal year 1969, and its overall distribution was nineteen percent federal, thirty-four percent state, and forty-seven percent local. This varies from state to state as indicated by the figures in Table 1. The state of South Dakota used the heaviest proportion of its expenditure from federal funds, with 38.4 percent of its total investment for vocational-technical education derived from that source. The heaviest proportion of total expenditures from state funds was found to be in the state of Delaware (74.3 percent), while the largest proportion of its total expenditure from local funds was spent by the state of Massachusetts (85.9 percent). In spite of the considerable variation in the distribution of the sources of funds, it is clear that the three sources are now extant in occupational education (Vocational and Technical Education: Annual Report/Fiscal Year 1969, 1970).

Another kind of national influence upon curriculum planning has to do with textbook authors. In the past, certain textbooks have found strong acceptance among the faculties of specialized subjects in vocational education. These authors had an indirect effect upon curriculum planning in that many of the faculty would design their courses and even curriculums in some cases around the context of these textbooks. No precise estimate of this kind of effect is available, but it has been and still is considerable in many of the occupational areas.

REASONS FOR NATIONAL CONTROLS

Although the tradition is to maximize local autonomy, some educational leaders believe national planning would be helpful in the improvement of the overall quality of American education. Among the reasons given for favoring national controls is (Keppel 1966):

> Careful planning and concerted action can keep our educational strategies from degenerating into spasmodic responses to the alarms of the moment. But failure to move ahead with all speed can result in our becoming second rate, lacking in trained manpower, lacking in the development of economic resources, and as a result lacking in influence, prestige, and strength among nations.

The trend away from local and toward state-federal control in education grew as the nation developed, as indicated in the following statement (AASA 1953):

> The new school objectives were not at all within the scope of small district schools, with their single curriculum and often untrained teachers. There was in truth educational chaos into which order had to be brought. And so state, city, and district school systems were evolved to correlate and coordinate the services of the individual schools. The principle that the wealth of a state should be taxed to afford equal educational opportunity to all children became mandatory standards. Compulsory attendance laws, fixed length of the school year, regulation of school building construction, statewide certification of teachers, determination of teachers, determination of the general curriculum, establishment of minimum salary laws gradually became the order of the day.

The above points to the extent to which attitudes favoring individual responsibility, so characteristic of the American home during the seventeenth and eighteenth centuries, have increasingly been supplemented by an attitude that stresses group interdependence. The proponents of more national involvement point to these societal changes, particularly with regard to the labor force, which is increasingly a national rather than local concern. This trend was felt early in vocational education, as manifested by the series of legislation which provided support to elements within it for over a hundred years (Venn, 1964: Udell 1971). More recent indications of increased involvement of federal level agencies with education are cited in the literature (Palola 1971; Spitzberg 1971). Advocates of increased federal involvement also indicate a concern for the effect of provincialism in curriculum planning, as seen in the following statement (McMurrin 1961):

> We must free ourselves from the constant temptation of a provincial posture with reference to the function proper to our education institutions. Our past isolations are gone and the isolation of our nation is gone. What we now do in our schools has importance not only for our immediate communities but for the nation and the world.

Another reason set forth for advocating federal level subvention for curriculum planning is that allocations of funds for curriculum research and development are most likely to happen with the provision of federal monies. Program research and development is needed to help arrange a priority of generalizations for occupational curriculums and provide impetus to close the gap between the rapidly expanding knowledge dealing with occupations and the contents of the programs in which people for these jobs are prepared. Many of the most recent federal acts relating to vocational education have provided funds for curriculum research and development (Udell 1971) and these monies have been used to provide some real program improvements in many states (Perkins 1971).

Summarizing, the major reasons for being in favor of federal involvement in curriculum planning are as follows: (a) increased chances of securing sufficient funding for program research and development; (b) a greater assurance that new curriculum planning will relate to national and large regional occupational education needs; (c) a minimization of the danger of developing new curriculums based on provincial and short-sighted goals; (d) an increased likelihood that a greater amount of skill and expertise will be brought to bear upon curriculum planning.

REASONS FOR STATE AND LOCAL CONTROLS

A certain amount of curriculum planning at the state level already exists in every state (Glenny 1959; Palola 1971; Berdahl 1971; Chambers 1970). In some states, it is treated as an integral part of local control as far as curriculum planning goes because responsibility for it is delegated back to the local level (such as to the local board of trustees of the local two-year college). Three of the major arguments given for favoring local controls are: (1) national curriculum planning is contrary to democratic principles because it tends to centralize education and is considered not in the tradition of American education; (2) some believe that real curriculum changes come about most naturally with local experimentation (which is complicated by the fact that finances and physical facilities for true experimentation are rarely provided at the local level); (3) some educators believe that curriculum changes come about best through the involvement of people in the change process, and feel the frequency with which people involvement occurs is reduced at the federal involvement level. These arguments are apparently not too effective, since there are clearly observable trends that point to increased state control and coordination (Berdahl 1971; Palola 1971).

There are some educators who believe, however, that it is entirely feasible to utilize resources from all levels (national, state, local-regional) to develop occupational curriculum plans best suited to meet middle level worker needs. To achieve this goal, a five-point strategy is worthy of consideration: (1) Federal aid to the states should be continued and increased for the improvement of education in general. Special monies earmarked for occupational education as a whole should also continue to increase and be funneled back to the states on the basis of a formula which rewards expansion of programs for preparing middle level workers in occupational areas where the greatest need exists; (2) departments of education and curriculum leadership at the state level should be strengthened; (3) high standards for those involved in curriculum leadership should be sought with greater vigor; (4) an increased effort, reflected in the form of larger financial commitments, should be made in research and occupational curriculum development, turning more to the vocational education departments of various universities for impetus in this direction; (5) There should be more serious involvement by certain professional associations in developing curriculum planning leaders.

Decision Making in Curriculum Planning

Decision making usually rests with the chief administrative officer, but the initiation of ideas upon which action is taken often originates with persons below the top leadership level in the hierarchy of the organization (Caplow 1964; Blau and Scott 1962; Etzioni 1964). Another possibility would be to utilize results of some university-based research endeavor, but to bring in new ideas from the "outside" introduces special hazards (Rogers 1962; Bice 1970). In a new institution, responsibility for the design and planning of a new curriculum will likely be delegated to persons who have competency in the specialized portion of the programs. When a new occupational curriculum is being planned for an existing college, the established administrative machinery that assigns responsibility for making decisions at various levels in the planning process is utilized (such as curriculum committees). Organization policies are generally made by the governing board (Caplow 1964; Hartnett 1969), which would be the board of trustees or board of education for a two-year college. The administrator then delegates responsibility for decision making to subsequent lower levels in the hierarchy, who in turn must make decisions that are within the framework of the established organization policies (Etzioni 1964). A good administrator lays out the lines of interest within which the curriculum planner is permitted to make decisions. Generally, these decisions fall within four broad categories, which are: (1) curriculum policies; (2) curriculum content selection; (3) actual development of the overall curriculum; (4) the arrangement of the learning opportunities within the curriculum.

Ideally, the program designer will use data and information that deal with (a) student characteristics, (b) characteristics of society at large, (c) the world of occupations, (d) types of knowledge and skills relevant to the program being designed, (e) principles, functions and objectives of learning, (f) parameters of the student population, (g) administrative and academic framework of the schools, and (h) facilities and finances available. When one views occupational program design from this angle, it appears to be a very complex task. In addition, there are a variety of forces which exert influences on curriculum planning. Some of the more significant ones are: (1) national efforts in the same educational area; (2) effects of tradition (constraints and incentives); (3) accreditation policies, regulations, and requirements; (4) kinds and number of colleges and universities in the region and state; (5) the nature of the regional business-industrial community; (6) regional public opinion of higher education in general and post-secondary occupational education in particular; (7) kinds and strengths of special interest groups; (8) the availability of textbooks and publishers of materials in that curriculum area; (9) regional critics of education and the focus of their criticism; (10) findings from educational research relevant to the curriculum area; (11) attitudes of the education profession as a whole and of occupational educators in particular toward the program being considered.

UTILIZATION OF EDUCATION RESEARCH

Until recently, very little curriculum planning has been performed with utilization of education research. In vocational education, because of the rapid changes being experienced in just about all occupational areas, curriculum planning must become increasingly dependent upon the findings of sound educational research. Chapter 10 deals with the importance of institutional research in this regard and Chapter 11 examines ways in which new ideas can be successfully injected into occupational education.

CONSIDERING STUDENT CHARACTERISTICS IN CURRICULUM PLANNING

Curriculum planning should take cognizance of the students and the social group that provides funding for the school. The rationale for considering students in curriculum planning is: (1) each student should be developed to his maximum potential; (2) every individual is truly educated only when he develops his talents and capabilities to his optimun; (3) the welfare of our society hinges on the maximum development of all individuals; (4) the welfare of our society hinges on the skills, insights, knowledge, and other characteristics of the individuals within it; (5) the individual's motivational syndrome is one of the chief bases for selection and development of learning experiences in the school setting; (6) programs and learning experiences must be adapted to the maturity, capacities, and abilities of the learners; (7) student evaluation must be based on the individual's own capacities, abilities, talents, and potentialities.

Certain kinds of information are absolutely necessary about people if we are to take them into account when planning curriculums. First is the student population. This would include enrollment and enrollment trends, classification of all kinds of students, the deviation from the norm of the student body to be serviced (such as poverty or minority groups), past attrition rates, the characteristics of dropouts, history of graduates, characteristics of transfer students, marriage rates, mobility patterns, projected regional population, composition of the population by age groups, trends in higher education (including all aspects of occupational education), projected future enrollments, enrollments and projected enrollments of special occupational and adult programs.

The growth and developmental characteristics, and status of youth and adults must also be considered. This includes their physical, emotional, social, and intellectual progress. We should also consider their developmental tasks at various age and ability levels; their psychological needs, interests, and problems, as well as their personality characteristics such as self-concepts, values, beliefs, ideals, morals, behavioral patterns, attitudes, aspiration plans, vocational choices, and motivational driving needs. The abilities, talents, potentialities, achievements, intellectual capacity and patterns of development, creativity, talents, exceptional needs of a typical youth, and educational achievement of potential students must come into focus in curriculum planning too.

Not to be overlooked are the considerations found in the home, immediate neighborhood, and the larger community—the socioeconomic status of the family, cultural and intellectual climate of the home, family aspirations, parents' occupations, previous occupations of adults to be served by the programs, social, cultural and economic characteristics of the region, characteristics of the youth's peer culture, educational level of community adults, possibilities for part-time and summer jobs, and characteristics of the labor force (distribution of types of occupations, trends in employment by occupation, trends in demands for workers by occupations). Last, but by no means least important while planning curriculums, is to be cognizant of the learning process, including the nature of learning, learning theories, factors conductive to learning, motivation, perception, and self-concepts in learning. Incorporating all these kinds of information would enhance the possiblity of building curriculum most relevant to students' needs.

Summary

Curriculum planning is treated in a general fashion. The major aspect considered are levels of curriculum planning, the rationale for national and local controls, the decision making process, utilization of educational research, and incorporation of knowledge of student characteristics in designing programs.

Certain elements within curriculum planning already go on at national, state, local, and regional governmental levels. Federal influence has evolved primarily from federal funding for occupational education over the past hundred years. Local control, considered most desirable by many educators, is becoming less important as the other two forms of financial support (which to some extent determine who controls the curriculum) become more evident. Reasons for and against each type of control are presented. No one form of control has all the advantages or is completely devoid of virtue. While national controls may increase the possibility that curriculum planning will be done with a view of national needs (particularly in occupational programs), it tends to bring an increased impersonalization that many educators dislike. Local controls, while increasing the chances that local educators will control their own curricula, run the risk of developing programs that are poorly designed and provincially oriented. Therefore, it appears that the eclectic approach is most desirable, with efforts made to minimize drawbacks of each mode of control.

The decision making process in curriculum planning is examined, indicating that program designers make decisions in four broad categories and use over eight kinds of data and information. Eleven factors that can influence the process of curriculum planning are examined. The last section deals with the importance of utilizing educational research findings and designing curricula with full consideration of the characteristics of future students.

REFERENCES

Berdahl, R.O. *Statewide Coordination of Higher Education.* Washington, D.C.: American Council of Education, 1970.

Bice, G.R. *Working with Opinion Leaders to Accelerate Change in Vocational Education.* Columbus, Ohio: Center for Vocational and Technical Education, Ohio State University, 1970.

Blau, P.M. and Scott, W.R. *Formal Organizations: A Comparative Approach.* San Francisco, Calif.: Chandler, 1962.

Caplow, T. *Principles of Organization.* New York: Harcourt, Brace and World, 1964.

Chambers, M.M. *Higher Education in the Fifty States.* Danville, Ill.: Interstate Printers and Publishers, 1970.

Cohen, A.M. and Roueche, J.E. *Institutional Administrator or Education Leader? The Junior College President.* Washington, D.C.: American Association of Junior Colleges, 1969.

Etzioni, A. *Modern Organizations.* Englewood Cliffs, N.J.: Prentice-Hall, 1964.

Glenny, L.A. *Autonomy of Public Colleges: The Challenge of Coordination.* New York: McGraw-Hill, 1959.

Hartnett, R.T. *College and University Trustees: Their Backgrounds, Roles, and Educational Attitudes*. Princeton, N.J.: Educational Testing Services, 1969.

Keppel, F. quoted in Saylor, J.G. and Alexander, W.M. *Curriculum Planning for Modern Schools*. New York: Holt, Rinehart and Winston, 1966.

McMurrin, S.M. "Education and the National Goal." An address delivered at the annual Harvard Summer School Conference on Educational Administration, Harvard University. Cambridge, Mass.: July 20, 1961. Mimeograph.

Palola, E.G.; Lehrmann, T.; and Blischke, W.R. "The Reluctant Planner: Faculty in Institutional Planning." *The Journal of Higher Education* Volume XLII, No. 7. Columbus, Ohio: Ohio State University Press. 1971.

Perkins, C.D. *Reports on the Implementation of the Vocational Education Amendments of 1968*. Washington, D.C.: U.S. Government Printing Office, 1971.

Public Law 415, 87th Congress (Manpower Development and Training Act of 1962).

Public Law 751, 89th Congress (Allied Health Professions Personnel Act of 1966).

Public Law 576, 90th Congress (Vocational Education Amendments of 1968).

Public Law 516, 91st Congress (The Environmental Education Act).

Public Law 210, 88th Congress (Vocational Education Act of 1963).

Public Law, 347, 64th Congress (Smith-Hughes Act).

Public Law 586, 79th Congress (Vocational Act of 1946—George-Barden Act).

Rogers, E.M. *Diffusion of Innovations*. New York: The Free Press, 1962.

Spritzberg, I.J., Jr. "Current Federal Financing of Higher Education and a Proposal." *The Journal of Higher Education* Volume XLII, No. 9. Columbus, Ohio: Ohio State University Press, 1971.

Udell, G.G. *Laws Relating to Vocational Education and Agricultural Extension Work*. Washington, D.C.: U.S. Government Printing Office, 1971.

Venn, G. *Man, Education and Work*. Washington, D.C.: American Council on Education, 1964.

*Vocational and Technical Education: Annual Report/Fiscal Year 1968 (OE-*80008-68). Washington, D.C.: U.S. Government Printing Office, 1970.

"What Schools Are For." *AASA American School Curriculum*. Washington, D.C.: American Association of School Administrators, 1953.

Chapter 5 STUDENT CHARACTERISTICS

Educational techniques and programs need to be developed which help students overcome limitations that stand in the way of completing an occupational program and entering the work world. Knowing about students also helps in recruiting them for and placing them in occupational programs. In order to aid students in this way, much needs to be learned about their characteristics. A number of significant research efforts have been made in this direction, and several salient findings of this research on the occupational student are reported in this chapter. Studies have looked at the occupational student and his background and have also compared him with his other college peers (those in preprofessional and academic programs).

Demographic Characteristics

Gillie (1969) found that 42 percent of occupational students are employed full-time and another 21 percent have part-time jobs. These figures are consistent with those found by the Educational Testing Service (CGPP 1968), which also reported that 40 percent of the students in vocational institutes and community colleges derived support from their parents. Thus a sizable fraction of two year college occupational students are financially on their own.

A relationship between father's occupation and student's program was found by Lindsay, Hoover, and Kepler (1968a). Fifty-four percent of the associate degree candidates at The Pennsylvania State University (all in occupational programs) have fathers with occupations in the skilled labor and semiskilled labor categories, compared with only 42 percent in those classifications for the entire university freshmen male student body. (The comparisons are made for males because there were no females in the occupational programs examined here.) Twenty percent of the fathers of the occupational students have professional and managerial occupations, while 32 percent of the entire freshmen male student body fathers are in that category.

Father's education as related to college programs was also reported by Lindsay, Hoover, and Kepler. The educational mean for the fathers of the male occupation students is 11.2 years, while for the entire freshmen male student body it is 12.2 years. These findings are similar to those reported earlier by Astin, Panos, and Creager (1967), Medsker and Trent (1965), and Cross (1968). The means for the mother's education are similar, 11.4 years for the occupational students and 12.0 years for the entire freshmen group.

Annual family income as a function of programs was also examined by Lindsay, Hoover, and Kepler. For all occupational students, the 1966 mean was about $6,800 and the 1967 mean was just under $7,100. For the entire freshmen group, these figures were about $7,900 and $8,200 respectively. Annual family incomes of over $9,000 were found for 24 percent of the occupational students and 38 percent of the entire male freshmen group. These averages run considerably below the findings reported by Cross.

The religious preferences of the occupational program candidates are not markedly different from those of the overall university freshmen group. About 50 percent indicated a Protestant preference, and just over 40 percent were Catholic.

Home communities of the occupational students are slightly different from those of the overall male student body of the university. While the same proportion for both groups came from cities (roughly 25 percent), a smaller percentage of the occupational students came from the suburbs (14 percent as opposed to 20 percent for the overall male freshmen group). Perhaps this finding indicates a tendency for the upper-middle class parents from the suburbs to favor four-year programs for their youngsters. Approximately the same percentage of students from the two groups examined here come from communities in which the major economic activity is industry, commerce, or mining (about 47 percent).

Educational Choice and Aspirations

The college entrance examination board obtained biographical data on incoming two-year college students. The information permits examination of differences between occupational students in three types of institutions: in the public community college, the private junior college, and the vocational-technical institutes (CGPP, 1969). In the public community college occupational group, main reasons for attending that institution are strength in intended major (27 percent), closeness to home (22 percent), inexpensiveness (18 percent). For vocational-technical institute students, major reasons are strength in intended major (39 percent), general academic reputation (17 percent). The private junior college occupational students give the following main reasons: closeness to home (23 percent); general academic reputation (20 percent); good impression of campus and students (19 percent); and strength in intended major (16 percent). Thus, strength in intended major appears to be an important basis for selection of an institution by occupational students, particularly those who enroll in vocational-technical institutes.

Differences in educational aspirations between vocational-technical institutes and community college students were also found: 60 percent of vocational-technical occupational students indicated that the extent of their educational plans was to complete a two-year special training program, whereas only 39 percent of the community college occupational group indicated they would be satisfied with this objective. A greater proportion of community college occupational students aspired to completing work for a bachelor's degree. The private junior college occupational group displayed a spectrum of educational aspirations somewhat similar to that for the public community college students.

Intellective Characteristics

The intellective factors identified by Lindsay, Hoover, and Kepler (1968b) point to some clear-cut differences between the overall university male freshmen population and the occupational student freshmen. The occupational male SAT average is about 120 points below the all university male average. The high school averages of the occupational students have a mean between C and C+, while the university group mean is between C+ and B. On the English Placement Test, the occupational student mean is about 39, while the overall university male freshmen average is 51, a sizable difference. Substantial differences are also found in mathematics and chemistry tests. In algebra, the all university group mean of 11.3 leads the occupational degree student mean by 5.6 points. The occupational student mean for trigonometry is 4.9, while the all university group mean is 8.8. In chemistry, the occupational student mean of 14.3 lags behind the all university group mean by 5.3 points.

The core battery test scores of the comparative guidance and placement program (CGPP 1969) enable us to compare occupational students in public community colleges, private junior colleges, and vocational-technical schools. The occupational students in the public community colleges and private junior colleges consistently scored lower than the overall college population in most of the core battery tests. But the reverse is true for the occupational students in the vocational-technical institutes. Furthermore, the occupational students in the vocational-technical institutes earned battery test scores that were the same as or above those of the overall student body in the public community colleges. If the sample is typical, the vocational-technical institutes are attracting occupational students with relatively high scores on these tests. It would be interesting to learn whether this is the result of selective admissions or student attraction to the vocational-technical institute programs.

Attraction to and Success in Post-Secondary Occupational Education

Secondary school counselors tend to overestimate the proportion of high school graduates who will go on to vocational programs in post-secondary vocational institutions. In one study (Fenske 1969) the high school counselors surveyed said that they expected 40 percent of the graduates to go on to post-secondary occupational programs, whereas only 19 percent of the students did so. One wonders if this discrepancy is not at least partially due to the fact that secondary school counselors have difficulty in identifying those student attributes and background characteristics that can be strongly associated with attraction to and success in post-secondary occupational programs instead of traditional baccalaureate programs.

Several relatively well known characteristics of two year college students need to be mentioned here since they relate to the problem of determining who will go into post-secondary occupational programs. A number of studies described by Cross (1968) show that the two-year colleges attract pragmatic students basically in search of vocational preparation. The two-year college seems to be less attractive to talented students who have the intellectual capacity and academic orientation to go into traditional baccalaureate programs. Also, students who expect to take part in a wide variety of activities while in college are not attracted to the two-year colleges when a choice of college (junior or senior) is available to them. In addition, the two-year college student is very likely to be the first person in his family to attend college. And most important, college for this student is his primary vehicle for achieving upward social mobility.

To turn to students in post-secondary occupational programs specifically, Cross (1968) and others report that students planning to go into these programs rate somewhere between the academically oriented college-bound students and the terminal high school graduates in terms of class standing, interest in school work, and satisfaction with their high school experiences. Many of the students who end up in occupational curriculums in college were relatively unsuccessful in high school and found their high school experience uninteresting. Furthermore, they had unrealistically low views of their scholastic and intellectual abilities. Many of the less academically oriented students admitted to baccalaureate programs probably share these characteristics and would be best served by going into occupational programs instead. Careful counseling in this direction can bring them into programs where they will gain the successful experiences they need.

An important factor to keep in mind when assessing which students are likely to enroll in occupational programs is the availability of facilities offering such programs. In communities where technical institutes are readily available, many of the high school seniors who score in the bottom 30 percent of their classes in scholastic ability and achievement indicate they plan to enroll in a post-secondary occupational curriculum. This, interestingly enough, is not the case in communities without such institutions. This verifies what two-year college authorities have claimed for the past several decades: the presence of a two-year college within easy reach of people in a community can exert considerable influence upon the plans made by those high school graduates whose scholastic records do not clearly recommend post-high school education of the conventional type. Other studies in various parts of the country have also shown that the presence of post-secondary institutions that offer occupational programs provides opportunities for those individuals who perhaps normally would not consider a post-secondary educational experience.

Two discernible types of graduating high school seniors are disposed toward occupational programs: (1) those seniors who rank in the highest 30 percent of their high school class but whose parents have low educational and occupational status. These youngsters tend to select occupational programs as the most realistic post-secondary education for them because they believe a four-year college program is beyond their economic means. (2) Those seniors who are in the lower 30 percent of their graduating class but whose parents have both high educational and occupational status. These youngsters have the means to go to college, but their low grades discourage them from going into traditional baccalaureate curriculums. Their parents send them into post-secondary occupational programs rather than have them not go to college at all.

If these discernible trends were tested and verified, they would provide a useful hypothesis both for high school counselors helping youngsters to decide where to go after high school and for those persons involved in planning their curriculums. This could be a very good starting point in developing a realistic way of predicting which secondary school students are most likely to be attracted to post-secondary occupational programs.

Other relationships between variables that influence the occupational plans made by these youngsters need to be researched carefully. Is the decision to enter an occupational program in fact only a reluctant personal compromise made because of the difference between scholastic abilities and parental support possibilities, or do other factors enter in? What differences, for example, exist between boys and girls in post-high school occupational ambitions? Since it is commonly accepted that women will work for a significant portion of their lives, we need to determine whether parents in certain social economic levels are reluctant to send their daughters into post-secondary occupational programs, just as they have been reluctant to send their girls to traditional colleges as evidenced by the almost two to one ratio of male to female students in colleges (Lerner 1970).

We need also to discover the implications of the fact that many so-called under-achievers have a stronger tendency to enroll in post-secondary occupational programs than do those seniors who are above them in scholastic rank (Fenske 1969). Low academic performance may be largely an indication of a student's dissatisfaction with those aspects of his academic program in high school that seem to prepare him only for going on to college rather than for some practical and immediate job. Some youngsters are attracted to a program which is short and is clearly directed toward a visible and easily attainable occupational goal. If such differences in terms of interest exist, they certainly have a tremendous significance for student recruitment and for the building of curricula and occupational programs. The current trend toward an increased general education component in occupational programs may reduce the attractiveness of these programs. Taking all these background variables (such as aptitude, achievement, and social economic status) in combination seems to be a promising approach to obtaining usable information for predicting student plans for post-secondary occupational education.

Let us look briefly at predicting success in occupational programs. A number of research studies have established and confirmed that grades in specific courses and overall grade averages of community college students are predictable with satisfactory accuracy by use of American College Testing Scores and high school grades. The standard aptitude measures (test scores) and high school grades still seem to be among the best predictors of success in general for the occupational program student (Cross 1968). Somehow knowing that students who succeed in high school will also succeed in occupational programs in two-year colleges does not seem too consoling. How can we take the non-academically oriented youngster, after a series of relative failures in high school, and match him with a post-secondary occupational program that will bring him success? We still have no good answers to that query.

One way of identifying students who will benefit from post-secondary occupational education is through use of a rear-view mirror approach. We can study the characteristics of those students who have successfully completed occupational programs in post-secondary institutions. A number of places have embarked in this direction by conducting follow-up studies of their graduates. The results of such studies (Gillie 1970, 1970b, 1971c) can be the basis for program evaluation in terms of what the graduates are doing and also what they say about their programs in retrospect.

Summary

One of the main reasons for occupational students' choice of institution is quality of occupational program offered. This finding seems to imply that they make career decisions either before enrolling or shortly thereafter. Along with this tendency is their feeling that the completion of a two-year occupational program will be the extent of their college education, at least for a time.

Regarding intellectual abilities, studies show that two-year college students score lower than senior college students on intellective tests, such as the SAT and subject matter tests. This chapter reports the differences between occupational student and senior-college freshmen on these test scores. These differences are probably greater in those institutions that offer occupational programs at lower academic levels than in the institutions examined here. These differences are not brought out to disparage the academic abilities of the paraprofessional student but to enable us to recognize his intellectual characteristics. Because the occupational student is intellectually different from both his two-year college peers and senior-college students (Lindsay, Hoover, Kepler; 1968b), it behooves us to continue to learn more about these differences so that we can improve the quality of occupational education. We shall never match people in programs with complete perfection, but significant progress is being made in this direction.

REFERENCES

Astin, A. W.; Panos, R. J.; and Creager, J. A. "National Norms for Entering College Freshman—Fall 1966." *ACE Research Reports.* Washington, D.C.: American Council on Education, 1967.

Comparative Guidance and Placement Program: Progress Report. Princeton, N.J. Educational Testing Service, 1968.

Comparative Guidance and Placement Program: Program Summary Statistics 1968. Princeton, N.J. Educational Testing Service, 1969.

Cross, K.P. *The Junior College Student: A Research Description.* Princton, N.J.: Educational Testing Service, 1968.

Fenske, R.H. "Who Selects Vocational-Technical Post-High School Education." In *Monograph 2: The Two-Year College and its Students: An Empirical Report.* Iowa City, Iowa: American College Testing Program, 1969.

Gillie, A.C. *Selected Community College Intellectual and Environmental Factors: A Three College Study.* University Park, Pa.: Department of Vocational Education, Pennsylvania State University, 1969.

———. *Geographic-Job Mobility of the Pennsylvania State University Two-Year Graduates.* University Park, Pa.: Department of Vocational Education, Pennsylvania State University, 1970.

———. *Associate Degree Technicians' Judgments on Quality of Instruction and Course Relevancy.* University Park, Pa.: Department of Vocational Education, Pennsylvania State University, 1971a.

——. *Employment Characteristics of The Pennsylvania State University Associate Degree Graduates.* University Park, Pa.: Department of Vocational Education, Pennsylvania State University, 1971b.

——. *Pennsylvania State University Associate Degree Technician Graduates: Some Demographic Variables.* University Park, Pa.: Department of Vocational Education, Pennsylvania State University, 1971c.

Lerner, W. *Statistical Abstract of the United States: 1970.* Washington, D.C.: U.S. Bureau of the Census, 1970.

Lindsay, C.A.; Hoover, T.; and Kepler, B. *1967 Fall Term Pennsylvania State University Freshmen Class: Profile of Demographic Variables.* University Park, Pa.: Office of Student Affairs, Pennsylvania State University, 1968a.

——. *1967 Fall Term Pennsylvania State University Freshman Class: Profile of Intellective Variables.* University Park, Pa.: Office of Student Affairs, Pennsylvania State University, 1968b.

Medsker, L.L. *The Junior College: Progress and Prospect.* New York: McGraw-Hill, 1960.

Medsker, L.L. and Trent, J.W. *Factors Affecting College Attendance of High School Graduates from Varying Socioeconomic and Ability Levels.* Berkeley, Calif.; Center for Research and Development in Higher Education, University of California, 1965.

Munday, L. A.; "A Comparison of Junior College Students in Transfer and Terminal Curricula." In *Monograph 2: The Two-Year College and its Students: An Empirical Report.* Iowa City, Iowa: American College Testing Program, 1969.

Venn, G.; *Man, Education and Work.* Washington, D.C.; American Council on Education, 1964.

Chapter 6 DETERMINING THE NEED FOR PROGRAMS

Sources of Pressure for Starting New Programs

Using the broad considerations dealing with the relationships between local, state, and federal controls as a basis, we can examine a more specific strategy for determining whether or not the inauguration of a new program is justifiable. Many new programs have been started without the benefit of a systematic assessment of their need, perhaps because their instigators did not know how feasibility studies ought to be conducted. Pressure for starting a new program by various groups can develop with only minimum concern about real need. Since they typically spend less than one work day per month on matters related to being college trustees (Hartnett 1969), such governing boards may take the easy way—grant tentative approval for programs and then leave it to the college officials to implement them. The danger of falling victim to this easy accommodation is illustrated by the fact that trustees generally believe that decisions relating to the starting of programs should be made by them or jointly by them and the administration; most of them agree that these kinds of decisions are not for the faculty to make (Harnett). It is quite clear that trustees see decision-making concerning the starting of new programs as working its way down from the higher echelons of governance (Rauh 1969). In light of these findings, strong demands need to be made upon the board unless a systematic way of responding to them is devised. Before delving into how the college should respond to new program demands, let us consider the major groups that can seek to influence a college to consider new programs.

CITIZEN-CIVIC-PROFESSIONAL LABOR GROUPS AT THE LOCAL LEVEL

Individuals and various groups at the local level sometimes seek to press the college for a particular program or group of programs. Reasons for their actions are quite diversified and provide an interesting area for research. Sometimes these demands are self-seeking while at other times they are completely altruistic. Example: Business-Industrial concerns, particularly small ones, sometimes honestly overstate their needs for certain kinds of occupational preparation. When the college accepts such demands at face value, the difficulty in placement of the first group of graduates reveals the serious discrepancy between the originally expressed need and the actual number of these graduates actually employed. An individual may press for the start of a new program with the belief that he detects an emerging need for a certain type of middle worker presently not available. Local chapters of professional, business, and labor organizations can also bring pressure to bear upon a college for starting new programs. There is seldom any consistent correlation between the intensity of a demand for a new program and its validity. This point is well worth remembering, particularly when intense pressure by certain groups is brought to bear upon the President and the Board of Trustees.

CITIZEN-CIVIC-PROFESSIONAL LABOR GROUPS AT THE STATE LEVEL

These are generally the same kinds of groups described as functioning at the local level, with the difference that they sometimes are able to command more attention from state level educators who have influence upon the college's operation. Pressures from the state level can more likely urge a board of trustees to approve a new program without subjecting it to the proper examination and evaluation, especially when it appears the pressure source has an orbit of influence that includes the source of state level funding for the institution as a whole or the agency which monitors federal-state funding for occupational programs. Also, since the demand originates from the state level, a Board of Trustees might assume that it has been made only after careful study of the request. Such assumption should not be made. The college should request copies of whatever feasibility study attempts have been made by others and should then feel entirely justified in conducting its own feasibility study if the previous one fails to meet minimum criteria for such studies.

CITIZEN-CIVIC-PROFESSIONAL LABOR GROUPS AT THE NATIONAL LEVEL

Various groups at the national level occasionally exert pressure on two-year colleges to consider certain occupational programs. An example is the encouragement which was provided for starting technician-type programs shortly after the Soviet Union launched Sputnik. Pressures of the same variety develop in the areas of medical care and delivery as well as in some of the social-service-related occupations (Manpower Report of the President, 1971). In some cases, the national pressures are coupled with the availability of federal funds for the start of certain programs (PL 89-751 and PL 91-516, for example), which increases the tendency to inaugurate such programs without a good systematic examination-evaluation of the need for such graduates in the region served by the college. National professional associations can have a marked influence on the initiation of new programs also, often indirectly. The National League for Nursing and the American Society for Engineering Education, for example, have had profound effects on the middle level occupations related to their professions.

LOCAL GOVERNMENTAL SOURCES

County boards of supervisors, city councils, mayors, etc., sometimes spearhead drives to get a new occupational program or programs going in a two-year college. Quite often this is coupled with an overall attempt in "uplifting" the community so as to make it a more attractive place for potential businesses and industries and to reduce or stop the out-migration of middle class workers and their families.

STATE GOVERNMENTAL SOURCES

Pressures at the state governmental level can result after identification of serious deficiencies in certain kinds of workers in terms of labor market needs for the entire state. Many states have bureaus which conduct on-going studies of labor market needs in conjunction with federal government data. These manpower studies serve as a partial basis for signaling both shortages and surpluses for certain types of workers (BLS 1606, 1969; McNamara and Franchak 1970).

FEDERAL GOVERNMENTAL SOURCES

When the need for certain kinds of education is strongly felt at the federal level, it can result in congressional appropriation of money to support it, as shown by the array of vocational-education-related acts during the past several generations (Udell 1971). Recent examples are the Manpower Development and Training Act of 1962 (PL 87-415), the Vocational Education Act of 1963 (PL 88-210), the Allied Health Professions Personnel Training Act of 1966 (PL 89-751), the Vocational Ammendments of 1968 (PL 90-576), and the Environmental Education Act (PL 91-516). The fact that funding is available does not alter the requirement to carefully ascertain the relevance of a given program in a particular region served by the two-year college. Some colleges, if they were completely honest in such evaluation, would find that they should not offer certain programs in spite of the fact that money is available. Proceeding on any other basis could result in unwise spending (Perkins 1971). The results of starting programs in an unplanned manner can include having graduates for whom jobs are not available.

THE FACULTY AND ADMINISTRATION OF THE COLLEGE

Faculty members and administrators, in their contacts with the business-industrial community, are sometimes alerted to their special needs. In this capacity they serve as important sources for identifying needed programs in the region served by the college.

Evaluation of Request for New Programs

Having examined the possible sources, how should these requests be dealt with? Concrete negative or affirmative answers must be based on considerable thought and planning. A final answer ought to be based on a systematic investigation of all factors related to the need for and the feasibility of starting the new program. Included in the criteria should be reliable indicators that there are job openings for persons interested in preparing for these jobs. These basic human determinants have to be tempered by the feasibility of starting and maintaining support of the new proposed program. Occupational programs are generally more costly to start and continue in their operation than academic programs (Kaufman, Hu, Lee, and Stromsdofer, 1969). Some reasonable estimates of these costs must be arrived at early enough to be used in reaching a decision as to whether the college is able to conduct the program at the proper financial level.

Let us examine a suggested generalized sequence of activities for decision-making.

INITIAL INQUIRY BY COLLEGE AUTHORITIES

The first response to a request could be the appointment of several administrators and faculty members to briefly review the plausibility of the request. This would consist of a careful perusal of the data and information offered by the petitioners, and rejections at this point would be limited to those that are patently unjustified. A common approach to forming this committee would be for the president to appoint an ad hoc committee, whose members are selected from those faculty and administrators most closely related to the occupational area in question. The president should follow this up with a suggestion that the group convene and render the initial judgment to him by some definite date. A second type of committee, particularly useful in larger colleges, is a standing committee consisting of administrators and faculty who are to conduct the initial review requests for all new programs. This formalized committee has a distinct advantage in that such an assignment results in the members allocating a certain portion of their "committee time" for this activity. A possible drawback to the formalized committee is that certain program requests deal with occupational areas in which no member of the committee is familiar. A wise committee would offset this weakness by calling upon a qualified person for assistance in the review of such specialized program requests.

REVIEW OF INITIAL INQUIRY BY THE BOARD OF TRUSTEES

This review can be made by a sub-committee, thereby sparing the entire board this chore each time a program request is received. In this way, only the most reasonable requests come to the attention of the entire board. The initial college screening committee will provide a concise and accurate report of its findings to the board. This report should be prepared so that it provides the board with information dealing with: (a) the source of the request (a local business, a faculty member or group, the town council, etc.); (b) the overall employment possibilities for graduates of the programs (this would be a gross estimation based on the number of businesses and industries that would be interested in employing such graduates); (c) the overall potential student interest in such a program (based on the number of high school graduates in recent years and the fraction of them presently drawn to the college); (d) a rough approximation of new facility requirements, particularly new kinds of shops and laboratories; and (e) the overall additional costs to the college. The terminology within the report should be couched in laymen terms (not educational jargon) that specify that the report is tentative in nature. The purpose of such a report is to provide the board with a basis on which to render a decision.

CONDUCT OF A COMMUNITY-REGIONAL SURVEY

Occasionally, the board members may feel that a more penetrating probe should be made before rendering a final decision, and they should then appoint a group to design and conduct the survey and present a synthesized report to them. The people selected for this important task should be well qualified and should include: (1) a faculty member, (2) a college administrator, (3) one or more lay persons, all of whom are knowledgeable in the occupational area in question, and (4) a researcher competent in the design, conduct, and interpretation of survey studies. The role of the faculty member is to assist in identifying program objectives that are consistent with the overall instructional and educational goals of the college. The administrator provides the know-how concerning the feasibility of obtaining laboratory-classroom facilities and equipment, and in the scheduling of activities contained within the program. One or two lay persons would provide insight to the important aspects of the business-industrial sector. The researcher has the task of obtaining the kinds of information deemed important by this group. The kinds of data and information that should be obtained for any new program feasibility study include: (a) determination of potential job vacancies appropriate for the graduates; (b) identification of potential students (this could include students in local secondary schools, older workers who need to be prepared for new jobs, and women returning to the work force after their children reach school age); (c) identification of the major components of the proposed new program. Rather than resorting to the traditional job analysis approach (Gillie 1970a), a careful assessment of the work modes should be made (Gillie 1970b). These are later translated into broad topic areas which eventually become the basis for establishing the content of the courses. (This is one of the most difficult parts of the survey to design and conduct); (d) arrival at accurate estimates of program costs, preferably stated on a per student basis (example: the two-year program in a given occupational area may have a net cost of X dollars for the college district, Y dollars for the state, Z dollars for the student and his parents, which result in a grand total of X + Y + Z dollars to society); and (e) a tentative cost-benefit analysis. Based on the cost described above, which would consider the income *not* received by the student while in college, a complete cost estimate per student can be computed. This estimate may be computed by comparing the differential incomes expected for the graduates who complete the program with the income of those who go directly to work from high school. Careful preparation of such data can provide governing boards with greater perception and increased appreciation of a proposed new program's real investment worth. The survey designer is intimately involved in the entire survey process from the very first meeting to the final presentation of the results. His overall task is to determine *what* is needed in the way of data and information, *who* it should be obtained from, *how* can it be obtained, synthesis and analysis of the data, and to then produce a final report in a form suitable for the board of trustees' decision-making purposes. He may be given a final task of helping to present the findings in laymen terminology to the board.

How are potential job vacancies in a certain occupational area determined? A common approach taken has been to ask various employers. This has many serious inadequacies. To ask potential employers about future employment possibilities is requesting information which they often don't have. Since the first graduates won't be available for at least two to four years, the employers can not predict the state of their business or industrial concern in terms of the number of certain kinds of middle level workers they will need. Therefore, such information needs to be supplemented by data from other sources. A considerable amount of data and information related to manpower projections is available at the national level (see BLS Bulletin 1606, and *Manpower Report of the President,* 1971, which include national projections for selected occupational areas). Longer term predictions are also available (see *Monthly Labor Review,* 1970). In addition, some of the professional associations conduct frequent surveys of employment in specific areas (Alden 1970). Many states now prepare manpower projections which are largely based on federal data. A typical example is the *Pennsylvania Department of Labor and Industry Bulletin.* The feasibility survey designer should utilize these kinds of sources in extracting information to be used in arriving at employment projections. Coupling this information with the results of direct queries to the major potential employers in the region would provide the best available estimate of potential employment. When preparing a summary of findings related to this aspect of the survey, the tentativeness of the estimates should be clearly indicated. The identification of students is most accurately accomplished in two steps. Initially, a brief opinionnaire may be given to the tenth, eleventh, and twelfth year students in the regional high schools. As an introduction, the student should be provided with a realistic description of the program and concrete portrayals of typical occupational modes of the program which graduates may anticipate. The results from this opinionnaire provide a gross indicator of potential enrollment interests. The information should be coupled with enrollment trends found for similar kinds of programs in the college (if there are such curriculums) and in other two-year colleges in the surrounding region. Considering the fact that high school graduates have a number of post-secondary education options at their disposal, the gross approximations obtained from the above approach probably provide the best estimate available at this point in time. The second phase of student identification is based on student abilities (as evidenced by high school grades, for example), student orientation, program orientation, and cognitive levels required for satisfactory performance in the program. However, these program components are not known to any degree of accuracy until the details of the program are worked out, and this doesn't occur until it is decided that the program is to be offered. This second step in student identification is considered in greater detail in the next chapter.

Identification of the major program components requires an approach that is separate from other aspects of the survey. First, the faculty members of the committee can search for similar programs offered by other two-year colleges so as to get some idea of how others have framed out their programs. Much can be gained from this effort since it is only on rare occasions when a college will be considering a program so new and innovative that no one else in the country has a similar one. Of course, slavish incorporation of another college's entire program should not be encouraged or accepted. On the other hand, locally designed programs should not be so different that they might be in danger of preparing people for non-existent kinds of jobs. Therefore, caution is recommended with regard to these two extremes. The overall content of the program will include those things that relate to the kinds of jobs the graduates are expected to enter. This is where the layman members of the committee can make their major contribution. They can point to those components they think belong in the program, and can also point to other sources where this kind of information can be obtained. The reader may feel this should be a matter for actual program design rather than a part of the feasibility survey, but queries of this kind are valuable at this point because the answers indicate whether the cognitive-physical skills needed are sufficiently different from what is offered in other curriculums to justify the introduction of a new program. This aspect of the survey may show, for example, that an existing curriculum, with perhaps some modification or replacement of several of its occupational courses, would suffice to meet the job requirements. This would also provide some idea about the level of cognitive and physical skills needed by people working in these kinds of jobs. A reasonably accurate awareness of this provides a beginning basis for determining which students would be suitable for the program. (The actual translation of this information into curriculum content becomes an integral part of program design, discussed in the following chapter.)

A part of the survey should gather, synthesize, analyze, and summarize information about program cost. Using federal, state, and regional employment data (see Lerner 1970, for example), an estimate of expected beginning salaries can be made, and data on the cost of the program, including actual dollar outlays at the federal, state, local, and personal levels, plus estimated "deprived incomes" during the time the student was in attendance can be gathered. Combining the costs and the income differentiation (also an estimate) would provide a cost-benefit statement of the program on both the individual student and overall program basis. Several approaches to cost-benefit analysis have been devised (see Kaufman, Hu, Lee, and Stromsdorfer, 1969).

After all the above have been done, the most important part of the feasibility study lies ahead: the synthesization and interpretation of the findings. Although the temptation always exists to present findings and conclusions in language heavily couched in statistical and research-type jargon, this tends to destroy the decision-making usefulness of the entire effort. Most members of boards of trustees are not acquainted with such jargon, and do not read the literature in higher education (Hartnett 1969), therefore it is vital that the final report be made available in a form somewhat consistent with the reading level of intelligent laymen.

The researcher can prepare the first report in a traditional way where he states the problem, describes what was known at the onset and the methods used to seek information, and presents the results. Then, and most important in terms of utilizing the fruits of the entire effort, the researcher should write a second report which is in everyday language, carefully pointing out the findings in a simple and concise manner. The conclusions should present to the board straight-forward recommendations for action and methods by which such action can be taken. This laymen's report could be simply prefaced with a statement that the statistical-research backup for the statements in the report they have before them is available in the other report. The research report would, of course, be drawn upon if and when someone should challenge any of the findings presented in the laymen's report. Both should be accepted by the feasibility survey committee and submitted to the president.

REPORTING OF SURVEY RESULTS TO THE BOARD OF TRUSTEES

This is the feedback aspect of the feasibility study and is the climax of the whole effort. Who should officially present this report falls within the rubric of the president's responsibilities, though it would be hoped that he would have the feasibility committee chairman and the researcher on hand at the meeting to provide whatever details the board might require. In large colleges it is likely that the president would designate the task of reporting the results to a dean or a member of the committee. The chairman of the committee usually serves as spokesman for the group and would rely on other members for support. The researcher should always be available for a dispassionate presentation or explanation of findings questioned by the president or the board.

Much can be said in favor of oral presentations of feasibility study results. Board members often prefer predigested information (the president and feasibility study committee serving as the digestive organs) on matters of this type. The recommendations of the president are often of greater interest to the board members than the details leading to the recommendation. Several investigators of the characteristics of trustees have implied this in their writings (Rauh 1969; Hartnett 1969). A wise administrator would map out his strategy accordingly.

THE DECISION

Eventually, the board of trustees will render a decision, hopefully based on intelligent consideration of the information presented to them under the auspices of the president. The arrival of the decision signals the dissolution of the feasibility study committee, with official acknowledgement of and appreciation for their efforts. If the decision is a negative one, then the study reports are filed away for possible future use. When a positive decision has been made by the Board, then a new mechanism needs to be activated—the program committee, who will be charged with the responsibility of designing the curriculum.

Summary

The chapter is subdivided into two major segments. The first deals with the source of pressures for starting new programs, and the second part examines approaches to evaluating requests for new programs. It is stated that the major groups that seek to exert pressure on a college to start new programs include citizen-civic-professional labor groups at the local, state, and federal levels, sources from within the local, state, and federal governments, and elements from within the professional staff of the college itself.

Considering the many potential sources, the likelihood of groups seeking such consideration are great, particularly in large urban centers. Therefore, systematic techniques for evaluation of these requests are in order. A suggested approach to determining whether or not a new program should be offered is described, which incorporates a sequence of activities including an initial inquiry by college authorities, a review of the results of that inquiry by the board of trustees, authorization by the governance board of a community-regional survey, and finally, the report of the survey findings to the board of trustees. Based upon the report, the board of trustees then makes the final decision as to whether or not the requested program should be inaugurated by the college.

REFERENCES

Alden, J. D. *Prospects of Engineering and Technology Graduates.* New York: Engineering Manpower Commission of Engineers Joint Council, 1970.

Department of Labor and Industry. *1960 Census and 1970, 1975 Projected Total Employment: By occupation, by residence, by state, by major areas and counties in major areas, and selected smaller areas.* Harrisburg, Pa.: Commonwealth of Pennsylvania, 1969.

Gillie, A. C. *Essays: Occupational Education in the Two-Year College.* University Park, Pa.: Department of Vocational Education, Pennsylvania State University, 1970a.

———. *Geographic-Job Mobility of The Pennsylvania State University Two-Year Technician Graduate.* University Park, Pa.: Department of Vocational Education, Pennsylvania State University, 1970b.

Hartnett, R. T. *College and University Trustees: Their Backgrounds, Roles and Educational Attitudes.* Princeton, N.J.: Educational Testing Service, 1969.

Kaufman, J. J.; Hu, T.; Lee, M. L.; and Stromsdorfer, E. W. *A Cost-Effectiveness Study of Vocational Education.* University Park, Pa.: Institute for Research on Human Resources, Pennsylvania State University, 1969.

Lerner, W. *Statistical Abstract of the United States 1970* (91st edition). Washington, D.C.: U.S. Bureau of the Census, 1970.

McNamara, J. F. and Franchak, S. J. *Planning Vocational Education Programs in Pennsylvania.* Harrisburg, Pa.: Bureau of Educational Research, Pennsylvania Department of Education, 1970.

Manpower Report of the President. Washington, D.C.: U.S. Department of Labor, 1971.

Perkins, C. D. *Reports on the Implementation of the Vocational Education Amendments of 1968.* Washington, D.C.: U.S. Government Printing Office, 1971.

Public Law No. 751, 89th Congress (Allied Health Professions; Personnel Training Act of 1966).

Public Law No. 516, 91st Congress (Environmental Education Act).

Rauh, A. "The College Trustee—Past, Present, and Future." *The Journal of Higher Education* Volume XI, No. 6. Columbus, Ohio: Ohio State University Press, 1969.

"The U. S. Economy in 1980: A Preview of BLS Projections." *Monthly Labor Review.* Washington, D.C.: U.S. Department of Labor, April 1970.

Udell, G. G. *Laws Relating to Vocational Education and Agricultural Extension Work.* Washington, D.C.: U.S. Government Printing Office, 1971.

U. S. Department of Labor (Bureau of Labor Statistics). *Tomorrow's Manpower Needs* Volume 1: Developing Area Manpower Projections. Bulletin # 1606, Washington, D.C.: U.S. Printing Office, 1969.

Chapter 7 SOURCES OF EDUCATION AND TRAINING

Middle level workers are traditionally trained in both educational and business-industrial settings. The basic rationale and characteristics of each type of training are examined in this chapter.

Training on-the-Job

Many middle level workers are trained outside the framework of formal educational institutions. In some occupational areas, especially in the newly emerging types of occupations, workers are trained outside of school. This agrees with the observation that the curricula of educational institutions sometimes lag behind progress in technology and other facets of the business-industrial community. In some cases, the lag is associated with strong resistance to certain curriculum changes by certain controlling elements within the educational institutions (faculty, administration, etc.). If a new type of training is needed by the business-industrial community, on-the-job training programs are likely to be established. Such programs are generally developed after failure of the educational institution to address itself to that need. This has recently resulted in the emergence of several contract-learning companies on the educational scene.

The business-industrial public service community has consistently shown more flexibility than the public education institutions in devising training programs to prepare people for emerging occupations. This has been true for occupations at levels ranging from semi-skilled to professional. Such a statement is not meant to be an indictment against public institutions as it is generally impossible for public educational institutions to adjust their curricula to accommodate an emerging occupation at the middle worker level until it is obvious that a new type of middle level occupation is in fact needed. Even after approval is given by the governing board, a further delay often occurs due to the time required for designing the curriculum, gathering of appropriate faculty and staff, and the enrollment of students. Because of these bureaucratic delays, it is expected that the business-industrial community will continue to prepare a large segment of newly emerging occupations until the educational institutions can respond to these needs.

One problem brought about by responding too rapidly to industrial-business job training needs is mistraining and over-training. The public two-year colleges must guard themselves against this hazard by taking time to analyze reported needs and demands made upon them. The role of the school is perhaps best seen as providing a foundational training that would be supplemented or topped off by specific training after the student has accepted an actual job (as described later in the chapter). Some of the specific training tasks can be taken on by the business-industrial community for those who have obtained a good foundational training in that occupational area. A major advantage of this approach is that it provides an easier vehicle for job mobility, both horizontally and vertically. If all jobs were perfectly ascertained and filled at the moment they became vacant, the opportunity for advancement or job change would be drastically reduced, resulting in a more static occupational force (Duncan and Blau, 1964). Further crystallization of the work force at the middle levels would create added job dissatisfaction problems. Fortunately, the possibility of this occurring in the American occupational structure is remote as long as technology and other elements in the business world continue to grow and change.

The business-industrial public service community has demonstrated remarkable adaptability in making adjustments to their worker shortage situations, so that their available worker pools suffice for the tasks that need to be done. This doesn't happen in an accidental or haphazard manner. The adjustments frequently made include (Hooper 1969): (a) training selected employees for the new paraprofessional duties; (b) changing specifications of the job; and (c) subdividing the particular job into several categories that can be more easily managed by people already in their employ.

By having such flexibility business-industrial organizations accrue several advantages: (1) They can better adjust to changes brought about by advances in technology, demands made of them by the community at large and by other industrial conditions. (2) The job mobility paths remain open for a substantial number of workers who are expected to transfer out of one job into another (PL 90-576). Thus, flexibility of this kind provides occupational "escape hatches" for those who are either dissatisfied with their present job or are seeking occupational advancement. (3) Training on the job, especially when it is a topping-off process for persons who have a sound foundation in that occupational area, insures greater relevance of the training to what is needed. Of course, there is also the hazard that such training can become strictly a tool of industry, with relatively little concern for the individual worker, but safeguards against this danger can be provided. Educational institutions require at least several years to formulate a program, and several more years to graduate the first group of students from it, which already places them at least four years behind the time the program was inaugurated. Industry often cannot wait that long and must train people for specific tasks on the job or send them to a skill center for such specific training. (4) A fourth advantage for individual organizations which adjust to their own unique worker problems and shortages is that on-the-job training tends to minimize the penalty an individual suffers if he decides he is in the wrong job. This is particularly true for those workers who have a foundational preparation in the same work area, since the topping-off skills needed for another position within that occupational area would not take long to acquire. Naturally, this doesn't help those who elect to leave their occupational area completely. Such changeovers are usually costly in both time and money, and it is doubtful if a curriculum model could be devised to overcome this difficulty.

Another phase of on-the-job training is sponsored by the Department of Defense. It is called the *transition program* and is aimed at returning veterans (Manpower Report of the President, 1971). Its objective is to provide career development for returning military personnel who have academic deficiencies (one out of five returning veterans fails to qualify for civilian employment). The transition program provides counseling, on-the-job training, and employment assistance. Four million dollars in Manpower Development and Training Act (PL 87-415) funds were spent in 1970 for 11,800 servicemen. Much of this was used in job training by private employers, including more than fifty large firms and one thousand smaller firms. Job training has been provided in occupational areas such as law enforcement, water pollution control, carpentry, bricklaying, and stone masonry. Since its beginnning, about 125,000 servicemen have been trained and 800,000 of them have been counseled under the auspices of this program. Although this effort is limited in scope and effectiveness (Manpower Report of the President 1971), it is an illustration of one way on-the-job training is sponsored.

The Manpower Development and Training Act programs are also a source of funding for both institutional and on-the-job training. In 1970, they provided 91,000 people with on-the-job training. Over 38,000 of this group were in middle level type jobs (professional, technical, managerial; clerical and sales; service; farming, fishing, and forestry). This illustrates how the federal government is involved with on-the-job training (Manpower Report of the President, 1971).

Secondary School Preparation

Although in the past not many middle level workers were prepared in the secondary schools, much of vocational education has traditionally been going on at that level. That occupational education should continue to be an important function of the secondary schools in the future is indicated by the school retention rates. In 1960, seventy-five percent of the students who entered fifth grade completed high school (Lerner 1970). This indicates (1) twenty-five percent of the students who enter fifth grade never graduate from high school and therefore should be prepared for an occupation in the secondary schools; (2) only half or less of the seventy-five percent who do complete high school will go on to a post-secondary institution. Specifically, thirty-four percent of the students who enrolled in the fifth grade in 1960 went on to enroll in college in 1969 (Lerner). The sixty-six percent of those enrolling in the fifth grade who do not go on to a post-secondary institution are in need of occupational preparation in high school.

About 850,000 youngsters drop out of high school each year. These persons are in the sixteen- to seventeen-year-old age group, which had an average unemployment rate of 16.9 percent in 1971 (BLS 1972). The National Advisory Council on Vocational Education has recommended that special effort be made in the secondary schools to occupationally prepare potential dropouts *(Second Report 1969)*, thus reducing the amount of money needed for unemployment and welfare programs.

Turning to the secondary school situation as a whole, there were about 13.3 million youngsters enrolled in 1971, of which only 5.5 million were in vocational education programs (DVTE 1972 estimates). If the present rate of college enrollment continues (about one-half of high school graduates), then seven to eight million high school students should be in occupational programs. Combined with the projected enrollment in occupational education programs in the two-year colleges, the number of students who would be served by programs in occupational education equals eighty percent of the total. This is based on the fact that about twenty percent of the population is the estimated maximum needed for entry into the professions (DVTE 1972 estimates).

In the face of the youth unemployment and job preparation crises is a philosophic debate relating to where vocational education should be provided. The stronger supporters of occupational education feel non-college bound youngsters should not leave high school until they are prepared to enter an occupation. On the other side of this philosophic fence are those who say that the entire high school experience should consist of general education and should serve as a type of experience which broadens the intellectual horizons of all youngsters. This latter group feels that the preparation for work should be delayed until the person is actually on the job or has enrolled in a two-year college or some other type of post-secondary institution. The manner in which occupational education is provided ought to be determined by the individuals' capabilities and interests, as well as the kinds of occupations needed. No single kind of educational institution or mechanism is likely to emerge as the sole vehicle for the preparation of people for the world of work. Those youngsters who do not graduate from high school, along with those who terminate their education with high school graduation, are clearly in need of vocational education during their secondary school years.

It appears highly unlikely that the secondary schools will be a major source of middle level worker training. At the moment, the major thrust in secondary school vocational education deals with skill level occupations rather than with middle level jobs (DVTE 1971), and unless there is a national reduction in the years of education offered to the population in general, secondary schools will become increasingly less involved with the preparation of middle level occupations.

At the present, students are being prepared for middle level occupations in several kinds of institutions. The first is the private type, and the second (usually much larger than the first) is the public-supported variety. The secondary schools that have some involvement with middle level occupational training are of several kinds: (1) the comprehensive high school; (2) the vocational high school; (3) the combination of the academic high school and area vocational school; and (4) the area vocational school.

Preparation in the Area Vocational School

What is the nature of this institution? First, its most important impetus was derived through the Vocational Education Act of 1963 (PL 88-210) and the Vocational Education Amendments of 1968 (PL 90-576). These acts allow for several kinds of schools to be categorized as area vocational schools if they meet certain requirements. These include specialized high schools, high schools with a department which offers programs in at least five occupational fields, a technical or vocational school, and a two-year college or university with a division which offers programs in at least five occupational fields. This demonstrates that area vocational schools, at least from the federal funding point of view, can offer programs at the secondary and/or post-secondary level. This has created some confusion. The Vocational Education Amendments of 1968 provided that at least fifteen percent of its funds be used for students who have either graduated from or left high school. It also provides allocations for special and disadvantaged students, which are largely utilized by two-year colleges. Many two-year colleges, because they offer vocational programs in five or more occupational areas, qualify for and accept funding as area vocational schools, but identify themselves as community colleges and not as area vocational schools (Perkins 1971). A number of senior colleges and universities do the same. In these cases, the general public and even the majority of their faculty and administrators do not view these institutions as area vocational schools (see Table 7-1).

The most visible type of area vocational schools are those institutions called area vocational technical schools, technical education centers, or board of cooperative educational service centers (the name varies from state to state). Their first major characteristic is their physical and academic separation from other kinds of educational efforts. This is educational separatism, which has been criticized by Dewey and others as long ago as the turn of the century (Curti 1935) and is still considered undesirable by some educators (Kerr 1970). But the philosophic reasons for the continued thrust toward separatism are intricately intertwined with the long-standing dissatisfaction of many vocational educators with the way academic and general educators have viewed and conducted occupational programs in the past (Venn 1964). Evidence of the strength of this movement is the number of area vocational schools in operation which is (as defined by PL 90-576) 1,889

TABLE 7-1

Distribution of Area Vocational Schools

State	Total AVS[a]	Sec. Level	Post-Sec. Level	PS Sec.[b]	Two-Year AVS[c]
Alabama	50	23	27	0	1
Alaska	9	6	2	0	2
Arizona	14	3	11	0	10
Arkansas	19	3	16	0	3
California	105	13	102	0	87
Colorado	13	13	13	13	5
Connecticut	19	5	14	0	4
Delaware	5	3	2	0	1
District of Columbia	6	4	2	1	0
Florida	31	14	17	14	10
Georgia	42	18	24	0	1
Hawaii	16	10	6	0	6
Idaho	6	6	0	0	2
Illinois	47	22	25	0	23
Indiana	30	20	10	0	1
Iowa	25	0	25	0	21
Kansas	14	14	14	14	1
Kentucky	57	44	13	0	0
Louisiana	32	23	32	23	0
Maine	21	13	9	1	3
Maryland	81	72	9	0	7
Massachusetts	66	54	27	9	9
Michigan	61	28	41	8	26
Minnesota	32	1	32	1	3
Mississippi	56	30	26	0	11
Missouri	55	45	28	18	7
Montana	5	5	5	5	0
Nebraska	10	2	8	0	2
Nevada	6	3	5	2	1
New Hampshire	24	15	9	0	1
New Jersey	35	35	17	17	0
New Mexico	8	6	8	6	2
New York	70	70	0	0	0
North Carolina	52	0	52	0	52
North Dakota	6	3	4	1	4
Ohio	126	105	21	0	15
Oklahoma	17	17	17	17	0
Oregon	18	4	14	0	13
Pennsylvania	62	62	27	27	1
Rhode Island	8	7	1	0	0
South Carolina	45	30	15	0	11
South Dakota	6	5	6	5	0
Tennessee	31	5	30	4	6
Texas	127	87	40	2	32
Utah	12	8	11	7	5
Vermont	15	15	0	0	0
Virginia	161	140	20	0	16
Washington	31	9	28	6	20
West Virginia	37	30	27	20	0
Wisconsin	37	37	37	0	10
Wyoming	7	4	7	4	7
American Samda	1	0	1	0	1
Guam	1	1	1	1	0
Canal Zone	0	0	0	0	0
Puerto Rico	16	16	0	0	0
Trust Territories	1	1	1	1	0
Virgin Islands	2	2	0	2	0
Totals	1,889	506	931	227	443

Notes: (a) Totals in Column 1 taken from *Directory AVS: Fiscal Year 1972* (USOE-mimeograph).
(b) Totals extracted from the same source.
(c) Schools identified as AVS in *Directory AVS: Fiscal Year 1972* (op. cit.) and also classified as a two-year college in *Directory: American Association of Junior Colleges.*

(Directory Area Vocational Education Schools: Fiscal 1972). Table 1 lists them by state with their classifications (secondary and post-secondary).

A second characteristic of area vocational schools is that those which offer vocational preparation programs to students in grades 10 through 12 emphasize occupations in the trades and crafts. Although in most states the programs are concentrated at academic levels compatible with the maturity and abilities of secondary school students, there are signs which indicate that they are moving toward offering programs for post-secondary type students, particularly on a part-time and evening basis.

A third characteristic, which also relates to curriculum, deals with the general education component of the program, which accounts for about half of the AVTS secondary level programs. In many cases, it is provided at the home high school from which the student was sent. General eduation is offered on a daily basis in many places where the AVTS is located close to the high schools they serve. In other cases, where the students must travel considerable distances between their home high schools and the AVTS, general education is offered in the home high school on certain days while the vocational courses are offered in the AVTS on the other days. Some of the area vocational technical schools offer the general education component within their own facilities. In most cases, regardless of the mode adopted, there is a clear separation of general and vocational education.

A fourth characteristic of area vocational technical schools is the latent potential they possess for the preparation of middle level workers. If legal mechanisms can be found whereby they can be disassociated from secondary schools and brought within the rubric of a new educational configuration consisting of grades eleven through fourteen (including the two-year colleges), they would become the most viable instruments for occupational education. Such an institution might be called a "universal college" (see Chapter 15).

In summary, the area vocational school at this time is sort of a splinter movement off the mainstream of secondary education. However, it has tremendous potential, particularly when coupled with the two-year colleges in a new configuration, to make occupational education both possible and attractive to eighty percent of the secondary students and to the even greater number of adults who are in need of retraining, and upgrading, or updating their occupational skills.

Post-Secondary School Preparation

Most middle level training in educational institutions occurs in post-secondary kinds of schools, but a great range of diversity is found in the ways the programs are designed and conducted. One common characteristic found among many middle level occupational curriculums is that graduates are awarded the associate degree. The post-secondary institutions in which most of the middle level associate degree programs are conducted can be identified by several broad generic types (Kerr 1970; Belitsky 1970; Harper 1972): (1) the public and private community junior colleges; (2) proprietary schools; and (3) senior colleges and universities. Among these three, the most visible thrust emerges from the public two-year colleges and is expected to increase further. The enrollment in two-year colleges was about 2.7 million students in just over eleven hundred institutions in 1971 (Harper 1972). Seventy-six percent of the 206,753 associate degrees awarded in 1969-70 by 1,107 of 1,296 higher education institutions were conferred by the public two-year colleges. About 124,000 associate degree awards were made in middle level occupational programs, divided among business (37 percent), engineering (23 percent), and health service (22 percent) (Hooper 1971). About half of the beginning community college freshmen complete a two-year program in two years, with some variation by program and college (Harper). Thirty-eight percent of the two-year degrees were occupationally oriented, resulting in 79,000 vocational-type associate degrees awarded in 1969-70 (Hooper). As the need for middle level workers becomes greater, this output should greatly expand (Manpower Report of the President, 1971).

While the two-year colleges experience continued growth, they are drifting toward a crossroad in their evolution. The equalitarian trend in education, where each individual is provided with the chance to obtain as much schooling as he can benefit from, may force many community colleges to come to the realization that for the majority of their clientele, this means more occupationally-oriented courses with a corresponding reduction in the kinds of academic work that senior colleges and universities traditionally offer. Until the full "switch-over" from academic to occupational programs is made, enrollment increases may level off. This is indicated in the rate of growth of two-year colleges in the past couple of years (Harper 1972). The increase in public financial demands is prompting state legislators and county and local political leaders to question priorities and the benefits derived from expenditures. Accountability in higher education is being bantered about in earnest. The indications are that this will become an integral factor in determining the amount of funding allocated to all institutions in higher education (McConnell 1971; Silverman 1971; Peterson 1971). Because the universities have had public attention drawn to them by their phenomenal budget increases and student agitation, they have been the first to come under this type of scrutiny, and many of them have fared rather badly. The community junior colleges are being subjected to the same treatment, especially in those states where a portion of their support is derived from direct real estate taxes. They will be increasingly confronted with the emerging duality of purposes between themselves and the area vocational technical schools. In some instances, the area vocational schools are encountering considerable difficulties in recruiting students. Although many of them were originally established to serve the vocational needs and interests of secondary school youngsters only, their facilities and potential capacity can easily accommodate post-secondary programs. The fusion of community colleges and vocational schools into a "universal colleges" is both logical and practical, but unfortunately, such a proposal is not attractive to educators in either. However, as the demand for the tax dollar continues to be more competitive, such fusions may be forced by the boards of governance. The equalitarian thrust in education would be enhanced by such mergers in that greater opportunities for the preparation of middle level occupations would be more readily available.

The Spectrum of Institutions Granting Post-Secondary Associate Degrees

A wide spectrum of institutions provide associate degree training for middle level workers. Of 1,296 institutions of higher education that offer associate degrees, 808 are under public control and 488 are private (Hooper 1971; Wade 1971). Also, 446 of the total (196 public and 255 private) are four-year institutions (93 universities and 353 other senior colleges). Furthermore, there are many technical schools and other institutions offering programs for middle level occupations that are not eligible for listing in the higher education directory (OE-5000-71) and are therefore excluded in these figures (many of them are private vocational schools and are examined in Chapter 13). The impact of different types of institutions can be observed by comparing the number of associate degrees, diplomas, and other awards granted by them (Hooper 1971). First, about 207,000 associate degrees were awarded, of which 26,000 were given by universities and the remainder by two-year institutions. Comparing public and private schools, 171,000 associate degrees were granted by public colleges that year. In occupational programs two or more years in length, senior colleges and universities graduated 21,000 of the total 108,000 and 70,000 of the total completed their programs in public colleges. These statistics indicate that although the community colleges provide the major thrust in this area, there are other institutions involved in the effort and we shall look at their characteristics briefly.

The variety of schools in the Commonwealth of Pennsylvania which grant associate degrees is a microcosm of the kinds of colleges that offer middle level occupational programs nationally. An examination of the Pennsylvania spectrum serves to reveal the diverse middle level occupational program possibilities found in various sections of the country. In June 1970, about 8,000 associate degrees were granted by 43 institutions, providing an average of 186 graduates per school (Hummel 1971). With the exception of the state university, typical middle level occupational training colleges have small enrollments. There are six generic types of associate degree granting institutions in Pennsylvania (Gillie 1970), including (a) public community colleges; (b) private junior colleges; (c) commonwealth campuses of The Pennsylvania State University; (d) private colleges and universities; (e) proprietary schools; and (f) private state aided institutions.

Taking an overall view of the institutions, it is found that the number of schools offering associate degree occupational programs is expected to continue increasing because new community colleges are still emerging in the state, and a substantial number of proprietary schools are being authorized each year to grant associate degrees. More than seventy will have been authorized to do so by 1973. No substantial growth in associate degree granting programs by universities, other senior colleges, and private two-year colleges is expected. About half of the associate degree candidates in the community colleges and private two-year colleges are in middle level occupational programs, while all of the university and proprietary school graduates are in that category. The Pennsylvania State University, with its nineteen campuses located throughout the state, also serves a two-year (nonvocational) function in that a large number of preprofessional students complete the first two years of their baccalaureate programs there and then transfer to the main University Park campus for their junior year. The preparation of middle level occupational workers is not the major focus of the commonwealth campuses of PSU whereas the proprietary schools focus exclusively upon occupational-type programs.

Another indicator of institutional and program diversity is reflected in the fact that eight types of associate degrees are offered by various Pennsylvania institutions: (1) Associate in Applied Arts (AAA); (2) Associate in Applied Science (AAS); (3) Associate in Arts (AA); (4) Associate in Science (AS); (5) Associate Science Technology (AST); (6) Associate Science in Business (ASB); (7) Associate Degree in Specialized Curriculum (AD); (8) Associate in Career Studies (ACS).

There is even greater diversity in post-secondary occupational programs that lead to diplomas and certificates (not associate degrees), many of which are offered by proprietary institutions. There are 122 licensed private business schools and 126 private trade schools (Bureau of Private Schools and Veterans Education, Pennsylvania Department of Education 1972). Therefore, the private sector is providing a considerable input to the post-secondary occupational education effort in the commonwealth.

Another major area of difference among these types of schools is the way in which they are controlled and financed. The public community colleges obtain their financial support in a manner unlike any other higher educational institution in the Commonwealth. Support for physical facilities is obtained on a matching basis between the State Department of Education and the community college district (which is a voluntary formation of school districts in a given region). Support for programs (other than facilities) is obtained from the student, the community college district, and the state (Pennsylvania Community College Act of 1963, Act 484), with each element contributing about one-third of the cost. Local taxation, based upon real estate assessment, is the means of obtaining local funding. Tuition (September 1970) averaged $350 per academic year for Pennsylvania residents or $700 for the entire two-year program.

Eighteen of the commonwealth campuses of The Pennsylvania State University receive their support from within the overall budget of the university, with no support from direct local taxation. The university receives about forty percent of its operating funds by state appropriations, forty percent from research and other contracts, and twenty percent from student tuition. Tuition at the commonwealth campuses is higher than at the community colleges (about $900 per academic year for in-state residents, or $1,800 for the entire two-year program).

There are thirteen private junior colleges, seven of which are independent, nonprofit, three of which are Roman Catholic, and three of which are under other religious affiliation (Church of Christ, Wesleyan, and Baptist). Tuition is considerably higher in these colleges than in the public community colleges. There is one exception which has a very low tuition of $320 per year, but others range from $960 to $1,350 per year. The average tuition was found to be $1,340 per academic year or $2,680 for the entire two-year program.

The proprietary schools, like most of the private junior colleges, rely almost entirely upon student tuition and fees for financial support. The greatest number of post-secondary institutions offering programs in occupational education are found in this group. The licensed proprietary schools in Pennsylvania are generally small in enrollment. In 1967, the 248 licensed institutions' total enrollment was 22,700 full-time students, an average of about 92 students per school. This is considerably smaller than in the other kinds of institutions. About 8,550 graduated from business-type proprietary schools in 1967, 1,706 of which were classified as being in the two-year category. Of the 6,035 proprietary trade school graduates that year, 2,973 were in the two-year category (Pennsylvania Department of Education, 1970). Tuition in these schools is higher than in the public institutions but generally lower than in the private junior colleges. Consider the cost per hour of instruction for associate degree programs (Pennsylvania Department of Education, 1971): (a) Business schools average 82.5 cents per hour of instruction or $1,485 for an 1,800 hour program; (b) trade and technical schools average $1.20 per hour of instruction or $2,160 for an 1,800 hour program; (c) computer schools average $2.00 per hour of instruction. An 1,800 hour program has a total cost of $3,600; (d) aeronautics schools average $1.20 per hour of instruction, and a 2,200 hour program costs $2,640.

What about the students in these institutions? In the private-independent junior colleges a substantial proportion of students come from fairly affluent socio-economic backgrounds and most are residential students. The SAT is used in admissions procedures in most cases, although there is a recent trend toward replacing it with the ACT. The average incoming student is usually average to a little below average in terms of high school graduation-class standing and test scores. Many of these students originate from homes outside the commonwealth, and in some of these schools sixty percent or more of the students are out-of-state residents. Some of these institutions are coeducational while others are for female students only. About sixty percent of the private junior college students are women. The average full-time student is slightly less than eighteen years of age upon entry and has gone directly from high school to college with no interruptions.

The students found at the commonwealth campuses of The Pennsylvania State University are slightly different in characteristics. Admissions tend to be more selective than in the other three kinds of institutions, with quotas established for each curriculum. Admission requirements are uniform throughout the university system and applicants are selected from those who have demonstrated adequate preparation for university work (based on SAT results and high school performance). Admission is offered first to those with the highest qualifications. Applicants with less impressive academic credentials are advised of associate degree occupational programs. The socio-economic background of the typical student is in the middle range (Lindsay 1970). Most of the students come from Pennsylvania, and there are more males than females (3,500 males to 300 females) in associate degree programs and in September, 1970, there was a ratio of about 2:1 (6,800 males to 3,500 females) in the commonwealth campuses as a whole. The associate degree curriculums are largely in male-type occupations, although several associate degree curricula recently introduced should reduce the male-female student ratio. Twenty-one percent of the associate degree candidates are over twenty-one years of age (Gillie 1971), which indicates some interruption in their education between high school graduation and college entry.

The admission requirements of community colleges are more liberal than those of the Pennsylvania State University, as liberal as those of the private junior colleges, and less liberal than those of the proprietary schools. High school graduates and other adults who are considered able to profit from the offerings are generally accepted. Most use ACT scores as an aid in program placement rather than for screening purposes (Sheppard 1970). Admission into specific curricula is based on space availability as well as on previous scholastic records and indicated aptitudes. About thirty-five percent of community college students are female. The majority of the applicants come from the region in which the school is located, and live at home while attending school. Some of the entering students have experienced interruptions in their education between high school and college, and come from families in the lower to middle class sector of the socio-economic spectrum.

Admission requirements for proprietary schools are more pragmatic than those found in the other kinds of institutions. A high school diploma or its equivalent is required for entrance into the associate degree programs. In other curricula, applicants are accepted on the basis of their predicted chances of completing the program and becoming a successful worker in that chosen field. This is a characteristic of admissions for proprietary schools throughout the country (Belitsky 1970). Many of these schools are geared to drop and add curricula much more quickly than the public institutions. The potential of the proprietary institutions to initiate and alter middle level occupational programs to meet changes in societal demands is one of their strongest assets.

A New Institutional Model for Preparing Middle Level Workers

The first step in preparing a new institutional model is the consideration of manpower needs. As explained in Chapter 2, this need is determined by studying past trends in the labor market and attempting to make an educated guess as to what the state of the national economy will be in the years ahead. Because of the great number of variables involved, and the frequency with which they are subject to change, prediction of occupational needs is a hazardous venture, particularly when making projections for a five- or ten-year period. However, the probability of making accurate predictions as to the number of workers needed in certain job groups is increased when the groups examined are broadened to encompass broader occupational groups or clusters. For example, the projections become more accurate when we look into the nation's work structure and predict future jobs that relate to such broad areas as health, government jobs, service-related jobs, business-commercial-related jobs, industrial-manufacturing jobs, and agricultural jobs. Present day predictions of tomorrow's job market should be limited to general occupational clusters (which reinforces the idea that the foundation of all vocational programs should be broad enough to encompass the entire group of jobs contained within one of these clusters). The model proposed here is based upon that conviction.

Let us consider the individual's basic needs that are directly related to the education and training of middle level workers. First, suitable jobs must be found for those in search of work. Matching the individual to an existing job is of secondary importance. Secondly, employment is important both as a source of income and also as a basis for achieving self-wants and social status. Studies reveal that the status element is just as important as income to the individual (Cross 1968). A third need is to keep open the opportunity to increase one's earnings, improve one's employment status, and to be able to adapt to the changes going on in the employment environment. No job or group of jobs should be "dead-end." Fourthly, an individual needs a maximum number of options and alternatives in terms of immediate employment and future advancement. Occupational programs should be designed to accommodate this. A fifth need is that every student, in order to make intelligent vocational decisions, should learn about the world of work. This can be the major focus of the social science part of every occupational program and should be granted the same prestige and importance as is traditionally given to courses in English and the humanities.

A further case for supporting a new institutional model for preparing middle level workers is the fact that several studies (Alden 1970; Gillie 1971) have found that many associate degree graduates do not go into full-time employment in the field of their preparation upon graduation. Thus, we need to adjust the occupational curricula so that graduates are better prepared for such eventualities.

In addition to these needs, another reason for establishing the new model is the trend toward more cognitive jobs and increased frequency in job changing (Manpower Report of the President, 1971). The most significant change in the nation's occupational structure has been a shift toward white collar jobs (Lerner 1970), particularly in human services occupations (Manpower Report of the President, 1971). Furthermore, the expectation is that the average twenty-year old in the work force today will change jobs four to six times during his working life (PL 90-576). These factors have obvious critical implications for adults in vocational education. In the new model perhaps the main effort should be to provide a broad type of occupational education up to the point where the student no longer benefits from that type of instruction, at which time he would be placed in a job. After accepting a particular job, the specific skills required would be indicated by the employer, and the student would then receive his training at a skill center associated with this model. Therefore, the last part of an individual's occupational program would be a *topping-off* process and would serve to meet immediate skill needs of the graduate. This approach simultaneously provides the student with a solid foundation in a middle level occupational area, and training for a specific job in that occupational group. An added advantage is that workers with good basic preparation can be referred back to the skill center for acquisition of additional skills later on. This approach meets the five personal occupational needs stated earlier.

In order to determine who ought to be eligible for this kind of occupational education, we need to remember that the national rate for college entry is about thirty-five percent of those who enter the fifth grade (Lerner 1970) and it is expected that the college entry rate may approach fifty percent of high school graduates by the year 1980. Indications are, based on previous years, that not more than thirty percent of college freshmen (fifteen percent of those who enter the fifth grade) will end up with a bachelor's degree (Lerner 1970). Therefore, we can assume that all other persons are in need of some kind of occupational education. This group includes both younger and older elements in our population. The younger group would consist of: (a) high school dropouts (presently about twenty percent of students who enter high school); (b) high school graduates who are not expected to go beyond high school immediately after graduation (fifty percent of high school graduates, which is another forty percent of these students that enter high school). The high school dropouts and graduates who don't go on to college make up sixty percent of the students that enter high school (Lerner 1970); and (c) about seventy percent of entering college freshmen (which is another thirty-five percent of all the high school graduates). The older groups that would benefit from the proposed occupational education model would include persons in need of upgrading or updating their skills, and/or complete retraining for new jobs. With a labor force of more than eighty million (Manpower Report of the President, 1971) the need for these kinds of occupational services is great. Vocational education can be made to meet the needs

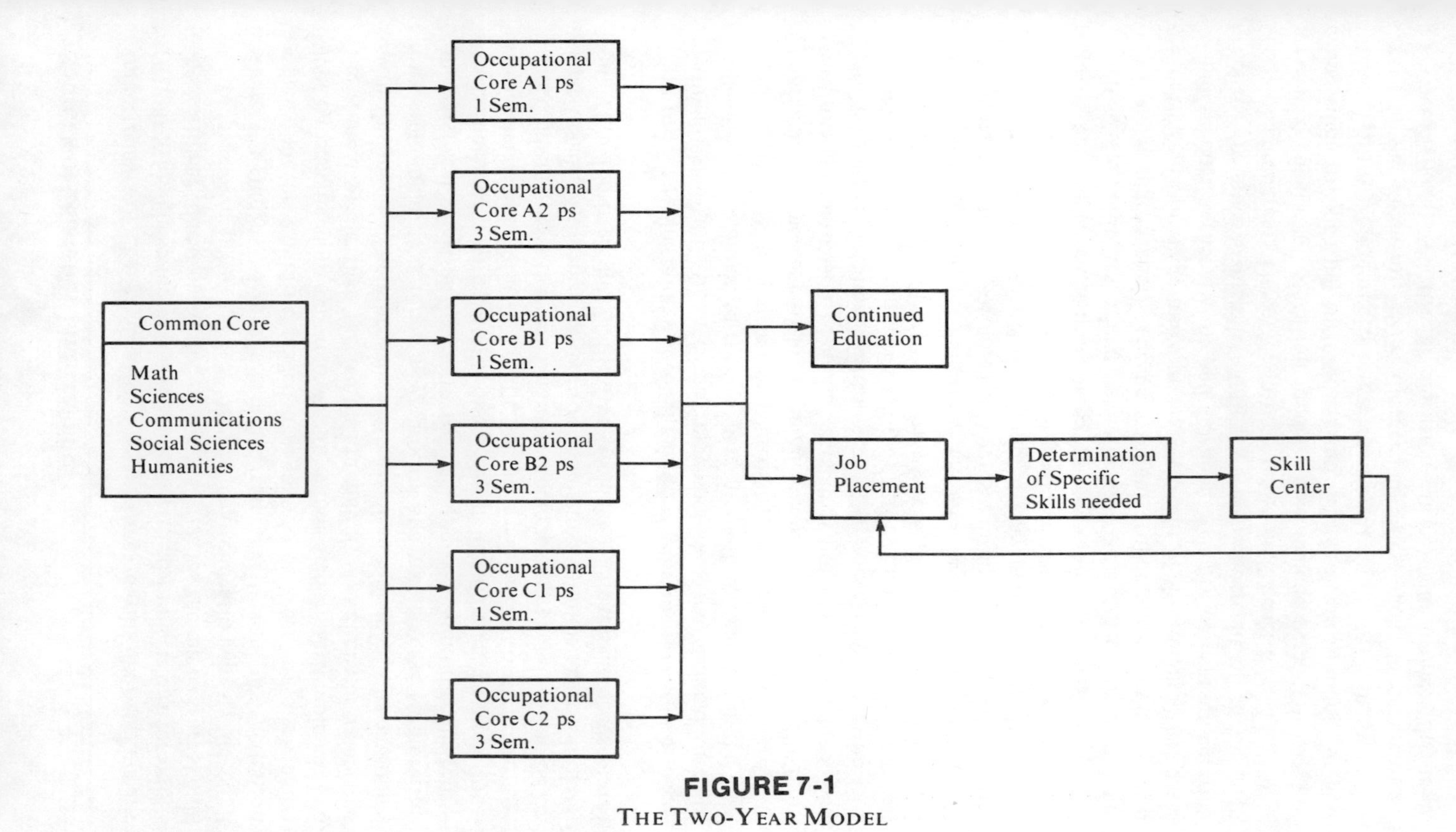

FIGURE 7-1
THE TWO-YEAR MODEL

of these diverse labor groups by adopting new modes of organization and instruction. The proposed models, with their skill centers, provide the setting to serve them.

THE TWO-YEAR MODEL

The two-year model (illustrated in Figure 7-1) would have a dual student input of: (al) youngsters at high school graduation age who are not admitted to baccalaureate programs; and (bl) adults who are out of school and are returning to be retrained for a new occupation. This proposed model would be a truly "open door" type of institution, with provisions for admission into one of several core curricula (three multilevel occupational cores are displayed in Figure 7-1). The term "open door" here means that all persons would be admitted to the college, but the program in which an individual would be placed would be the one deemed best suited to his potentialities and interests. Admissions would include: (a) a counseling process that would be a confluence of student interviews, examination of test results and other records; (b) a careful assessment of the multiple assets associated with each person's abilities, personality, and background; (c) utilization of the above to predict the broad occupational areas in which an individual would most likely succeed. This heavy reliance upon counseling and testing would require a larger admissions team than is customarily found in post-secondary vocational schools (a counselor/student ratio of 1/100 would be ideal).

Another input for the model would be associated with the skill center (see Figure 7-1). This is the part of the model where specific skill development, upgrading, and updating would take place. The nature of the skill center would provide for a continuous entering and exiting of job holders in it, as described later.

For the placement of students in the model, a group of individuals with a predicted spectrum of abilities in each occupational core would be organized so that they could benefit from group instruction (traditional classroom-laboratory type activities). However, this would be augumented and strengthened by the availability and intensive use of individualized instructional techniques. The successful development and blending of these approaches could result in each student achieving a common basis (or minimum level of achievement) in his own time, hopefully sooner than if reliance was placed solely on the traditional type of instruction. Students with higher levels of academic abilities could utilize individualized instruction to move ahead of the instruction provided in the conventional modes. The individualized instructional modes would enable the less academically inclined student to proceed at his own rate in areas not dealt with in the conventional classroom-laboratory approaches. Academic failure would not be a consideration because each individual's progress would be in keeping with his own abilities and interests, and with reference to his starting point. Standards would be based on relative individual progress, and not on group averages.

The model has a common element that pervades throughout the curriculum called the common core. This would offer preselected aspects of mathematics, sciences, communications, social sciences, and humanities. Topics would be carefully extracted from the traditional subject areas and taught with an eye toward how they relate to the world in which the students find themselves. The rational-abstract approach used in the more traditional baccalaureate-oriented programs would be avoided. Based on the admissions process previously described, each student would be placed in a class with others that are at his level in each of the common core topics. Placed on a similar academic level, students could be instructed in the traditional manner for a considerable portion of the common core topics, thereby providing a savings to help offset the high cost of counseling services. Each student would "spin-off" and proceed at his own rate later on in the common core courses by utilizing various individual instructional techniques. A student's time and abilities for a given topic would largely determine when and where he finishes. Therefore a well thought-out and administered combination of the group and individual instruction techniques can bring each student to his maximum level of performance.

How are the occupational cores determined? The model has to address itself to several problems: (1) It should offer a sufficient variety of programs so that the interests and needs of most students will be met: and (2) it also should offer each type of program at more than one academic level, thereby permitting students to prepare for entry into an occupational area at several job levels. Problems can be best overcome if a minimum enrollment of only one-thousand is required for the establishment of each school. This would indirectly mandate the development of regional schools for rural areas, which might have to provide residential facilities for those who come from great distances. The suburban and urban schools would be able to provide a rich variety of occupational cores. In order to insure a minimum enrollment at all times, the institution should draw students from a population base of at least one-hundred thousand. The smaller schools should provide a minimum of three occupational cores, each at a dual level, in the areas of health-related, social service-related, and manufacturing-related occupations. The larger institutions could easily splinter these three into more specific cores (see the typology presented in Chapter 2 for some of the possible arrangements). Each occupational core would consist of those kinds of informative-cognitive courses that would be common to all or most of the jobs found in that core. A special sequence of courses would be especially designed for each occupational core level; therefore, the courses for the higher academic level would be different in length, content, and presentation from those designed for the lower level occupational cores. At each level—but not across several levels—the common core and occupational core courses would be intermingled.

The lower level occupational core would be limited primarily to basic aspects of communications, computations, and a brief overview of its unique elements. Not more than one-third of a semester should be allocated to the common core subjects. The remaining two-thirds would be utilized for treatment of the occupational core materials. In the high level track, the three semesters would be evenly divided between common and occupational core subjects. A more precise determination of time allocation is made for each program by the curriculum designers (See Figure 7-2).

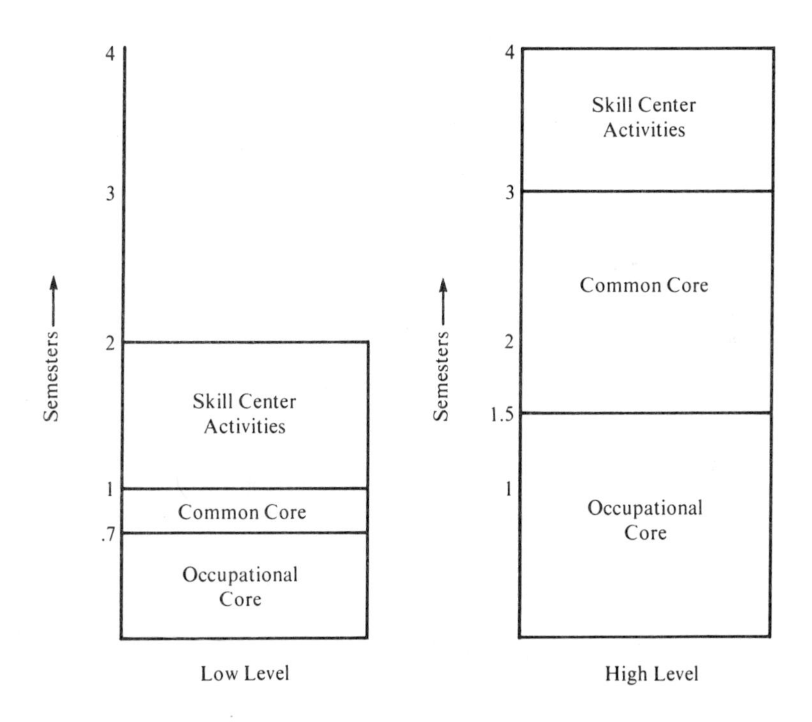

FIGURE 7-2
DISTRIBUTION OF TIME FOR COURSES AND
SKILL DEVELOPMENT FOR MODEL OCCUPATIONAL PROGRAMS.

Information and subject matter in the occupational core would be treated in a cognitive and broad manner with no specialization toward particular jobs. The basic rationale for not specializing at this point is to allow each student maximum flexibility in terms of future job selection, thus reserving his specific skill training for the skill center.

Because of the great amount of individual instruction required, teacher aides should be well familiarized with individual instruction modes. Teacher aides could be utilized at four levels: (1) to perform tasks at the housekeeping level; (2) to be paper and assignment readers; (3) to serve as individual tutors; (4) to teach certain course topics. The introduction of a hierarchy of teacher aides (to the extent proposed here) would pose a threat to conventional teachers in an established school, therefore it should be introduced only after careful consideration of the idea with the faculty. In a new institution, the faculty should be selected with prior understanding of the proposed roles and activities of teacher aides.

An integral and vital part of this plan is evaluation. This should be based primarily on the measurement of behavioral outcomes that were carefully predicted before the program began. Methods for ascertaining the extent to which the desired course objectives were achieved and what problems were encountered should be devised prior to starting the program. The objectives of the common core offerings should be to provide the student with a concept of himself in the work society, thereby inproving his chances of dealing with his world at large. The occupational core objectives should include improving the student's abilities to interpret certain principles and functions, and developing his ability to translate his newly acquired knowledge into actions relating to a selected occupational core. Evaluation strategies must also be established that review and assess the long term effectiveness of the program and determine where the program should be modified or whether it should be discontinued. Several follow-up techniques could be utilized.

The heart of the entire model relates to job placement in a manner opposite the traditional approach. A basic element in the philosophy of vocational education has been to prepare people for job entry which is then followed by a search for a job that fits the training. In this model the student proceeds with no commitment beyond the overall occupational core. Upon its completion, the student is connected with a specific job, from which his specific training is determined.

This leads us to the skill center aspect of the model. Once the student has a job, the guesswork associated with what skills are needed is done away with. The employer is requested to submit a descriptive list of the entire skills needed by the new worker, who then undergoes a training period in which he acquires the required skills. Ideally, the skill center would consist of a large cluster of laboratory and shop areas where a multitude of skills at many levels could be taught, practiced, and mastered. It would be an open-ended, task-oriented activity where the new worker would remain only long enough to master the skills demanded for his entering position. The skill center activities would be equated with academic credits which could contribute toward a future certificate or degree. Methods for granting academic credits could follow the guidelines used in laboratory and shop courses offered in traditional curricula.

A potential problem in operating the skill center is scheduling. At times there may be tendencies for a larger number of people to require a certain group of skills than the center is capable of handling at that particular time. Difficulties of this nature require imaginative scheduling of available resources. The skill center could also be a "diagnostic clinic" for older workers to teach them how to update and/or upgrade their specific skills. This could reduce, if not eliminate, the unemployment time between jobs for many persons. Once business and industry knew that the skill center was available for such tasks, perhaps they would assign workers (who might otherwise be laid off) to the center and have them return to prescribed new jobs with no period of unemployment. Such arrangements require relatively close liaison between the skill center and the business-industrial community.

A reasonable question at this point is: Who will finance the skill centers? They will obviously be expensive because of the great amount of machinery, equipment, and instruments needed, which must be kept up-to-date so that they reflect what exists "out there" in the world of work. However, professionally administered, and if a large enough group of old workers and new workers are serviced by it, a long term cost per student hour of instruction could be lower than what is now spent on the laboratory courses in many of the area vocational schools and community junior colleges. The key to low cost is maximum utilization, which requries some kind of a regional cooperative effort. The business-industrial community must be willing to hire new workers *before* they have acquired specific skills, based on their potential. After employing the individual, the employer should specify the skills required for that job. Then the new worker must return to a skill center for acquisition of the needed skills. The employee would report to his place of work upon completion of his training in the skill center. Inducements to industry to participate in such endeavors could include special tax concessions. This approach could also be effective for older workers, and would reduce the humiliation and frustration associated with drawing unemployment compensation while assisting them in making the transition to a new job. Support from the business-industrial community, with heavy subsidization by federal and state funds, would be imperative in order for this aspect of the model to work. Both older and first-time workers could be paid while enrolled in the skill center. There are already several federal programs that provide this type of financial support for selected individuals (PL 87-415).

Another question is: Who will manage the skill centers? There are several management possibilities. (1) The school where the student receives the common core-occupational portion of the program might establish the skill center (an area vocational-technical school or community junior college). (2) A special consortium of community college districts could sponsor a skill center with its own campus in a location that is near the population center of the consolidation. (3) Proprietary school-controlled skill centers are possible. There were over seven thousand private vocational schools which served more than 1.5 million students in 1966 (Belitsky 1970). (4) Another possibility is management of skill centers by profit-making learning corporations (commonly associated with the term "contract learning"). There are a number of viable industries of this type already on the scene, and the kind of learning activities that go on in the skill center lend themselves to "contract learning." There are subtle indications that public educators are a bit uneasy about this trend, but it seems their entry into the education business could have a tonic-like effect on education as a whole.

The inauguration and proper administration of the proposed model could be a major advance toward equal educational opportunity. The emphasis upon college transfer-type curricula for some high school graduates is now known to actually deter their movement toward equal educational opportunities. Permitting students with low academic abilities in such programs leads to a very high percentage of failure, and tends to turn them away from other forms of education entirely. Well over half of high school graduates ought to be counseled into the kinds of programs proposed here. There is reason to believe that providing more alternatives for students (as demonstrated by this model) could be a significant method for reducing the number of school dropouts (twenty percent of high school students and fifty percent of college students).

THE FOUR-YEAR MODEL

The two-year model, which is post-secondary in nature, can be expanded into a four-year model, as illustrated in Figure 7-3. The last two years are essentially similar to the two year model (see Figure 7-1). The first two years extend into grades eleven and twelve (see Figure 7-3). Non-academic type students (potential dropouts and non-college bound high school graduates) would be counseled into the model at the start

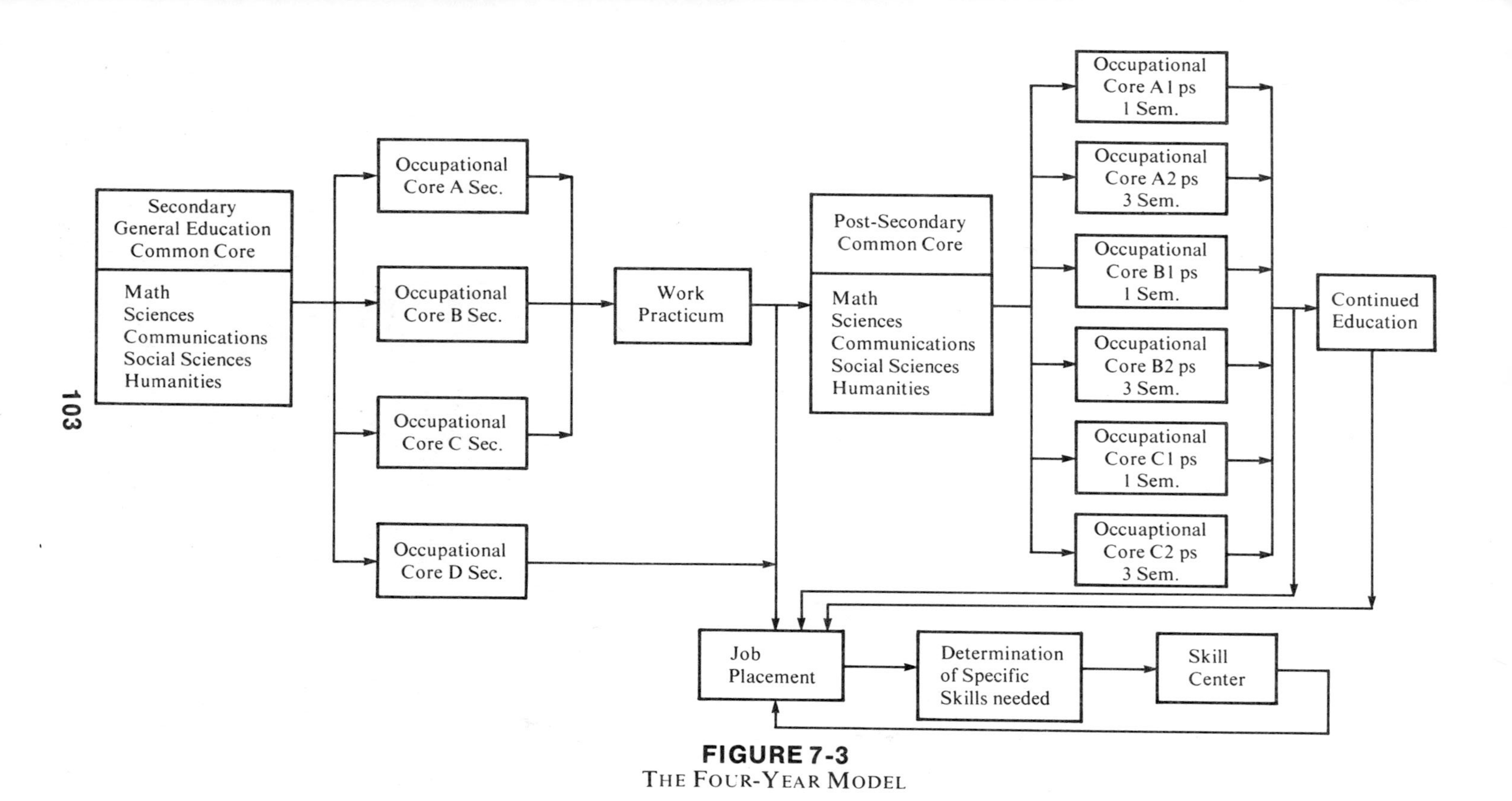

FIGURE 7-3
THE FOUR-YEAR MODEL

of grade eleven. Student selection, as indicated in the first model, would be based on a wide combination of testing, interviewing, and past performance. The search would probably begin in grades nine and ten.

Some of the serious drawbacks obstructing the full development of many secondary area vocational schools are avoided here. Many traditional programs draw the nonacademic student out of the secondary school mainstream and launch him into specific job preparation. Because many youngsters in their first two years of high school do not have clear occupational plans, this approach is not attractive to them. The first two years proposed here would be clearly exploratory in order to help the nonacademically inclined youngsters come to grips with their job-decision dilemma.

This model would also have a general-education common core, with about half of the entire curriculum allocated to it. It would consist of selected aspects of the liberal arts subjects extracted from traditional courses and taught as pragmatic application courses. One of the crucial necessities of this approach is to select faculty who are sufficiently competent to extract the topics which are germane to the nonacademically oriented youngster, and who at the same time believe in this kind of teaching. Such instructors are not common and initially it may be necessary to recruit some nontraditionally prepared teachers into the effort. Successful development of this would result in general education elements truly permeating throughout the entire two-year secondary part of the program.

The secondary school portion of the model would also have occupational cores. (Four are illustrated in Figure 7-3). The number of occupational cores would vary with school size—the smallest schools might not have more than one or two, whereas the larger ones could have as many as ten or more occupational cores. In any event, there should be at least one occupational core which deals with clusters of low-skilled type jobs. This core would provide a unique type of educational treatment for potential dropouts, and would not attempt to keep them within the academic areas for too long a time. Youngsters from this core would move rather quickly into job placement. The sequence described earlier is then followed: the employer specifies the needed entry skills, the student obtains them at the skill center, then he reports to the first job, fully qualified. This scheme extracts the potential dropout from the unsuitable academic situation as early as the eleventh grade. Some of them could be prepared for job acceptance and entry into the skill center in six months, and many will be functioning on their first job within seven or eight months. These individuals will likely return to the school for retraining, skills updating or upgrading, later on. Successful implementation of this aspect of the model would result in very few youngsters leaving school without a job. This approach for potential high school dropouts has several difficulties. Foremost is the present hesitancy of business and industry to employ sixteen- and seventeen-year-old youngsters, particularly those not holding a high school diploma. Some mechanism for inducing business and industry to hire them must be found, such as granting a tax credit (state and/or federal) to those who employ them. Another possibility would be partial subsidization of their salaries until they are able to earn a "living wage." An extension of civil rights legislation to require employment of younger workers is another mechanism worthy of consideration. This aspect of the model rests upon the belief that potential high school dropouts develop into functional and valuable workers when provided with this kind of occupational shelter.

One difference in the secondary school occupational cores is the provision of the work practicum. This can be a part-time work situation in which the student works up to fifteen hours a week for varying lengths of time. For the more cognitive individuals, the work practicum could be much more limited, perhaps restricted to only one semester of the program. It is important that the work practicums be designed to meet the particular needs of each student, since some individuals need considerably more practice in work than others. The activities should be under the supervision of a work practicum coordinator. This person, with the assistance of a good counseling team, and in cooperation with the local businesses and industries, would place students in those jobs that would best meet the needs and characteristics of each. He would be in close and frequent contact with every student in his work practicum placement, and would be responsible for placing students in other situations whenever a mismatch of students and jobs occurred.

The work practicums have the following overall objectives: (1) to introduce the student to a successful work experience from which he can begin to develop positive attitudes toward work in general (many youngsters don't believe they can hold a job, and others feel that working is basically an unpleasant experience); (2) to enable the student to acquire practical on-the-job experiences which might enable him to develop an interest in a specific occupation; (3) to provide him with a limited income, which gives the student some verification of his ability to earn; (4) to provide him with experiences that would make the classroom-laboratory activities more relevant.

At the end of two years, a youngster completing any one of the occupational cores would have two options: (1) he could seek job placement, or (2) he could enter a post-secondary level occupational core program. Those electing the latter option would proceed to one of the occupational cores at the level most consistent with their interests and abilities.

It has been demonstrated that the major objective of the models is to provide an ideal learning environment for those youngsters not likely to enter the professions. The four-year model (which encompasses the two year version) would serve as the major "finishing" educational institution, since it would serve all but the small fraction of youngsters who are presently served by the traditional secondary schools and community colleges. Perhaps this approach would reduce the disproportionate emphasis upon preparation for the professions and the acquisition of a bachelor's degree. Looking back upon the past trends in educational attainment, it appears likely that the completion of 14 years of schooling will soon become as common as high school graduation is today (Hooper 1971). At the same time, the proportion of the population acquiring bachelor degrees may not increase at such a rapid rate. The post-secondary vocational schools might best serve their clientele by becoming "universal colleges," incorporating grades eleven through fourteen, and steering most of the students into occupational programs. The four-year model described is an attempt to demonstrate how such an institution could be initially designed. Many of the additional problems associated with trying to alter school systems so that such models can be established are discussed in the last chapter. The two-year model is more practical since it could evolve out of the present community junior colleges and area vocational schools in some places.

Summary

The major sources of training and education of middle level workers are examined. Training on-the-job is perhaps the major source of occupational education in many of the middle level occupations, particularly in some of the newly developing ones. Educational institutions frequently do not establish a curriculum for a new occupation until it becomes abundantly clear that the need for such a program exists. Ironically, the lag also exists on the other side of the continuum—educational institutions tend to not alter or terminate programs until they are clearly outdated. One of the major disadvantages of on-the-job training is the tendency to restrict instruction to those elements needed by that particular business or industrial concern, which may provide only short term benefits for the employee. On-the-job training also has a number of advantages: it provides flexibility for the industrial business community; it keeps job mobility paths open; it tends to be more relevant to job needs; and it minimizes the penalty a worker sometimes accrues when he switches from one job to another.

High school preparation for jobs is the second most common way in which vocational education is offered. The need for occupational education in secondary schools will continue well into the future, as evidenced by the high rate of secondary school dropouts and by the great number of high school graduates who do not immediately go on to some post-secondary education or training.

Post-secondary preparation of middle level workers is discussed. Several broad generic types of institutions are involved, including public and private two-year colleges, proprietary schools, senior colleges and universities. A specific example of the distribution of types of school involved in these efforts is offered by examining the Pennsylvania experience.

A new model for preparing middle level workers is examined. The proposed model has two versions, one two years in length which relates to two-year colleges most directly, and the second, which is four years, and encompasses both secondary schools and two-year colleges and could be the basis for developing a "universal college."

REFERENCES

Alden, J.D. *Prospects of Engineering and Technology Graduates: 1970.* New York: Engineering Manpower Commission of Engineers Council, 1970

Belitsky, A.H. *Private Vocational Schools: Their Emerging Role in Post-Secondary Education.* Kalamazoo, Mich. W.E. Upjohn Institute for Employment Research, 1970.

Blau, P. and Duncan, O.D. *The American Occupational Structure.* New York: John Wiley, 1967.

Cross, P.K. *The Junior College Student: A Research Description.* Princeton, N.J. : Educational Testing Service, 1968.

Curti, M. *Social Ideas of American Education.* New York: American Historical Association on the Social Studies, 1935.

Directory Area Vocational Education Schools: Fiscal 1972. Washington, D.C. : Department of HEW DOE, Bureau of Adult, Division of Vocational and Technical Education, 1972.

Education Directory, 1970-71, Higher Education. Washington, D.C.: Department of Health, Education and Welfare, OE-5000-71.

Employment and Earnings. Washington, D.C.: Bureau of Labor Statistics, U.S. Government Printing Office, 1972.

Gillie, A.C. *Pennsylvania State University Associate Degree Technician Graduates: Some Demographic Variables.* University Park, Pa.: Department of Vocational Education, Pennsylvania State University, 1971c.

______. *Post-Secondary Occupational Education: An Overview and Strategies.* University Park, Pa.: Center for the Study of Higher Education, Pennsylvania State University, 1970a.

Harper, W.A. *1972 Junior College Directory.* Published by the American Association of Junior Colleges and the ERIC Clearinghouse for Junior Colleges, with assistance from the Research Division, National Education Association, Washington, D.C. : AAJC, 1971.

Hooper, M.E. *Associate Degree and Other Formal Awards Below the Baccalaureate: 1967-68.* Washington, D.C.: National Center for Educational Statistics, 1969.

———. *Associate Degree and Other Formal Awards Below the Baccalaureate: 1969-70.* Washington, D.C.: National Center for Educational Statisitcs, (OE72-48), 1971.

Hummel, R.C. *Our Colleges and Universities: Degrees and Other Formal Awards Conferred by Pennsylvania Institutes of Higher Education 1969-70.* Volume 8, No. 2, 1970-71. Harrisburg, Pa.: Bureau of Educational Statistics, Department of Education, 1971.

Kerr, C. *The Open Door Colleges: Policies for Community Colleges.* A special report and recommendations by the Carnegie Commission on Higher Education. New York: McGraw-Hill, 1970.

Lerner, W. *Statistical Abstract of the United States: 1970,* 91st Annual Edition. Washington, D.C. : U.S. Bureau of the Census, 1970.

Lindsay, C.A.; Hoover T.; and Kepler, B. *1967 Fall Term Pennsylvania State University Freshmen Class: Profile of Demographic Variables.* University Park, Pa. : Office of Student Affairs, The Pennsylvania State University, 1968.

McConnell, T.R. "Accountability and Autonomy." *The Journal of Higher Education,* Volume XLII, No. 6. Columbus, Ohio: Ohio State University Press, 1971.

Manpower Report of the President 1971. Washington, D.C. : U.S. Government Printing Office, 1971.

Perkins, C.D. *Reports on the Implementation of the Vocational Education Amendments of 1968.* Washington, D.C.: U.S. Government Printing Office, 1971.

Peterson, M.W. "The Potential Impact of PPBS on Colleges and Universities." *The Journal of Higher Education,* Volume XLII, No. 1. Columbus, Ohio: Ohio State University Press, 1971.

Public Law No. 415, 87th Congress (Manpower and Training Act of 1962.)

Public Law No. 210, 88th Congress (Vocational Education Act of 1963.)

Public Law No. 576, 90th Congress (Vocational Education Amendments of 1968.)

Second Report. Washington, D.C.: National Advisory Council on Vocational Education, 1969.

Sheppard, R.L. *Directory Listing Curricula Offered in the Community Colleges of Pennsylvania.* Harrisburg, Pa. : Department of Education, 1970.

Silverman, R.J. "Accountability." *The Journal of Higher Education,* XLII, No. 8, November 1971. Columbus, Ohio: Ohio State University Press.

Venn, G. *Man, Education and Work.* Washington, D.C.: American Council on Education, 1964.

Wade, G. *Fall Enrollments in Higher Education 1970.* Washington, D.C. : Department of Health, Education and Welfare, OE72-57.

National Study of Educational Statistics. Washington, D.C.: U.S. Department of HEW. Oe-54056-68, 1969.

Chapter 8 DESIGN OF PROGRAMS

Since programs are frequently initiated at the local level in two-year colleges, a discussion of some general steps for designing new programs is in order. The pattern of two-year college control varies from state to state, which makes it difficult to specify a simple step-by-step procedure for initiating new programs that could fit all situations. However, the overall procedure for assessing the need for new programs presented in Chapter 6 is sufficiently general to be applicable in most places. As the trend toward injecting public funds into private colleges gathers momentum, the control characteristics of independent two-year colleges will become more like the public two-year colleges. In most public two-year colleges, there is a pattern of decision making relative to new programs that operates at three levels. The first or "grass roots" level is the local group (frequently an ad hoc committee consisting of lay citizens, faculty, and administrators) that proposes to the local governing board of the college that a new program be offered or not offered. Using this group's recommendations as a basis, the local board of trustees (which is the second level in the decision-making structure) accepts or rejects the proposed new program. Should the Board decide to accept the new program, they make provisions for it in their state level budget requests (which is the third level in the decision-making structure). State level control is indirect in some states (a matter of approving the requested budget increase which provides for the new program) or may be more direct (where a state level board makes the final decision as to whether or not the new program can be offered).

While much can be said in favor of designing programs at the local level, such an approach is also fraught with hazards, such as (1) calling upon persons with inadequate preparations to design the new curriculum; (2) designing a provincial curriculum so unique that no business-industrial concern outside that locale is attracted to the graduates; (3) excessive concern with the academic syndrome (always a danger with a program committee which has a preponderance of non-vocational educators on it), resulting in a program which requires a pre-engineering or pre-medical type student to get through the required academic courses; (4) proposing studies within the curriculum that are not relevant to the overall occupational area; (5) creation of serious imbalances between the three major components of an occupational curriculum (the vocational, support, and general education courses); (6) selecting verbiage in describing courses and the program that inaccurately portrays the curriculum and its objectives. Designing a new program is a task which should be assigned to professional personnel associated with the two-year college for which the request was made.

The sequence suggested for designing new programs includes ways to: determine subject content; decide whether the program should be broadly or narrowly based; determine the most appropriate cognitive level of the courses; achieve optimum balance of specialty, general education and support courses; effectively utilize a college-wide curriculum committee; inaugurate evaluation provisions, including a biannual program review; establish liaison between potential employers and the college; and recruit students.

Determination of Behavioral Objectives

The subject-content areas to be included in a new occupational program should relate directly to program objectives, which in turn should directly deal with student-oriented outcomes. New curriculum objectives should be concerned first with providing a vehicle for middle level occupational preparation for all those who can benefit from it and who want it; secondly, the "open-door" concept should be implemented into a program admission mechanism that provides a reasonable and realistic approach to selection and rejection of applicants. Rejecting some applicants for a program superficially appears to be in contradiction with the egalitarian admission goal of the college, but is actually in agreement with it. Admission into occupational programs, whether they are well established or newly designed, should be based on careful study of individual abilities and interests. Selecting students for programs in this way actually enhances their chances for successful completion of their curriculum and eases their entry into occupations that match their capabilities and interests.

There should be no serious attempt to select subject matter until the objectives of the new curriculum are clearly established and agreed upon. Once the objectives are established, they should be put in behavioral terms. There is a substantial amount of available literature related to the business of building behavioral objectives, much of which stresses the necessity of stating objectives in ways that can be measured (Mager 1962; Moss 1968; Lessinger 1970), but sometimes this literature fails to provide sufficient concrete examples for the faculty member who is unfamiliar with behavioral methods. Perhaps the provision of an in-service training workshop for faculty members would be the most direct way to help them develop behavioral objectives. Such endeavors can be quite effective when conducted by an educator who is a specialist in the specific occupational area to be dealt with in the curriculum and has had previous experience in drawing up behavioral objectives (Gillie 1970). When this is not possible, a satisfactory alternative is to provide special training in drawing up behavioral objectives for one of the specialty faculty members of the future curriculum who then, with special assistance, can learn to develop behavioral objectives in specific occupational areas. After being trained, he could return and teach his fellow faculty members how to do the same. In a workshop-type setting, they could together draw up behavioral objectives for the new program.

Determination of Subject Matter Content

It should be emphasized that the major goal of occupational programs is to prepare people for jobs in a certain middle level occupational area, and curricular subject matter should be subservient to that goal at all times. When this is truly the case, subject matter identification does not merit serious consideration until student outcomes have been established in behavioral terms.

The ideal approach to selection of subject matter content, after identification of the behavioral objectives, is to carefully sort out the academic skills and techniques needed to achieve them. Once they stop *building* courses and begin *searching* for courses, the creative aspect of curriculum design ends. When this happens, much of their thinking regresses into trying to decide how to "parley" various courses found in other places, resulting in a mere amalgam of courses. Curriculums developed in this fashion often end up with new objectives based on the courses, and the original program objectives are subverted. This is an example of the *means* (completing courses) becoming the *end* (Merton 1957).

Successfully designing a curriculum in which the subject matter is limited to those things needed for the achievement of the established behavioral objectives is most likely to happen when: (a) one or more faculty members competent in the occupational area also knows how to develop behavioral objectives; and (b) when it is clearly specified by the administration that a program designed in this fashion is the only acceptable one. Strong administrative support, coupled with obvious enthusiasm by the program designers, could help to gain the unified support of new programs by all the faculty members.

When a new program is to be offered in more than one college in a district or state, it should be designed with this more diverse area and population in mind. The new program could be essentially the same in each of the colleges and could also be used by colleges within that region or state that might want to bring the new program into their group of offerings a year or two after its design—in fact, they could benefit from the experiences gained by the earlier offerers of the program. It is unnecessary, and sometimes wasteful, to "re-discover" a program when a very similar one is successfully functioning in another college with a similar geographic and population base. In such instances, adoption of an established program (with some modifications to compensate for institutional differences) is certainly acceptable. However, design of a completely new program is recommended when no similar program is available or when present programs of the same type appear to have serious deficiencies or flaws. (Sometimes it's easier to start from the beginning than to try to patch up a poorly designed existing program.)

Determination of Curriculum Orientation—Broad or Narrow?

Intermeshed with the question of subject content is the question regarding curriculum orientation: Should the program aim at preparing graduates for specific jobs or for a broad occupational area? There is a tendency for many nonoccupational educators to automatically opt for programs that aim at broad occupational areas, since they feel this provides the students with

TABLE 8-1

DIAGRAMMATIC CHARACTERISTICS OF BROAD AND NARROW BASED CURRICULUMS

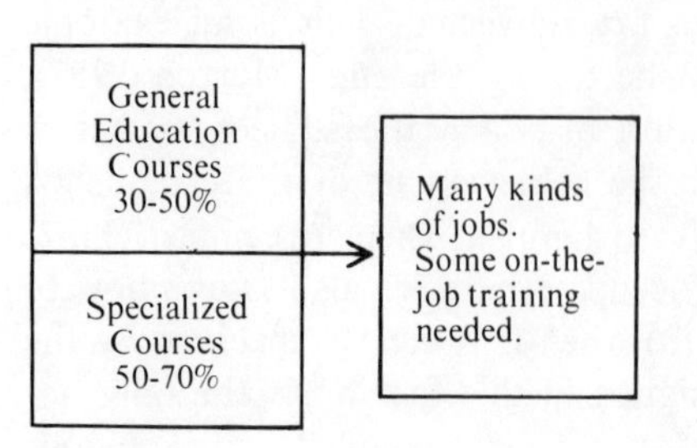

Other Characteristics

(a) Most courses (occupational and general education) conducted at a higher cognitive level.

(b) Most courses follow a more traditional "collegiate" format.

(c) Career Orientation limited to a general occupational area (not to specific jobs).

(d) Laboratory courses stress examination of principles, laws, etc.

A. Broad Based

10-30% General Education Courses

Specialized Courses 70-90%

Specific jobs. Little or no on-the-job training needed.

Other Characteristics

(a) Most courses (occupational and general education) conducted at lower cognitive levels.

(b) Most courses are designed around job preparation and are usually untraditional (in the collegiate sense).

(c) Career orientation is heavily accented to specific job preparation.

(d) Laboratory courses stress practice in skills needed for a specific job.

B. Narrow Based

more occupational options. While this makes for attractive reading in the college catalog and brochures, the question of curriculum orientation should not be decided on that basis. Before continuing, we should explore the characteristics of broad- and narrow-oriented programs.

THE BROAD-BASED PROGRAM

The broad-based program is designed to prepare people for a large number of jobs in a broadly defined occupational area. The occupation-related courses in such curricula emphasize the foundational aspects of the occupational area and deal primarily with cognitive applications. Typically, these occupational courses would be limited to one-half or less of the entire curriculum (in terms of credit hours). Specific skill development is either limited to a small part of the last occupational courses in the sequence or is omitted completely. The rationale frequently offered for designing such programs is that they increase the job-entry flexibility of the graduates. Having a sound cognitive foundation in a broad occupational area enables the graduate to more easily qualify for a larger number of jobs. The proponents of this approach contend that short term specific "on-the-job" training or using a skill center (as proposed in Chapter 4) would provide students with the necessary job entry skills. A diagrammatic display of the broad and narrow types of curricula are found in Figure 8-1.

THE NARROW-BASED PROGRAM.

Although equal in length to its broad-based counterpart, the narrow-based program is very different in several ways. First of all, most or all of its courses are directly oriented to preparation for specific job entry. Secondly, the courses are usually conducted at a practical level and are designed to deal directly with potential jobs. This orientation is not limited to the occupational courses, as the general education offerings (courses such as "report writing," "technical writing," "social problems in the world of work," "development of trade unions") are also centered around a future job. Frequently colleges offering narrow-based curricula offer a wide variety of these job oriented types of general education courses. A third difference between broad- and narrow-based programs is the purposes served by their laboratory courses. While they serve to examine principles and laws in broad-based programs, they are a place to develop and practice specific skills necessary for specific job entry in the narrow-based programs. A greater amount of time is spent in a laboratory shop environment in the narrow-based programs.

Briefly synthesizing the similarities and the differences between the two types of program orientations, we find: (1) They are both two-year programs and both award the associate degree. Indications are that the narrow-based program tends to have a lower drop-out rate (Bjorkquist 1968). (2) The broad-based version aims to occuptionally educate persons for a family (cluster) of jobs within a somewhat wide occupational area. Example: A broadly prepared electronics technician would have an adequate background to become an electronics middle level worker in a number of electronics related jobs such as computer customer servicing, radar and microwave work, various manufacturing jobs, communications industries, and others, whereas a narrow-based program in electronics would more likely prepare people for specific jobs such as radio television servicing, electronics maintenance in a particular industry, or specific electronics equipment servicing. (3) Long laboratory-shop sessions with heavy emphasis on skill development and practice is commonplace in narrow-based programs, whereas in broad-based programs these activities tend to be limited to examination and testing of basic principles and laws associated with the occupational cluster.

In the final analysis, the orientation of the program should be determined by the perceived job needs in that occupational area and the kinds of students available for entry into the program. One type of student is best fit for broad-based programs while a second kind of student is best suited for narrow-based programs. Job needs in the particular occupational area should be carefully analyzed to determine whether the needs of the business-industrial community would be best served by the broad-based or the narrow-based program. The two factors together, available jobs within the occupational area, and the kinds of students interested in those kinds of jobs, should be the major factors behind making a decision about program orientation.

Student Types

Although at first glance the broad-based program seems to offer maximum flexibility for the student, this is not always the case. There is some evidence that the narrow-based program has a lower dropout rate (Bjorkquist 1968). Probably the most important factor is the placement of students in programs in which the orientation is consistent with their occupational orientation.

Two-year college students can be divided on the basis of their reasons for enrolling in selected occupational programs. First, there are students who come to prepare for a specific kind of job; for example, an individual who enrolls in a dental assistant program because she intends to work in that capacity. Secondly, there are students who enter an occupational program to study the techniques, principles, and cognitive approaches that are essential to that occupational area, and who have little awareness of the specific work styles associated with jobs in that occupational area; for example, the student who enters an electronics curriculum because of his general interest in electronics, applications of physics and mathematics to the solution of electronic problems, and the overall cognitive style associated with this study, but who has not thought about or even considered relevant the specific kind of job he would enter upon completion of the program. Cross (1968) and Gillie and Impellitteri,

(1972), point out the validity of the notion that these two types of students do exist in two-year colleges. For the purpose of this book, these two groups can be designated as being *career oriented* students or *academically oriented* students.

It is common knowledge that two-year colleges have higher dropout rates than other kinds of colleges. Ironically, this phenomenon is also true for the occupational programs, even though their overall goal is to prepare people for entry into the world of work. The fact that the dropout rate is so high in the occupational programs indicates a serious failure on the part of the two-year colleges in providing programs in which students can successfully graduate and enter the work world with skills commensurate with middle level job objectives. Placing career oriented students in narrow-based programs, and academically oriented students in broad-based programs, would be a direct and probably successful approach to reducing occupational program dropout rates, since this would be matching student expectations with program orientation. Therefore, the selection of students should hinge primarily on program orientation, which is determined in large part by occupational need found by the feasibility study. For example, if it is found that electronics positions in very specific kinds of jobs with a high degree of specialization is required, then this should be given heavy consideration when designing the curriculum. This in turn would suggest that career oriented students would be sought for admission into the program.

The Distribution of Courses

The kinds of courses which make up the overall occupational program can be divided into occupational, support, and general education types. When new curricula are designed, a debate frequently ensues about how these courses should be proportioned in the curriculum. Faculty members tend to desire greater allocation of program time for their kinds of courses. Moderate tendencies in this direction are merely a healthy manifestation of a teacher's belief in the importance of his own specialty, but there are more sound approaches to deciding the portions of the program to be allocated for each. A better way would be to schedule course time according to the established objectives. Program objectives, if conceived in terms of the people in the program as well as the occupations in which they are to enter, will deal with some aspects of general education as well as the support and occupational type courses.

Furthermore, the college will likely have general education goals for all of its students which should be considered in any new program design.

A review of college catalogs shows considerable variation in the allocation of program time, with an observable trend in terms of institutional type. Single purpose institutions, which often call themselves "technical colleges" or "technical institutes" allocate a greater proportion of their total curricula to occupational courses and correspondingly less time to general education. This fits with the overall goals of such institutions, which emphasize occupational preparation as their primary function. At the opposite end of the spectrum are the more comprehensive public community colleges which allocate as much as 50 percent or more of their total two-year program credits to general education. Again, this coincides with the overall goals of those institutions, which seek to somewhat broadly educate a person for the world of work. There is no magic combination of the three generic course types, but it does seem reasonable to expect a sizeable part of broad-based curricula to be earmarked for general education. On the other hand, the narrow-based program tends to allocate a smaller portion of curriculum time to general education courses.

THE ROLE OF THE LABORATORY-SHOP EXPERIENCES

One of the more obvious distinctions between occupational curricula and academic-oriented programs is in the amount of time set aside for learning how to perform certain tasks that are related to the occupational area. There is also considerable variation in the kinds of things they do within various kinds of occupational programs. As stated earlier, the narrow-based programs usually have more hours per week allocated to the development and practice of job-related skills, and the laboratory activities are more directly aimed at specific jobs.

The laboratory-shop activities in the broad-based programs tend to have a different focus. They are often concerned with examining, testing, and proving the cognitive principles of the occupational area. Students in these programs may have little or no idea of the specific job they will eventually enter upon completion of the program. Actually, the laboratory-shop activities are often designed in such a way that concern for specific jobs would not be relevant to the tasks at hand. There are some broad-based programs in which some skill development and practice is permitted only in the last one or two occupational courses. Even when this occurs, the skill development and practices are of a broad nature and deal with a job type and not a specific job.

Evaluation of New Occupational Programs

The evaluation of occupational curricula is important, regardless of whether the programs are relatively new or of long standing. If the evaluation is soundly done, it points to the merits and shortcomings of the program, and these findings in turn become the basis for making decisions about the future operation of the curriculum. Considering the effect such programs have on the students who pass through them, the faculty who teach them, and the cost to the public which finances them, any advancement in the decision-making process that results in a better program is welcome.

Considering the varied meanings associated with "program evaluation" found in the literature (see Moss 1968; Lessinger 1970; Rouche et al. 1971; Medsker 1971), we should clarify just what is meant by the concept in this chapter. There are four aspects to new-program evaluation as used here. First of all, the evaluation of a new program must be comparative. By that we mean the actual curriculum outcomes should be compared to the expected outcomes. (It is obvious to see why development of behavioral objectives is essential when this approach to evaluation is employed.) An earlier section discusses behavioral objectives in terms of their development by faculty. With the intended program outcomes stated in behavioral terms, they are measurable, and therefore can be compared to the intended outcomes. This process can be refined by determining which outcomes are due to the characteristics of the curriculum and which outcomes are brought about by student characteristics, and which program outcome differences are attributable to the interaction of program and student characteristics. After all, each student walked into the program with his own repertoire of intellective-demographic characteristics, and these differences within the group could result in differences in the outcomes. Determining these things enables the evaluator to more accurately identify those program outcomes that are attributable to the characteristics of the curriculum itself, and having been isolated from the other outcomes, they can be compared to the hoped-for outcomers, and can be used for making judgements about the new curriculum.

The philosophy or value system of the new curriculum must be established in behavioral terms, just as the instructional components must be. Furthermore, anticipated outcomes can be stated at two or three levels of specificity, as illustrated in Figure 8-2. The most general (macro) level deals with broadly stated outcomes which express a philosophic or value position. These outcomers are not likely to be directly measurable in behavioral terms. At the next level, the stated outcomes would be an the form of measurable indices of the more general statements. Then there would be the most specific (micro) outcomes, which sample the behavioral outcomes. The outcomes in all three levels of specifcity must be consistent with the overall intentions (i. e. objectives) of the new curriculum. This point is stressed because original goals are sometimes displaced by the means used to reach them (Merton 1957). *Example:* Assume a new broad-based electronics curriculum has been in existence for just over two years and the first class has graduated. One of the general outcomes of the program was to improve the quality of electronics paraprofessionals available to regional and state industries. This is a broad philosophic outcome. A more specific outcome might be to increase the ability of electronics paraprofessionals in the use of certain electronic instruments in a variety of businesses and industries. A measurable index of this group of abilities would be the overall time required to prepare persons to operate and utilize these electronics instruments at predetermined skill levels. One of the several micro outcomes within this cluster might be the time needed to prepare students to operate an oscilloscope for a preselected variety of voltage and frequency measurements. The above example is a very limited one, since it is restricted to only one illustrative outcome at each of three levels. It should be noted that the administration can play a part in the development of the more general goals while the micro outcomes are determined by faculty. In actuality, the more specific outcomes are more numerous than the general ones. Therefore, a pyramiding of lower level outcomes under each philosophic or value statement would be found (see Figure 8-1).

A fourth consideration in the evaluation of new programs is the relationship of monetary values to program outcomes. This would involve an attempt to measure the cost per student for the program, after which a cost-benefit ratio could be established. This ratio would be useful in determining the cost of a particular program and would provide at least a partial basis for comparing its costs with other programs. Furthermore, cost-benefit ratios can be used to assess the relative efficiency of selected occupational programs—for example, the cost-benefit ratio of a new electronics program in College A can be compared to the same ratio in colleges B, C, etc., to determine which is most efficient. This approach has considerable implications for state-wide evaluation efforts. It may also be useful within a given college for examination of its various occupational program offerings. However, there are a number of inherent difficulties in assigning dollar values to all the outcomes of an occupational curriculum, and this approach has not been widely utilized up to now (only seven cost-benefit analysis studies were reported by Little 1970).

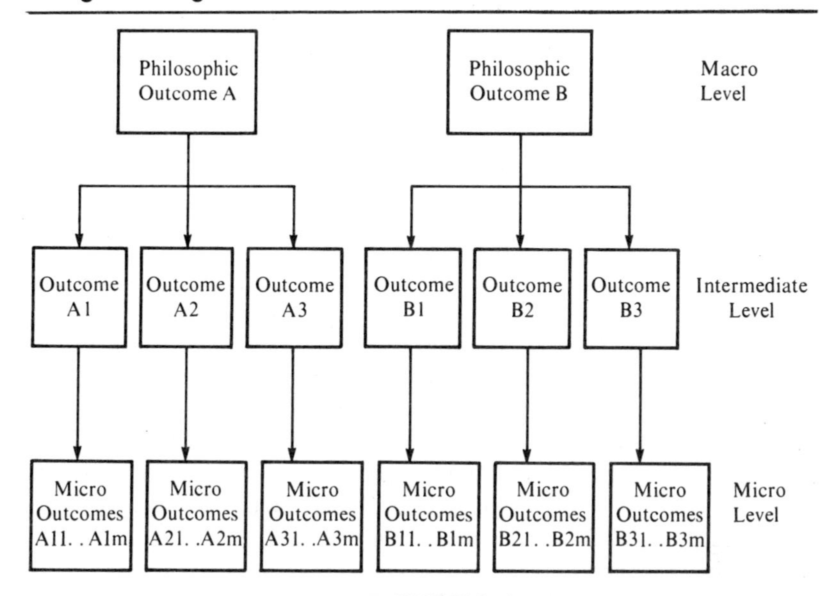

FIGURE 8-1

HIERARCHY OF EVALUATIVE OUTCOMES

Another increasingly common problem related to the evaluation of new occupational programs has to do with the fact that significant numbers of graduates from certain two-year occupational programs go right on into a baccalaureate program instead of entering the work force. This conflicts with the philosophic goal of preparing associate degree paraprofessionals but it agrees with another philosophic goal that more and more of these programs are embracing—to provide the first two years of a four-year occupational curriculum. What this reduces to in some cases is that those who do reasonably well academically in the associate degree program often have the option of continuing toward a baccalaureate degree or seeking employment. Some studies have found that surprisingly high percentages of associate degree graduates in certain programs elect to continue as full-time students in baccalaureate programs (Alden 1970). In spite of the fact that many occupational programs are embracing both philosophic goals, and although the idea of an advanced degree improves the attractiveness of the program to certain potential students, it is a contradiction in values and creates tension within the program. It was pointed out earlier that those outcomes that are attributable to some combination of curriculum and student factors should be discounted in the evaluation of that program. Applying this principle to this situation, it would be inappropriate to consider the percentage of students who transfer into four-year programs as a measure of program effectiveness—there is reason to believe the proportion of students who transfer has as much to do with the initial abilities of the student body as with the two-year program completed.

Selection of Students for the New Program

In addition to their orientation, students should be selected for a new occupational program on the basis of: (1) interest in the particular occupational area, and (2) a predicted reasonable chance of successfully completing the program. Both of these factors deal with the actual content of the curriculum so recruitment of students for a new program could begin when it could be described to potential students in terms of the behavioral objectives. Telling them about the things they will learn to do in the program and the kinds of work styles that they may expect to encounter when they graduate, would give them a reasonable basis for deciding whether or not they are interested in it.

This first phase of student selection can be implemented in a number of ways. The message can be directly provided to secondary school seniors, returning veterans, persons ready to switch jobs, and mothers preparing to return to work. The most desirable approach is the direct one—where someone who knows about the program tells others about it and remains on the scene to answer whatever questions they might have about the curriculum, job possibilities, and administrative details concerning enrollment. An enthusiastic presentation, particularly to high school seniors, can arouse considerable interest. Second best are announcements in the various communications media likely to be used by potential students, such as local radio and television stations, the local newspaper, etc. A third method is the use of brochures, booklets, etc., which describe the new program.

The second phase in student selection begins when a student indicates interest in the program. Before attempting to verify his interest in the program, it is wise to check into personal-academic characteristics relevant to his changes of success. The first such review can be merely a rough assessment, which will suffice to identify whether or not he is obviously underqualified or overqualified for the curriculum. (More consideration would be given to those who exhibit marginal success.) The most pronounced unqualified applicants should be counseled into occupational programs that impose lower cognitive demands. The overqualified applicants should be counseled in the other direction—into other occupational programs that are more cognitively demanding or into the more traditional academic programs in senior colleges and universities. Successful counseling of this type would probably reduce the dropout rate of the program from present rates (fifty percent and above in many two-year colleges) to less than one in ten.

Student selection requires a cooperative effort from competent counselors, faculty, and administrators. The counselor's role is to identify the academic-cognitive possibilities of those potential students indicating an interest in the new program; the faculty could assist in providing curricular details to them, and the administrators' role is to determine matters relating to class-laboratory scheduling, class size, meeting places of classes, and the like.

It ought to be mentioned that programs that are really good, both in terms of what happens during the two-year sequence in college and what opportunities await the graduates upon completion, eventually have little difficulty in attracting students into their curriculum. Usually, although it may be heatedly denied, programs that have difficulty in attracting students are bad programs and "the word is out" as far as the students and other faculty are concerned.

Liaison Between the New Programs and the Outside World

If the program is to attain its maximum success, considerable involvement between the educators and the potential employers of the graduates is necessary. Ideally, there should be a more or less continuous exchange between employers and educators. The representatives of employers could contribute ideas to help keep the program relevant. The faculty would then translate these into program activities that would result in improved student preparation.

The involvement between educators and employers can be at several levels (Gillie and Pratt, 1971). In some cases employers and educators may work together in an informal or ad hoc manner. More formal relationships in the form of advisory committees are sometimes established. There are three major types of advisory committees in common usage in two-year colleges (Riendeau 1967): (1) general advisory committees: (2) occupational advisory committees: (3) joint apprenticeship committees. As its name implies, the general advisory committee is usually charged with broad responsibilities, such as reviewing all the occupational programs offered by the college. The occupational advisory committee, on the other hand, is frequently asked to advise the educators in matters regarding a specific curriculum. Therefore, an occupational advisory committee should be appointed upon initiation of a new program. Such a committee can be helpful to (Riendeau 1967; Burt 1967): (1) serve as a communication channel between college and related occupational groups in the community; (2) assist in the identification of skills needed by the graduates; (3) suggest related occupational information that might be included in the curriculum; (4) assist in finding competent teachers for the program; (5) assist in evaluation of the program; (6) assist in improving the visibility of the program in the community; (7) assist in the recruitment of students; (8) provide internships and cooperative work-study positions; and (9) provide jobs for the graduates.

Summary

The initial step in the design of occupational programs is the establishment of behavioral objectives. Once these have been identified, the program designer has a sound basis for selection of subject matter content, which should be aimed at achieving the objectives. An important concern with regard to curriculum design is program orientation. The determination of program orientation should be made primarily on the basis of program objectives and the kinds of students most likely to enroll in the program. The kinds of students that should be sought for occupational programs can be divided into two categories, namely the career-oriented students (who would be best served by narrow-based programs) and the academically-oriented students (who would do best in broad-based programs). A broad-based curriculum is one designed to prepare students for a fairly large number of jobs in a broadly defined occupational area. A narrow-based curriculum differs in that its courses are usually conducted at a practical level and aim directly at specific jobs.

This chapter examines the distribution of courses in occupational programs. Course types can be categorized as occupational, support, and general education. There is no evidence at this time to indicate that an optimum ratio of these three types of courses exist. The laboratory-shop experiences are the heart of most occupational programs and differ according to program orientation.

A scheme for the evaluation of the program should be established and understood by the faculty before the new curriculum begins. A good evaluation strategy points to the program's merits and shortcomings and can be used as the basis for making decisions about the future operation of the program. A hierarchy of evaluative outcomes, which includes what are called the macro, intermediate, and micro levels, and a discussion of the cost-benefit aspects of evaluation, is included. In the selection of students for new programs, enrollment criteria should include: corresponding student and program orientation, student interest in the chosen occupational area, and a predicted reasonable chance for him to successfully complete the curriculum. The last section of this chapter stresses the importance of establishing interaction between the future employers and educators involved in the program, particularly through the use of advisory committees.

REFERENCES

Alden, John D., *Prospects of Engineering and Technology Graduates.* New York: Engineering Manpower Commission of Engineers Joint Council, 1970.

Bjorkquist, D. C. *The Education and Employment of Technicians.* University Park, Pa.: Department of Vocational Education, Pennsylvania State University, 1968.

Burt, S. M. *Industry and Vocational-Technical Education.*New York: McGraw-Hill, 1967.

Cross, K. P. *The Junior College Student: A Research Description.* Princeton, N. J. : Educational Testing Service, 1968.

Gillie, A. C. "Occupational Education in the Hawaiian Community Colleges." *Technical Education News* Volume 29, Jan/Feb. New York: McGraw-Hill, 1970.

Gillie, A. C. and Pratt, A. L. *Marine Technology Programs: Where We Are and Where We're Going.* Washington, D.C.: American Association of Junior Colleges, 1971.

Gillie, A. C. and Impellitteri, J. T. *The Differential Effects of Selected Programs on the Performance, Degree of Satisfaction, and Retention of Community College Women.* University Park, Pa.: Department of Vocational Education, Pennsylvania State University, 1972.

Lessinger, L. "Accountability in Public Education." *Today's Education.* Washington, D.C.: National Education Association, 1970.

Little, J. K. *Review and Synthesis of Research on the Placement and Follow-up of Vocational Education Students.* Columbus, Ohio. ERIC Clearinghouse for Vocational and Technical Education, 1969.

Mager, R. F. *Preparing Instructional Objectives.* Palo Alto, Calif. Fearon, 1962.

Medsker, L. L. "Strategies for Evaluation of Post-Secondary Occupational Programs." *The Second Annual Pennsylvania Conference on Post-Secondary Occupational Education.* A. C. Gillie, ed. University Park, Pa.: Center for the Study of Higher Education, Pennsylvania State University, 1970.

Merton, R. K. "The Role Set: Problems in Sociological Theory." *British Journal of Sociology,* Volume 8, 1957.

Moss, J., Jr. *The Evaluation of Occupational Education Programs.* Minneapolis, Minn.: Technical Report, Research Coordination Unit in Occupational Education, University of Minnesota, 1968.

The Role of the Advisory Committee in Occupational Education in the Junior College. Washington, D.C.: American Association of Junior Colleges, 1967.

Roueche, J.E.: Baker, G.A., III: Brownell, R.L. *Accountability and the Community College.* Washington, D.C.: American Association of Junior Colleges, 1971.

Part III CONSIDERATIONS FOR THE FUTURE

Chapter 9 IMPROVEMENT AND MODERNIZATION OF ONGOING PROGRAMS

One of the best ways to keep programs up-to-date is to maintain and utilize two-way communications among people most directly associated with the curricula, specifically graduates of the program and employers of the graduates. This statement is not a new one and has been made by vocational educators for years, but its translation into workable relationships has not been particularly successful. A first step in improving communications is to assess the effects of an occupational program by addressing prepared inquiries to employers of program graduates. An obvious drawback with this approach is the difficulty in determining the extent to which the employee's present "worth" as seen by his employer is in fact due to the experiences gained from his course of study or from the many other factors within his overall environment (Moss 1968). Studies have found that graduates of the same program often end up several years later earning different salaries, experiencing a different number of job changes, and doing considerably different kinds of things on their jobs (Gillie 1970, 1971a, 1971b, 1971c; Alden 1970). Therefore, there is a dilemma when it comes down to determining what we really need to know about the graduates and their jobs. In this chapter it is decided what should be ascertained and how it should be used in the improvement and modernization of occupational programs. The way in which the derived information can be fed back to the faculty and administrators for curriculum improvement purposes is illustrated. The last section deals with a topic that has been kept under wraps for too long in occupational education—planning for the burial of programs that have become disfunctional.

The Development and Utilization of Surveys

What is a survey? It has been described in a number of ways (Oppenheim 1966; Good 1963), but we will identify the term within the context of its use in occupational education. A survey is a preplanned scheme for obtaining data to be used in any of the following ways: (1) for describing what the graduates are doing and related characteristics; (2) for predicting what the future graduates may expect; and (3) for analyzing the relationships between certain factors.

In describing what the graduates are doing, and ascertaining some of their job related characteristics, we have the basis for assessing the relevancy and modernity of their particular curriculum. The careful collection of predetermined data in a longitudinal fashion could provide the ingredients for predictions of what the future graduates may anticipate. Such predictions are of considerable interest to students because they prepare them for the things they are most likely to encounter after graduation. An example is the prospect of the student continuing his education beyond the attainment of the associate degree. Skillfully designed and carefully conducted longitudinal studies can help to identify the certain kinds of graduates who go on to earn baccalaureate degrees (Alden 1970; Gillie 1971c). Predictions of such a trend and the kind of student involved, enables educators to make the necessary curriculum adjustments for switching to working toward the next degree, thus providing a substantial amount of upward job mobility (Alden 1970; Gillie 1971c). The use of carefully selected and obtained survey data would enhance the accuracy of such predictions. A good survey also can establish relationships between certain factors (Gillie 1970); for example, surveying the need for certain curricular topics on a job could be the basis for considering the removal of certain topics which are found to be unnecessary.

The design of a survey requires considerable thought before, during, and after it is conducted. The following sections discuss the general and specific considerations for planning and conducting surveys, and examine the process for designing follow-up studies.

PLANNING THE PROCEDURE

Before actually developing the survey, a number of points should be considered and satisfactorily answered, including:

1. What are the queries for which answers should be sought?
2. What issues can be wisely used in public opinion polls? Questions dealing with emotionally laden topics should be avoided.
3. Is the survey the best way to obtain the desired information? This calls for some careful thought about alternative ways to obtain the same data.
4. How will the results be used? The survey design should ask this of every potential question. If the answer received is vague or non-decisive, that item should be excluded. "Nice to know" kinds of items have no place in this kind of instrument.
5. Who will use the results? The answer to this question has considerable effect upon how the survey results are to be reported. As pointed out in the preceding chapter, if it is to be used by a layman group (such as the Board of Trustees), the original statistically oriented report should be supplemented by a second report which is a presentation of the results in a manner that is unencumbered by statistical and educational jargon.
6. Are the facts obtained in such a way that they will not be out-of-date or of no interest by the time they are obtained and tabulated?
7. Can the data to be obtained by the survey help solve the problem under consideration? (This relates to point four above.) No "side trip" queries should be allowed in the survey.
8. What finances are available for the conduct of the survey? The finances that can be allocated to the conduct of the study heavily determine the kind of instrument, sampling strategy, and follow-up on nonrespondents used.
9. Are there other resources available for assistance in conducting the study? It is important to know about computer availability, personnel assistance, etc., that can be used in the endeavor.
10. Would it be advisable to turn over the task of designing, conducting, and interpreting the survey to an outside group (such as a state university or a private research agency)? When the two-year college does not have the personnel to manage a survey, outside help should be sought. In many cases, university professors with an orientation for post-secondary occupational education are available to assist in such endeavors.

11. Is the survey seeking answers that are in fact already known? More than one survey has asked for data from respondents that was available from other sources. The survey should seek answers that are clearly not known at the time.
12. How will the information be obtained? Should a mail questionnaire be used? Or should it be some form of an interview? (This must be decided early because the approach taken will determine the structure of the survey.)
13. Are the people conducting the survey truly capable of doing so? (This relates to point number 10.) Because of its importance, this question *must* be answered candidly. It is well to remember that a willingness to design, conduct, and interpret the survey is not enough—a survey director must be competent in this kind of activity.

PRETEST

After the survey instrument has been designed, there should be a pretest and a pilot study of it (Oppenheim 1966; Good 1963) to point out defects in the original procedures, instructions, and schedules. Individuals similar to members of the group to be examined or questioned should be selected for the pretest or pilot study. The results of the pretest are used in the final improvements of the instrument.

COST ESTIMATES OF THE SURVEY

There should be a realistic cost estimate of the survey (Oppenheim 1966). This is particularly important when special funds will have to be solicited for the conduct of the study. One approach in estimating the budget for this effort is to divide it into three parts: (1) planning the survey, drafting schedule forms and instruction, etc.; (2) investigating in field, collecting of the data, and editing schedules; (3) coding, tabulating, analyzing data, and preparing of the final report. Each of these phases generally takes about one-third of the time and of the funds. If there is to be a large scale publication of the report, budgeting for that should be a separate consideration. This may be a sizable factor for survey reports that are to be distributed on a state-wide basis.

SETTING THE TIME SCHEDULE FOR FIELD WORK

Setting the date for field work is the next step. A flow diagram showing the duration and sequence of events should be constructed, and should include the following: (1) drafting the plans, and assembling all necessary statistical background data; (2) designing the schedule and framing the questions; (3) setting up the organization for conducting the study, providing work-office space supplies, selecting personnel, posisibly training interviewers, etc.; (4) drawing and testing the sample. This involves preparing a source list, selecting the sample cases, writing the sample card, preparing the master list, and conducting a dryrun; (5) collecting and processing the data; (6) tabulating returns; (7) analyzing results and writing the report; (8) publishing the findings; and (9) terminating the survey and disposing of the data.

METHODS TO OBTAIN INFORMATION

As indicated in an earlier paragraph, there are various ways of obtaining the desired data (Oppenheim 1966; Good 1963). Six general methods worthy of consideration are: (1) personal interview; (2) observation and recording devices; (3) telephone interviews; (4) mail questionnaire or ballot; (5) radio-television media appeal and; (6) panel technique. Let us examine some of these methods in a little more detail.

The Personal Interview. There are five basic types of personal interviews (Oppenheim 1966): (1) The interviewer asks questions in accordance with instructions that were prescheduled in advance; (2) the free-sharing technique, in which the interviewer urges the respondent to talk about the survey subject matter, and from this conversation obtains a general impression of the respondent's attitude or situation; (3) the focused interview, which is a modification of the free-sharing technique, where the interviewer has a list of questions about the subject matter to which the informer is to react; (4) unaided recall, whereby the informant is urged to tell what he remembers about a particular situation that relates to the information desired for the survey; and (5) aided recall, which stimulates cooperation from the respondent, recognition which consists of going over some of the material with the respondent and then asking him what he has seen, and identification.

The personal interview has a number of advantages. (1) A high percentage of returns is obtained; (2) an almost perfect sample of the desired population can be obtained (since practically anyone can be reached by this technique); (3) the information acquired by the personal interview tends to be more correct, since inaccurate responses can be cleared up by the interviewer on the spot; (4) the interviewer can collect supplementary information if so desired; (5) scoring and testing devices can be utilized; (6) the respondent can be made to react to visual material; (7) it is possible to have return visits to complete items if necessary; (8) the interviewer can sometimes obtain more spontaneous reactions by this approach; (9) the interviewer, being present, can control the responses of the respondent and keep them on the topic about which information is desired; (10) there is a greater opportunity for the respondent to become oriented to the topic being investigated; (11) sensitive questions can be sandwiched in by the interviewer so that the respondent does not become unduly upset by them; (12) more of the respondent's time can be obtained this way than through the mail questionnaire; and (13) the interviewer can alter his own language at the time of the interview in order to suit the ability and the educational level of the respondent.

The personal interview technique also has several disadvantages: (1) transportation cost and time; (2) the human equation element might distort the results if not carefully controlled; (3) the interviewers must be well trained, so that the data will be accurate and complete; (4) greater organizational details are required; (5) the cost per respondent will be higher than in the use of other techniques; and finally (6) the personal interview takes more time than any of the other techniques.

The Telephone Interview. Studies for middle and high income groups can easily be done by telephone. Several of the major advantages of this technique are: (1) it is the quickest of all survey methods; (2) the refusal rate tends to be low; (3) it is easy to train interviewers for this technique; (4) the approach and the questions are easy to standardize for all respondents; and (5) the cost is lower than for the personal interview approach.

The telephone interview technique does have a number of disadvantages, however: (1) it is difficult to obtain a representative sample in some kinds of surveys, particularly those that should include persons in the lower socioeconomic groups. (This would obviously not be a disadvantage when attempting to contact graduates of middle level occupational programs but could introduce shortcomings in a community-type survey.) (2) detailed data is sometimes difficult to obtain by way of the telephone; (3) the respondent cannot be observed visually; (4) only a limited amount and type of information about the respondent can be obtained by telephone; (5) attitude scales are not too dependable by this technique; (6) the respondent cannot orient himself well to the survey; and (7) misinformation is difficult to spot check in such short inquiries.

The Mail Questionnaire. Some of the advantages of questionnaires sent by mail are: (1) it is possible to cover a wide geographic area (a decided advantage for follow-up type studies; (2) mailing costs are generally lower than the direct or telephone interview approaches; (3) there is no need to train a staff of interviewers; (4) there is a tendency to be assured of more frank responses if the respondent can withhold his identity, which is possible in many mail type questionnaires (although not in most follow-up surveys); (5) mail questionnaires can reach groups normally protected from solicitors and the direct investigators; (6) no personal antagonism to the investigators can develop if the instrument is thoughtfully constructed; (7) a high rate of return can be obtained for a relatively low cost; (8) the questions are standardized for all respondents; (9) the respondent can answer the questionnaire at his convenience; and (10) it is easier to locate certain individuals by mail (although this is not always the case—in a recent survey by this author eleven percent of the sample could not be located).

The mail questionnaire also has a number of disadvantages that must be taken into consideration: (1) the respondents may not be entirely representative of the people to whom the questionnaire was sent, unless special statistical precaustions are taken (Gillie 1971a); (2) the returns are frequently low, sometimes as low as ten to twenty percent (Oppenheim 1966)—although a higher percentage of returns can be obtained if special strategies are used (Gillie 1971a), the questionnarie must be very interesting if a high response is to be obtained; (3) the respondent may misinterpret questions or omit essential items; (4) the questions must be simple and self explanatory because the respondent has no one to turn to for clarification; (5) the questionnaire must be brief, otherwise the respondent will lose interest and perhaps fail to complete the questionnaire; (6) it may be necessary to supplement mail returns with personal interviews of some nonrespondents in order to minimize or detect the type of bias present (Gillie 1971a; Oppenheim 1966; Cochran 1963); (7) checking the honesty and the reliability of returns is difficult when the respondent is not seen and known; (8) it is difficult (if not impossible) to return unsatisfactory or incomplete questionnaires to the respondent for correction; (9) up-to-date addresses and names of the potential respondents is sometimes very difficult to obtain; (10) certain questions must be avoided so as not to antagonize the respondents.

The Panel Technique. The advantages of the panel technique are: (1) if the same sample is surveyed over a period of time (that is, at the beginning and then again at the end), changes in the findings can be attributed with greater certainty to actual changes going on in the area being investigated; (2) the information obtained from the same persons over a period of time can be cumulated and a detailed picture of the factors underlying the shifts in the situation can be obtained; (3) the respondent provides more detailed information than would be obtained with the mail questionnaire; (4) assuming the group is cooperating in the endeavor, experimental situations which expose all the members to a certain influence can be established and the effectiveness of that influence can then be measured; (5) by being a member of the panel, the respondents get to learn how to adequately express themselves.

The panel technique, like the other approaches to obtaining survey information, also has a number of disadvantages: (1) there is a possibility of losing some of the panel members over a period of time in which the investigation is being conducted; (2) the mere fact that a person is participating in a panel investigation may change a person's attitudes and opinions and thereby make it more difficult to assess the situation realistically; and (3) the panel members have tendencies to remain with their originally stated attitudes and opinions.

SELECTION OF QUESTIONS FOR THE SURVEY

Following are several general suggestions that should be applied to the selection of survey questions. (1) Restrict questions to those matters that directly relate to the problem; (2) avoid those questions whose answers can be accurately found from other sources; (3) remember your tabulation plans when selecting questions, as many types of questions do not lend themselves to easy tabulation and should be avoided; (4) if possible, obtain comparable data—compare questions, terms, definitions, and quantitative units of measurement with those that were found to be meaningful in other completed surveys; (5) exercise care and caution when asking personal or potentially embarrassing questions; (6) ask factual questions whose answers the respondents can be expected to know. When asking respondents questions that deal with recall, keep in mind the principle factors involved with remembering, namely: recency—more recent actions are remembered best and more accurately; primacy—associations formed first by the respondents are better remembered than those that are formed later; frequency—a more frequent type experience is recalled more effectively and accurately; duration—the length of experience affects remembering; meaningfulness—it is easier to recall things that make sense: set—people have a set or a readiness to remember certain experiences more readily than others; mode—the mode of recall demanded by the questions affects the ability to remember. (7) Avoid questions that encourage inaccurate responses, either rephrase them or don't use them at all; (8) avoid questions that demand too much extra effort from the respondent; and (9) avoid opinion questions except when the questionnaire is surveying opinions.

FORMS OF QUESTIONS

Let us now consider seven forms of questions that deal with obtaining opinions: (1) Open-ended questions. These are most suitable for small studies or pilot studies. It should be noted that open-ended types of inquiries impose a heavy burden in terms of classifying and statistically handling the responses, and therefore should be avoided in large studies. (2) Free study and case method. In this method the interviewer conducts extended conversations with the respondent and records the significant results. (3) Coincidental, recall, and recognition questions. (4) Dichotomous questions. The responses for this kind of question consist of yes or no, agree or disagree, and so on. The chief advantage is its simplicity. However, it has the disadvantage that a respondent who misinterprets the question may give an answer that is reversed from what he really feels. (5) Check lists. The most common of multiple choice types of questions are check lists. For example: if prices go up, whose fault do you think it will be? And the possible responses might be: congress, everybody, big business, government officials, the present administration, labor unions, others, don't know. The respondent indicates his choice by an X or a check mark. (6) Ranking of items. This is also used in attitude measurement. For example: how important are the following features in a good suit? ( ) color, ( ) fit, ( ) style, ( ) quality. Place the number 1 inside the parentheses in front of the feature you consider the most important, and so on. (7) Multiple choice questions. The respondent selects from among several possible answers that one which comes closest to his opinion on the matter.

Rating or intensity scales are of several types: (1) Three point scales. For example: higher—same—lower; yes—depends—no. (2) The four point rating scales. For example: excellent—good—fair—poor. (3) The five point scales. For example: strongly approve—approve—undecided—disapprove—strongly disapprove. (4) Graphic rating scales. The strength of opinion can be indicated by the respondent on a line provided for him. The line could, for example, extend from plus 10 on the right, 0 in the middle, to minus 10 on the left. Then the respondent could be provided with directions as to which extreme would indicate strong approval, which would indicate strong disapproval, and so forth. The respondent would place his X mark in the appropriate position.

SUGGESTIONS FOR PHRASING QUESTIONNAIRE ITEMS

When attempting to work out questions for a survey instrument, the following suggestions might be of use. (1) Use simple words that are familiar to the respondents. (2) Be concise. (3) Construct the questions so that they yield exactly the information sought. (4) Avoid ambiguous questions. (5) Avoid leading questions. (6) Avoid catch-words, or stereotyped words with emotional connotations. (7) Avoid the use of phrases that may reflect upon the prestige of the respondent. (8) Decide whether you want to personalize some of the questions. (9) Allow for all possible responses, including the answer "I don't know". (10) Avoid the use of unrealistic choices in multiple choice questions. (11) Keep the writing required of the respondents down to a minimum. (12) Include a few questions that serve as checks on the accuracy and consistency of the responses as a whole. Two questions worded differently but asking for the same fact would be the type of approach suggested here. (13) Avoid questions that ask for responses toward socially accepted norms or values. (14) Avoid the risk of certain questions being considered unreasonable by prefacing them with a brief explanation which justifies the question.

The Use of Follow-up Studies for Program Evaluation

American society—and this includes education—undergoes cyclic fads. The latest rage in education is a demand for accountability from nursery school to graduate school. This has within it considerable potential for both good and bad. Looking at it negatively for a moment, taxpayers and legislators might demand answers for very difficult questions and then "punish" a segment of education for unsatisfactory answers by undercutting financial support (witness the present widespread pressure exerted upon higher education in the United States in the 70s.) All too often, a demand for accountability is not accompanied by a sound understanding of what the educational effort should produce. This vagueness can result in demands upon education which then develop wide breeches between requests for education and what legislators are willing to financially provide. However, it must be admitted that educators as a group have skirted the accountability issue for much too long; and a public that is being simultaneously badgered on two sides (by requests for more money via ever-increasing tax rates at a time when the overall economy is inflationary and is declining) must know more about what's happening to their tax dollars—hence a demand for accountability.

Looking at the problem more positively, a demand for accountability can result in long term improvements in education. Educational accountability has to do with what happens to people as a result of spending a portion of their lives within the influence of an educational institution. How can we assess the changes occupational students undergo during the time space between their initial enrollment and their entry into the work world? To what extent are the graduates "better off" for having completed their respective occupational programs? What are the relationships between the graduates, what they are doing now, and the occupational programs from which they graduated? These are central accountability questions.

The development of measurable objectives, on which course and program content are established, is a necessary first step in accountability. These behavioral objectives serve as one of the major bases in designing a survey instrument that can be used for program improvement. For preparing for the design of a follow-up questionnaire, objectives at the program level will generally suffice. It hardly needs to be said that the quality of the follow-up instrument is determined in no small part by the quality of the objectives obtained prior to the construction of the questionnaire.

DEVELOPMENT OF THE FOLLOW-UP INSTRUMENT

The follow-up instrument can take a number of forms. While the interview has the greatest overall flexibility, the economic advantage of the mail questionnaire is sufficiently great to result in most follow-up studies relying upon it. Therefore, we shall limit ourselves to the mail questionnaire in this section. A good follow-up questionnaire for occu pational programs is developed in this logical step- by- step manner.

1. Identification of program objectives. A small working group of faculty and administrators should identify those objectives that are to be examined by the questionnaire.
2. Verification of the objectives. It is recommended that the agreements arrived upon by the small group be fed back to the other faculty members and administrators concerned with this follow-up study to solicit their reactions to these topics for examination.
3. Determining what additional information should be sought. Follow-up questionnaires are quite often useful in obtaining information over and above testing program objectives.
4. Translation of objectives and desired information into questionnaire items. The designer of the study has the task of designing the items so that they are understandable to the person who will receive the questionaire.
5. Pretest of the questionnaire. The instrument should be tried out on a dozen or so individuals who are similar to the intended sample. The pretest should reveal most of the difficulties associated with responding to the questionnaire (Oppenheim 1966; Good 1963; Gillie 1971c)
6. Refinement of the instrument. Based upon the results obtained in the pretest, the questionnaire should be revised into its final form.

7. Selection of the sample. This can be done prior to any of the preceding steps, but is included here for convenience. The initial decision to be made is to whom the questionnaire should be sent. Some possibilities are: (a) all the graduates; (b) all graduates and non-persisters; (c) statistically selected graduates and non-persisters; (d) statistically selected graduates (Cochran 1963; Kendall 1964; Gillie 1971c). The decision should be made with regard to the number of students and the allocations of time, manpower, and finances available for the follow-up study.
8. Mailing of the questionnaire.
9. Development and implementation of a follow-up strategy. It is common knowledge that the usual rate of return for follow-up surveys is considerably less than 100 percent. A suggested remedy is a sequence of two or three follow-up letters, spaced out about ten days apart. This may bring the response rate to about fifty percent. Another measure which can increase the rate of response is to resort to telephone contact for the remaining non-residents or a randomly selected portion of that group when it is a very large group (Gillie 1971c).
10. Compilation and synthesis of the results. Sophisticated designs may utilize the computer for certain statistical analysis, whereas the more simple questionnaires may not need to do this. Most good questionnaires do rely on certain statistical approaches in order to identify correlations, relationships and so forth (Siegel 1956).
11. Reporting and interpreting the findings. This is obviously one of the most important parts of the entire study, and ironically, it is also frequently one of the most poorly designed.

The kinds of information that would be usable for program improvement could deal with factors such as (a) job characteristics of the graduates as they fall within the hierarchies of *people-related activities,* which are supervising, serving, mentoring, instructing, persuading, negotiating, and speaking-signaling; *data-related activities,* which are copying, synthesizing, comparing, compiling, coordinating, computing, analyzing; and *thing-related activities,* which are precision-working, tending, driving-operating, setting up, handling, operating controlling, and manipulating. (Dictionary of Occupational Titles 1965; Gillie 1971c); (b) job mobility characteristics, including the number of job changes and residence changes, and lists of residences in terms of distance from school graduated from (Monthly Labor Review 1963; Bjorkquist and Finch 1970; Ogden 1970); (c) evaluation of major course topics and objectives in terms of their usefulness for the graduates' present jobs; (d) the respondents' education and work history, including salary since graduation, to detect trends in education and job progression either horizontally or vertically over the period of time since the graduates left the institution. (Cost benefit statements can be developed from some of this information.); (e) aspects of the respondents' job satisfaction in terms of salary, job activities, possibilities for promotion, importance of job to their lives, etc.

INTERPRETATION OF INFORMATION

After all the data is collected, it must be compiled and synthesized in a predecided manner. Upon completion of this rather formidable task, the designer should translate the findings into statements and conclusions for faculty and administration consideration. The study designer-interpreter should inform them of the study's limitations as well. Special efforts should be made to prepare all the conclusions, implications, and resulting suggestions in simple, nonstatistical terms. To do this and still preserve accuracy is a difficult task, but is a "must" if the study outcomes are to be utilized by the faculty and administrators in the improvement of their programs.

Presentation of Information and Recommendations to Opinion Leaders and Decision-makers

After the preparations discussed in the preceding section have been carefully completed, arrangements should be made to present these findings to the opinion leaders and decision makers. Meetings with them for the purpose of providing them with the information would be the next step in the sequence. It is important that these individuals be correctly identified (Rogers 1962). Who are opinion leaders? They are the few individuals in the educational institution to whom the majority of the faculty (and perhaps even administrators) turn to for advice and information relative to that occupational program (Rogers 1962). Therefore, it seems logical to present the results and recommendations of the follow-up study to this select group of persons. The opinion leaders are often quite accurately identified by those administrators who are most familiar with the day-to-day operation of the college (Bice 1970). The decision makers are easier to identify. They are most likely the group of administrators directly associated with governance of the institution at the operations level (Caplow 1964).

Having identified the appropriate opinion leaders and decision makers, a meeting of these persons should be arranged for the purpose of providing them with a complete briefing of the information and recommendations emanating from the interpretation of the follow-up study. When these things have been completed, the stage is set for the conduct of the feedback conference (Gillie 1970a).

The Feedback Conference

The purpose of the feedback conference is to present the information and recommendations derived from the follow-up study to the appropriate faculty and administrators. This should be done in a dispassionate manner by the opinion leaders, actively supported by the decision-makers. The role of the follow-up study researcher is to serve as a resource person for the feedback conference. Clear identification of the role of the faculty in the feedback conferences is a decisive factor for enabling changes to be made. Hopefully, the feedback conference will also provide the initial impetus for faculty and administrators to respond to the recommendations in terms of curriculum changes and/or administrative procedures.

Following is a suggested generalized strategy for trying to incorporate changes identified by follow-up studies through the use of feedback conferences (Morgan 1966; National School Public Relations Association 1967; Gillie 1970a; Rogers 1962): (1) the opinion leaders and decision-makers associated with that program or aspect of college work should be "sold" on the idea or suggested change before convening the feedback conference; (2) the suggested change should be presented in such a way that it blends well with the cultural values and past experiences of those faculty members who are expected to incorporate the change; (3) the faculty and administrators who are expected to incorporate the changes must clearly understand the nature of the change and that its incorporation would result in a better program; (4) it should be made very clear that in addition to improving the program itself, the change will also enhance the competence of the teachers; and (5) the social consequences associated with making the change should be carefully anticipated and accommodated for in advance. For instance, if a recommended change called for an alteration in the size of the faculty, an acceptable strategy for doing this should be considered prior to the meeting. For example:

Assume a follow-up study was conducted of the graduates of a technology program. Also assume the program has had graduates for the past ten years. If the graduates were properly sampled, a cross-sectional view of both older graduates as well as the most recent graduates would be available. Let us further assume that one of the items examined in the questionnaire was the extent to which the graduates needed certain topics in mathematics on their present jobs (a list of mathematics levels in which they check the highest needed level would be one way such information could be readily found). For the sake of our illustration, assume the responses to this item revealed that the mathematics needed by the most recent graduates clearly ruled out some of the higher level mathematics presently being taught in the program, and that the older graduates needed even less mathematics. This information would be assembled in a simplified clear-cut fashion for presentation to the opinion leaders and decision-makers and later to the appropriate faculty members (probably the professors of technology and mathematics). The opinion leaders, with the support of facts by the conductor of the follow-up study would strongly urge for curriculum changes that would bring the program more in harmony with the needs of the graduates. At this point in the feedback conference it seems constructive action would most likely result if the appropriate faculty felt their role was not to decide *whether* a curriculum change was in order (since the results of the study clearly indicate such a change is in order), but how these changes could be made most efficiently and quickly.

The Inauguration of Suggestions Into the Curriculum

In the final analysis, actual curriculum changes are made by individual faculty members and/or administrators. These changes for program improvement should be reviewed and assessed at regular time intervals to see how effectively they have been made and what assistance is needed by those involved in making the changes. Another assessment should take place when the next follow-up study is conducted, the results of which may suggest recommendations for still more changes.

Burying Outmoded Programs

Let us examine the problem of outmoded programs, and some possible approaches to its alleviation. Educators are usually concerned with planning new programs but give virtually no comparable thought to discarding outmoded ones. Many two-year colleges have curricula that are "dead," but no one has the courage to give them their just due—a respectable burial. What are the signs of a moribund program? (1) a chronic lack of student interest to enroll in the program; (2) a lack of jobs of the type students are prepared for in the curriculum; (3) a preponderance of antiquated equipment and instruments in poorly functioning laboratories and shops; (4) a rigid, lockstep curriculum which is outdated; and (5) obsolete instructors. For example: A fifty-five year old instructor of electronics, with twenty years of teaching experience, is particularly expert in his knowledge of vacuum tube circuitry, but has demonstrated his inability to acquire sufficient new knowledge in solid state circuitry. His old program has been dropped in favor of a new one oriented toward the new electronics. What should be done with him? I believe the fairest solution, to the students and to the college as a whole, is to release him. For years industries have dismissed workers when their skills no longer coincided with their function on the job. Occupational teachers face the same risks as engineers and other professionals; if they don't stay up-to-date in their fields, they must be released from practicing in their profession. Furthermore, if the changing industries in the area result in a particular kind of program no longer being needed, the instructors should be released and the program discontinued. The idea of keeping an unneeded program going for the sake of one or a few faculty is absurd, to say the least; it's actually irresponsible. However, the college should make every attempt to help the displaced instructor find a suitable job.

Another problem in the elimination of outdated programs has been the injection of large amounts of federal and state funds for equipment and facilities in vocational education (particularly PL 88-210 and 90-576). Many administrators are haunted by the fear of being accused of unwise spending in the past years (Perkins 1971). Admittedly, it is a difficult task to look at costly equipment, sometimes not more than five years old, and issue the order to "get rid of it." Furthermore, getting rid of equipment purchased with federal and state funds is not so simple. Added to this is the reluctance of a governing board to honor a request for another heavy investment for replacing equipment that should be discarded. The dilemma can become not unlike the cycling of automobiles—one hardly completes the payments when it is necessary to purchase another one.

Looking ahead, problems of this kind can be minimized by not establishing laboratories and shops that have the "latest" in their particular specialty, since in a few years it will be outmoded. It's better to leave a high degree of specialization to the kind of skill center proposed in Chapter 7 or for actual on-the-job training. Careful selection of generic-type equipment for the laboratories and shops could greatly lengthen their useful life. For example, an electronics laboratory could select basic kinds of volt-ohm meters, oscilloscopes, signal generators and the like, and not purchase large numbers of the more specialized and exotic equipment.

What about the large amounts of funds—federal, state, and local—that have been invested in equipment and facilities no longer appropriate for the present state of the occupational area for which they were purchased? There is only one answer, and it is a painful one: The outmoded equipment must be done away with. Such a decision is unavoidable since it is based on the fact that the kinds of things the students are being prepared for are no longer appropriate. It is important that decision-makers admit to these things so that the program and its outmoded equipment can be quickly removed. Once the program and its outmoded equipment are removed from the students, and out of the college's offerings, the business manager can decide on the procedures to be used in disposing of the equipment.

It seems reasonable to plan a procedure by which we can determine when a program should be modernized or dropped. The pulse of the program is student interest and job availability. When student interest wanes, the program is in trouble. Should student interest decrease to the point that a certain minimum number of students cannot be enrolled, it's time to decide whether the program should be buried. Lack of student interest for several years in a row is an indication that curricular rigor mortis may have already set in and a quiet burial should be considered. A clear-cut procedure for removing programs should be established, including a standing committee with sufficient authority to do the job. The administration then makes the final decision, based on the facts, as to whether the program in question should be commissioned to the academic graveyard. In instances where a standing committee does not exist, an evaluation of the curriculum can be made by an outside expert in the specific occupational program, but this must be done carefully, because a consultant sometimes seeks to reinforce the feelings of those who employ him (Skaggs 1967). A third source of assistance can be the regional or specialized accrediting agencies, many of which are becoming increasingly more concerned with post-secondary occupational education (Southern Association of Colleges and Schools 1970a; 1970b).

The first step in program elimination is to stop taking students into the program. Then plans should be made to allow the present enrollees to complete the course, resulting in a full year between the decision and the complete stop of the program. During this year, several important things have to be done. The procedures for dispensing with the old equipment should be set in order, ready to implement as soon as the school year is ended. Also of importance and of greatest difficulty, is the finalizing of arrangements for displaced faculty. Unfortunately, pleasant arrangements cannot always be made—a reason why many schools have delayed discontinuance of a program until the involved faculty members retire. But I believe this is putting the wrong values first. Although it would be ideal to be able to place every displaced faculty member into another position (or into retirement), there are many instances when it simply can't be done.

The results of follow-up and longitudinal studies may be the harbinger of program obsolescence. If the signs of a dying program are there, they should be immediately heeded. Then, if it's apparent the program should go, it should be proclaimed as such and be done away with. There's no logic in carrying dead programs around when there is so much that needs to be done for live programs and real jobs.

Summary

Improving and modernizing ongoing occupational programs requires investigating what past graduates are doing, predicting what future graduates will need, and analyzing certain selected relationships. The survey is a pre-planned scheme to serve this purpose. The major steps in the survey include planning the procedure, pretesting the instruments' first design, arriving at a cost estimate for conduct of the survey, establishing the time schedule for conduct of the field work, determining the methods to obtain the desired information, selecting the questions for the survey, determining the form the questions should take, and deciding on the phrasing of the questionnaire items.

The use of follow-up studies for program evaluation is considered, and it is suggested that surveys used to meet a demand for evaluation of programs be designed to also obtain data that can be used in curriculum improvement. This chapter offers eleven suggestions for the development of a follow-up questionnaire for occupational programs.

Emphasis is placed on the fact that the most important aspect of conducting follow-up studies is the translation of the findings into suggestions that can in turn be utilized by the faculty and administration. A special process to accomplish this is suggested. Step 1 in the process is to identify the opinion leaders and decision-makers from among faculty that should incorporate the findings from such studies. It is important that the opinion leaders and the decision-makers be won over to accepting the translated results of the follow-up study. The next step is the feed-back conference, which is conducted by the opinion leaders and the decision-makers. The major purposes of the feed-back conference are to present the acquired information and recommendations to the appropriate professional staff, and to provide the initial impetus for accepting the recommendations for inaugurating the suggested changes. Finally, there should be a follow-up of the conference to see if the involved professional staff is incorporating the suggestions and to determine if they need special in-service training.

The final section of the chapter points to the chronic problem of removing outmoded programs from the college. The symptoms of an outmoded curriculum are given, and problems associated with this dilemma are discussed. It is strongly suggested that outmoded programs be discontinued with dispatch, in the interest of the beneficiaries of the college—the students.

REFERENCES

Alden, J. D. *Prospects of Engineering and Technology Graduates.* New York: Engineering Manpower Commission of Engineers Joint Council, 1970.

Bice, G. R. *Working with Opinion Leaders to Accelerate Change in Vocational-Technical Education.* Columbus, Ohio: Center for Vocational and Technical Education, Ohio State University, 1970.

Bjorkquist, D. C. and Finch, C. R. "The Relationship of Personnel Characteristics of MDTA Graduates to Geographic Mobility." *Journal of Employment Counseling* Volume III, No. 3. Reno, Nev: National Employment Counselors Association, 1970.

Caplow, T. *Principles of Organization.* New York: Harcourt, Brace and World, 1964.

Cochran, W. G. *Sampling Techniques: Second Edition.* New York: John Wiley, 1963.

Gillie, A. C. *Essays: Occupational Education in the Two-Year College.* University Park, Pa.: Department of Vocational Education, Pennsylvania State University, 1970a.

______. *Geographic-Job Mobility of The Pennsylvania State University Two-Year Technician Graduates.* University Park, Pa.: Department of Vocational Zducation, Pennsylvania State University, 1970a.

______. *Employment Characteristics of The Pennsylvania State University Associate Degree Graduates.* University Park, Pa.: Department of Vocational Education, Pennsylvania State University, 1971a.

______. *Associate Degree Technicians' Judgements on Quality of Instruction and Course Relevancy.* University Park, Pa.: Department of Vocational Education, Pennsylvania State University, 1971b.

______. *Pennsylvania State University Associate Degree Technician Graduates: Some Demographic Variables.* University Park, Pa.: Department of Vocational Education, Pennsylvania State University, 1971c.

Good, C. V. *Introduction to Educational Research: Second Edition.* New York: Appleton-Century-Crofts, 1963.

Kendall, M. G. *Basic Ideas of Scientific Sampling.* New York: Hafner, 1964.

"Job Mobility in 1961." *Monthly Labor Review.* Volume 86. Washington, D.C.: U.S. Bureau of Labor Statistics, 1963.

Morgan, J. S. *Practical Guide to Conference Leadership.* New York: McGraw-Hill, 1966.

Moss, J., Jr. *The Evaluation of Occupational Education Programs.* Technical Report Minneapolis, Minn.: University of Minnesota, Research Coordination Unit in Occupational Education, 1968.

"Occupational Classification." Volume 2 of the *Dictionary of Occupational Titles.* 3rd Edition. Washington, D.C.: U.S. Department of Labor, 1965.

O'Connor, J.J. *Follow-up Studies in Junior Colleges: A Tool for Institutional Improvement.* Washington, D.C.: American Association of Junior Colleges, 1965.

Ogden, G. L. "Upward Mobility of Licensed Vocational Nurses." *Junior College Journal.* Volume 40, No. 7. Washington, D.C.: American Association of Junior Colleges, 1970.

Operational Policies of the Committee on Occupational Education. Atlanta, Ga: The Southern Association of Colleges and Schools, 1970b.

Oppenheim, A. N. *Questionnaire Design and Attitude Measurement.* New York: Basic Books, 1966.

Perkins, C. D. *Reports on the Implementation of the Vocational Education Amendments of 1968.* Washington, D.C.: U.S. Government Printing Office, 1971.

Public Law 210, 88th Congress (Vocational Education Act of 1963)

Public Law 576, 90th Congress (Vocational Education Amendments of 1968).

Rogers, E. M. *Diffusion of Innovations.* New York: The Free Press, 1962.

Siegel, S. *Nonparametric Statistics for the Behavioral Sciences.* New York: McGraw-Hill, 1956.

Skaggs, K. G. *On Using and Being a Consultant.* Washington, D.C.: American Association of Junior Colleges, 1967.

Tentative Standards of the Committee on Occupational Education. Atlanta, Ga.: The Southern Association of Colleges and Schools, 1970a.

The Conference Planners. Washington, D.C.: National School Public Relations Association, 1967.

Chapter 10 INSTITUTIONAL RESEARCH: A MECHANISM FOR PROGRAM AND INSTITUTIONAL IMPROVEMENT

Stevens College, about fifty years ago, was one of the first higher education institutions to initiate institutional research. Even as recently as just after the conclusion of World War II, institutional research was fragmented and sparse (Dressel 1970). Since that time, colleges and universities have become more concerned with instructional effectiveness and efficiency (USOE 58042), and offices of institutional research have become more common. However, many colleges and universities still shy away from such efforts. Reasons given for not supporting institutional research are varied (Roueche and Boggs, 1968), but none of them are very convincing—some college authorities probably feel that a continuing research effort is costly; others see their institutional research departments as primarily collectors of all kinds of data, much of which is filed away and forgotten.

Institutional research is even less accepted in two-year colleges. This is unfortunate because occupational education, a major element of two-year colleges, is kept most viable and relevant by active institutional research. One study reported some startling facts about this (Swanson 1965). Nine percent of the 334 junior colleges sampled had a formal organization for instructional research and had specific budget items for that purpose; and *only four* of the 334 colleges had full-time personnel assigned to institutional research. A more recent survey (Gillie

1972) found an increase in the number of two-year colleges that have full-time personnel assigned to institutional research. Of the 633 public two-year colleges from forty-one states and one trust territory accounted for in the study, eighty-one had full-time institutional research personnel, or 12.8 percent of the total colleges included in this study. It should be pointed out that the 214 two-year colleges from the remaining ten states and two trust territories not accounted for here, could significantly alter this percentage. Table 10-1 illustrates the distribution of two-year colleges with full time offices of institutional research. Many of the state directors of community colleges indicated that some of the

TABLE 10-1

DISTRIBUTION OF PUBLIC TWO-YEAR COLLEGES THAT HAVE FULL-TIME PERSONNEL ASSIGNED TO INSTITUTIONAL RESEARCH OFFICES

State	A	B	State	A	B
Alabama	17	0	Nebraska	8	0
Alaska	7	0	Nevada	1	0
Arizona	12	1	New Hampshire	1	0
Arkansas	4	0	New Jersey	13	5
California	92	NA	New Mexico	9	0
Colorado	16	0	New York	43	20
Connecticut	14	0	North Carolina	54	0
Delaware	3	1	North Dakota	6	0
D. C.	1	0	Ohio	36	4
Florida	27	16	Oklahoma	14	6
Georgia	14	NA	Oregon	13	3
Hawaii	6	1	Pennsylvania	32	6
Idaho	2	NA	Rhode Island	1	0
Illinois	47	NA	South Carolina	21	0
Indiana	2	0	South Dakota	0	NA
Iowa	20	0	Tennessee	9	0
Kansas	20	NA	Texas	45	2
Kentucky	15	1	Utah	5	NA
Louisiana	7	NA	Vermont	1	0
Maine	5	0	Virginia	21	NA
Maryland	15	10	Washington	26	0
Massachusetts	15	0	West Virginia	4	NA
Michigan	32	0	Wisconsin	25	0
Minnesota	18	0	Wyoming	7	0
Mississippi	18	0	American Samoa	1	NA
Missouri	15	5	Canal Zone	1	NA
Montana	3	0	Puerto Rico	3	0
TOTAL	447	35		400	46

A— Number of Public Two-Year Colleges
Total: 847
B— Number of Full-Time Institutional Research Offices
Total: 81
Total Included in Survey: 633
Percent that have Full-Time Institutional Research Offices 12.79% (of 633)
NA—Not Available (Either the State Director did not know or no response was obtained from that state.)

Note 1: "Number of Public Two-Year Colleges" was taken from the *1971 Junior College Directory* (W.A. Harper, ed.) Washington, D.C.: American Association of Junior Collges, 1971.
Note 2: These figures were obtained by the author in a survey of all State Directors of two-year colleges in 1972 and are based on the responses to the question "How many public two-year colleges in your state employ at least one person on a full-time basis for the purpose of conducting institutional research?"

two-year colleges in their states had part-time institutional research efforts. These are not shown in Table 10-1 because of the difficulty in ascertaining the degree of commitment to institutional research in such cases.

Institutional research is misunderstood in many places. In some colleges, one person has a portion of his time allotted for the routine tasks of accumulating records and data on students and other kinds of information. Even though efforts of this sort often stop at this point, they are identified as institutional research by some colleges. Even colleges strongly interested in research tend to spend very limited funds on studying their own operations (Dressel 1971). The mere collection of sundry data is hardly a significant step in institutional research. The major criterion for the success or failure of institutional research is whether or not its findings are translated into improved institutional practices (instructional and other).

An office of institutional research can survive as a viable effort only when its purposes are understood and strongly supported by the administration and faculty of the institution. An office of institutional research requires the presence of a full-time director who is a competent applied researcher. The director's first task should be to identify the significant questions for which answers are most needed by the faculty and administration. Ideally, he should provide leadership and assist the faculty and staff in finding ways to improve instruction (Saupe and Dressel, 1971; Johnson 1971). This would require the involvement of everyone—students, faculty, and administrators—with the director of research. Although the institutional researcher must be concerned with the overall relationships between students, faculty, and the institution, he would most likely come to be more involved with the individuals rather than the organizational framework of the institution itself.

Much research is needed to determine the work modes of both graduates and early leavers, the differential effects of narrow- and broad-based occupational programs upon students of both orientations (career and academic), the differential effects of various instructional modes upon students while they are in school and later in the world of work (Mortimer and Leslie 1970; Thompson 1967: Suchman 1967; USOE 58042, 1970). The number of things that need doing are so great that the real problem is establishing priorities.

Using Research Findings to Improve the Institution

One of the basic purposes of institutional research is to study the structure of the institution in order to find weaknesses that block or impede efforts of the school to achieve its goals (Dressel 1971a). After this comes the all-important task of getting the institutional members to use the obtained data and to act on the findings. If the research findings are not used, the effort is a failure.

In setting the stage for the conduct of these studies, plans must be made to determine what needs to be collected. Then it should be collected, processed, and an accurate interpretation of the findings should be developed (Dressel 1971). A good office of institutional research should have relatively easy access to data and also would provide a method of joining together this data, resulting in a data band—a mechanism within the college (or a consortium of colleges in some cases) where a network of relationships necessary for access and communication is established. It can be regarded as a carefully designed environment for co-operation between data, access, and communication. The joining together of institutional data in the form of a data bank smooths the way for studies to be initiated, administered, evaluated, and incorporated by the faculty and administration. A readily accessible data bank would tend to minimize the tendency for a specific principle investigator or research director to launch into a project with no regard as to its applicability for the rest of the institution. A competent director of institutional research can assist in designing studies that dovetail into other efforts which result in some improvement in the operation of the college.

PROJECT VERSUS PROGRAM

Institutional research can take the form of a program, which is a broadly conceived experimental activity, and consists of a continuous, coordinated series of experiments that emanate directly from the office of institutional research, or it can take the form of a project is a more limited research effort with short term objectives, under the leadership of a project director or principal investigator. An institutional research effort should be well planned in advance (Dressel 1971b). It should begin with a clearly stated objective, which should then be translated into a research strategy. This can then be broken down into its several elements with sufficient specificity to permit successful conduct of an investigation. No institutional effort can succeed unless the right questions are asked in the right places so that their answers can be found. Ideally, the president of the institution ought to have knowledge of ongoing research in his college, and should strongly support the incorporation of the findings into the educational fabric of his institution. It is difficult to envision a research finding having an impact upon a college without this kind of support.

DATA, INFORMATION, AND KNOWLEDGE

There are important differences and interrelationships among these three terms. Data consists of symbolic representations of properties of objects or events; it represents facts. Data becomes useful only when it is translated from a symbolic state into a meaningful state, at which time it becomes information. The extent to which information is significant is determined by its relevance to the problems at hand. The data banks provide a pool of potential information. Knowledge is the act, fact, or state of *knowing* in terms of *understanding*. The office of institutional research has the major task of reducing data to information and converting it into knowledge.

The Importance of Institutional Climate

Projects and programs, not being self-sustaining, must be nurtured and encouraged with continuous support from the administration. This is no small task in those two-year colleges where antipathy toward research exists (Gillie, Leslie, and Bloom,1971). Strong continuing support from the college's power structure can help institutional research win acceptance from the faculty, especially when it is demonstrated by recognition and rewards for those who take part in it. Without active support, research in the two-year college will likely fall by the wayside, and research-oriented persons will drift toward performing disciplinary research (likely in another institution) or abandon all efforts to do research (with the emergence of an "anti-all-research syndrome"). The major indicator of research success would be whether or not it changed some aspect of institutional practice. Successes should be plainly announced, so as to provide encouragement to all involved. Some kinds of changes can be measured only indirectly, and come about in the form of new action proposed by the research outcomes. Such new action should be credited to the research effort. More successful research endeavors will tend to ease the way for more investigations and subsequently more changes in institutional practices.

Innovation

Innovation means many things to various people. One definition of innovation is (Miles 1964): "A deliberate, novel, specific change, which is thought to be more efficacious in accomplishing the goals of a system." Another is (Drucker 1958): "Man's attempt to create order in his own mind and the universe around him by taking risks and creating risks. It can be defined as the organized, indeed deliberate, seeking of risks to replace both the blind chance of modern times . . . and the certainty of the more recent but still outdated belief in inevitable progress, both chanceless and riskless." From our point of view, in terms of occupational education, it suffices to consider innovation as *a label attached to a change that is considered an improvement.* With regard to institutional research in occupational education, to be significant a change must be able to contribute in successive stages to putting to work an improvement in the college's endeavor in the preparation of middle level workers.

Need for Synthesis and Dissemination

Research has developed a large number of tiny bits of findings which are difficult to synthesize into results that can be translated into strategies for bringing about institutional changes and improvements (Cohen and Quimby, 1970). Dovetailing results so that they can be used in changing something for the better in that institution happens only when planned that way. Also, research findings from other institutions should be utilized and incorporated into new research. Information of this type is readily available from the federally financed Educational Research and Information Center system. Of particular value for two-year colleges and occupational education are the ERIC Clearinghouse for Vocational and Career Education at Northern Illinois University, ERIC Clearinghouse for Junior College Information in Los Angeles, and ERIC Clearinghouse for Higher Education in Washington, D.C.

Planning for Change

Planning for change is one of the most important objectives of institutional research. Three things have happened in higher education that make it necessary for changes to take place more rapidly now than has been the case of the past. They are: (a) student apathy; (b) the generally bleak financial condition of higher education; and (c) a tendency for the public to react against the performance of higher education. This situation can improve only when educational institutions conform to meet the circumstances. Changes should be made on the basis of solid study and research. Rather than waiting for each crisis to develop, and then reacting to it, we must take a far broader and more penetrating look at our institutions, the people they serve and those who work in them. One possible function of institutional research is to serve as a guide to determine what the problems really are and then to strategize ways to find solutions. Leaders in higher education have consistently asked the question *what should a university be?* We need to ask the same question in terms of post-secondary occupational programs. We need a protean definition of this role which would help the institution maintain realistic relationships with its social environment on a long term basis. Occupational education via the two-year college can serve as a catalyst in the articulation of the three major human resources in our society—education, industry, and government. They must be balanced in such a way that the values of one do not stifle the value of the others while maximum productivity is obtained from each by preparing people for middle level occupations. Achievement of a perfect balance may be impossible, but we can continue to strive toward that ultimate goal.

Managerial Efficiency and Instructional Effectiveness

Institutional research efforts toward identifying answers to two major problems should be made: (1) the development of greater managerial efficiency; and (2) the development of increased instructional effectiveness, which is one of the avowed concerns of educational institutions (OE-58042, 1970). Institutional research is a logical mechanism for demonstrating the interrelationship of institutional governance and the learning processes going on within the school. The tendency to separate these two (some researchers focus their efforts on institutional matters while others direct their endeavors toward the area of learning and learning resources) should be resisted. There is a need for both approaches, and the office of research is the vehicle for bringing these two elements together in the most functional way. There is also a goal conflict which has long been recognized: faculty goals are prestige-oriented whereas students' goals relate to achievement. Although this particular conflict might be less pronounced in two-year college occupational programs, it does exist. Perhaps institutional research can help in the search for ways in which rewards would be more related to student goal achievement.

Other Tasks for Institutional Research

It is common knowledge that innovative and creative changes are usually resisted (Rogers 1962). This resistance may be related to several major factors, including (1) the faculty reward system; the faculty is not hired or paid to improve the product—student knowledge. Rather, teachers are hired on the basis of their ability to teach so many hours a semester. Trends toward greater accountability may eventually change this, but for the time being there seems to be little evidence of movement in this direction, and (2) many two-year college faculty members have underlying feelings against research (Gillie, Leslie, and Bloom 1971) which may be related to vague feelings of inadequacies on their part. These instructors ought to be made to appreciate how they can become intelligent consumers of the fruits of research.

Not many colleges spend very much of their appropriations for research and development, and much of this is devoted to basic research at the university levels (Dressel 1971). In occupational education, the greatest part of the research effort should be made in the application of findings. Agricultural education is one place where a reward system for improvement has been established, largely through federally sponsored experimental and demonstration stations, although these have been subject to strong criticisms at times (PL 12-503 and PL 24-440). Some progress in post-secondary occupational education research is being made with federal funding assistance (PL 90-576), but much more needs to be done.

What are the areas that need to be researched? Some possible projects (Cohen and Quimby, 1970) are: (1) teacher and administrator information services; (2) assessing teaching effectiveness; (3) validating content of junior college curricula; (4) constructing a model of junior college schooling; (5) constructing program assessment models; (6) determining the effects of junior college schooling on students; (7) determining student characteristics in occupation-centered curricula; (8) assessing verbal skill dependency; (9) evaluating the impact of junior colleges on the communities they serve; (10) assessing organizational climates; (11) studying the attitudes of various educational factions; (12) polling community opinion. Each one of these topics is directly related to preparing people for middle level occupations. Institutional research by community colleges can serve as a catalyst in many of these efforts.

Summary

Institutional research does not appear to be supported by the majority of two-year colleges, based on the number of two-year colleges that have full-time personnel assigned to institutional research. This is unfortunate because occupational education, which should be the major thrust of two-year colleges, requires continuous investigation to remain relevant and attractive to students. The first step in establishing a viable office of institutional research is to allocate into the college budget the position of a full-time research director. Part-time positions, often cluttered with countless other responsibilities, result in little or no sustained effort to inaugurate meaningful institutional research. The purposes to be served by institutional research should be clearly established. Hazy notions of research possibilities may well be part of the reason for its lack of support.

Institutional research includes the study of problems connected with college operations, but its efforts should not stop there. It should have the responsibility and the resources to urge professional staff members to use the obtained data and to act on the findings. Finding solutions to problems is a prerequisite to institutional improvement, but establishing ways in which they can be put into operation within the college is the most critical task of the office of institutional research.

The *program* is considered to be a broadly conceived experimental activity, whereas a *project* is usually more limited and conducted in a shorter span of time. All institutional research efforts should begin with a clearly stated objective which relates to the institution. The office of institutional research, because it is contained within the organizational framework of the college, has the potential to be a successful vehicle for improvement of institutional climate and also to serve as the mechanism for the introduction of desirable innovations. The evaluation of programs, instruction, and students, are apt to meet with less resistance from the professional staff if they are conducted as "in house" activities. Areas in which institutional research efforts would be beneficial are listed. An effective office of institutional research would serve as a catalyst in the many efforts toward improving various elements within the two-year college.

REFERENCES

Cohen, A. M. and Quimby, E. A. "Trends in the Study of Junior Colleges: 1970." *ERIC Junior College Research Review: September 1970.* Volume 5, No. 1. Washington, D.C.: American Association of Junior Colleges.

Do Teachers Make a Difference? Washington, D.C.: U. S. Government Printing Office (OE-54042), 1970.

Dressel, P. L. and Associates. *Institutional Research in the University: A Handbook.* San Francisco, Calif.: Jossey-Bass, 1971.

———. "Nature of Institutional Research in Self-Study." *Institutional Research in the University: A Handbook.* San Francisco, Calif: Jossey-Bass, 1971a.

———."Planning and Executing Studies." *Institutional Research in the University: A Handbook.* San Francisco, Calif.: Jossey-Bass, 1971b.

Dressel, P.; Johnson, F. C. and Associates "Studying Teaching and Learning." *Institutional Research in the University: A Handbook.* San Francisco, Calif.: Jossey-Bass, 1971.

Dressel, P. L.; Saupe, J. L. and Associates. "Evaluating Outcomes of Instruction." *Institutional Research in the University: A Handbook.* San Francisco, Calif.: Jossey-Bass, 1971.

Drucker, P. F. *Landmarks of Tomorrow.* New York: Harper, 1959.

Gillie, A. C.; Leslie, L. L.; and Bloom, K. L. *Goals and Ambivalence: Faculty Values and Community College Philosophy.* University Park, Pa.: Center for the Study of Higher Education, Report No. 13, Pennsylvania State University, 1971.

Gillie, A. C. *A National Survey of State Directors of Community Colleges.* Unpublished survey, 1972.

Mayhew, L. B. "Keynote Address." *Institutional Research in the Community College: Process and Product.* Sacramento, Calif.: Junior College Association, 1965.

Miles, M. B. *Innovation and Education.* New York: Bureau of Publications, Teachers College, Columbia University, 1964.

Mortimer, K.P. *Accountability in Higher Education.* Washington, D.C.: American Association for Higher Education, 1972.
Education, Pennsylvania State University, 1970

Mortimer, K. P. *Accountability in Higher Education.* Washington, D. C.: American Association for Higher Education, 1972.

Public Law 503, 12th Congress (The Morrill Act).

Public Law 440, 24th Congress (The Hatch Act).

Public Law 576, 90th Congress (Vocational Education Amendments of 1968).

Rogers, E. M. *Diffusion of Innovations.* New York: The Free Press, 1962.

Roueche, J. E. and Boggs, J. R. *Junior College Institutional Research: The State of the Art.* Washington, D.C.: American Association of Junior Colleges, 1968.

Suchman, E. A. *Evaluative Research.* New York: Russell Sage Foundation, 1967.

Swanson, H. L. "An Investigation of Institutional Research in the Junior Colleges of the United States." Unpublished doctoral dissertation. Los Angeles, Calif.: School of Education, University of California, 1965.

Thomson, J. "Institutional Studies of Junior College Students." *Junior College Research Review.* Volume 1, No. 4, ED 013070. Washington, D.C.: American Association of Junior Colleges, 1967.

Chapter 11 DIFFUSION OF KNOWLEDGE, RESEARCH FINDINGS AND INNOVATIVE PRACTICES

The introduction of new ideas and concepts is an integral part of keeping occupational programs up to date, and therefore it might be fruitful to review how innovations can be diffused in occupational education. The issue is examined here by delving into the characteristics associated with diffusion of new ideas and practices, and then applying them within the context of two-year college occupational programs. The importance of this topic cannot be overstressed because real changes in the education of middle level workers occur only when those changes are accepted within the existing structure of two-year colleges and others who prepare middle level workers. Apathy and even antipathy toward the introduction of new ideas and concepts within institutions are often displayed by certain individuals; much needs to be learned about why such feelings hold sway, and more importantly, what can be done to reduce or eliminate these obstacles.

The Process of Diffusing a New Idea

Let us first examine the four basic elements involved in the process of spreading a new idea from its source to its potential users. They are: (1) establishing the new practice or idea;

(2) communicating it to the potential users; (3) spreading it among the individuals within a given social system; (4) continuing the diffusion of the idea or practice over a period of time.

As indicated earlier, the term *innovation* has a number of meanings to different people; it is used here to signify an idea or practice considered to be new by the person who came up with it. *Diffusion* is the process by which a new idea or practice is spread from the originator to its intended users (also called consumers or adopters). Diffusion occurs within a social system, which consists of the population of individuals who are potential users of the idea or practice. The faculty and administrators associated with middle level occupational preparation are in the social system in this case.

The ultimate goal of diffusing a new idea or practice is to have it adopted by its intended consumers so that the organization of which they are a part can better achieve its goals. The term *adoption* refers to a decision to continue the full use of the innovation. The process of adopting an innovation or research finding is the mental progression through which one must move from the time he first hears of the innovation to that moment when the decision is made to incorporate it on a permanent basis. Another term we need to deal with is *innovativeness*, and we shall use it to indicate the extent to which one individual adopts the new idea in advance of the general population within his social system. This leads us to the concept of adopter categories, which are classifications of individuals within the social system on the basis of their innovativeness.

The Adoption Process

The adoption process can be fragmented into five steps through which the potential consumer would progress: (1) the awareness stage, when he first learns that the innovation exists; (2) development of interest in the new idea or practice, when he considers the feasibility of utilizing it in his work; (3) evaluation of the innovation, to ascertain its usefulness to him and the practicality of using it in his work; (4) the conduct of a trial or test of the innovation, which may be in the form of a demonstration in some cases; and (5) the incorporation of the innovation on a permanent basis.

During the adoption process, the potential user considers the relationship of the innovation to his own mode of operation (Rogers 1962). There are a number of characteristics of an innovation that come under scrutiny during this phase of the process, including the relative advantages the new idea or practice offers to him—whether it is superior to the idea or practice it is designed to supercede; compatibility—it must be reasonably consistent with the potential adopter's past experiences and existing values; complexity—the new idea or practice must be simple enough to be readily understood and put into practical use by a potential adopter; communicability—the results brought about by the innovation must be in such a form that they can be spread to others with relative ease; and rate of adoption—if the new idea or practice is to gain hold in educational institutions within a regional or national basis, the speed with which it is adopted becomes important. Slowness in adoption results in fewer adopters.

Categorization of Innovativeness

Individuals within an educational system can be classified on the basis of their innovativeness. The distribution of adopters by categories follows a bell-shaped curve over a period of time and approaches normality (Rogers 1962). The continum of innovativeness, as shown in Figure 11-1, can be divided into five categories. They are listed below with brief descriptions of each.

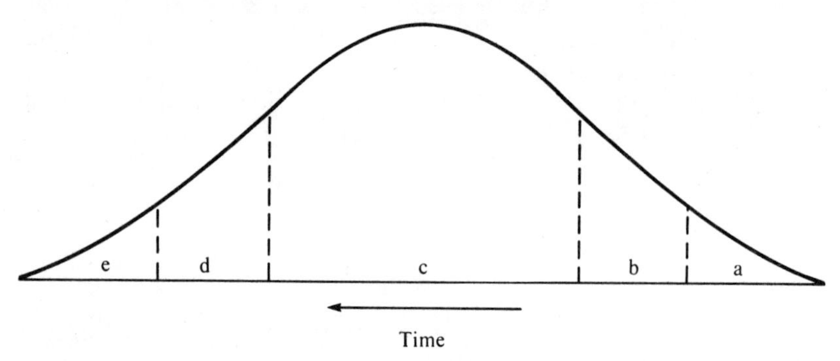

FIGURE 11-1
NORMAL DISTRIBUTION OF INNOVATION ADOPTERS

A. *Innovators*. Innovators are adventuresome and are perceived as deviants within their social system. The degree to which they are viewed as deviants depends to a considerable degree on (1) the social norms regarding innovativeness of their social systems (i.e. the position of their institution on the traditional-innovative spectrum) and (2) the adopter category of the person viewing the innovator (he is perceived as most deviant by the more conservative elements within his social system).

B. *Early adopters*. Early adopters are highly respected by their co-workers. They are younger, enjoy a higher social status, are better off financially, and are engaged in more specialized operations within their institutional setting. Furthermore, the early adopters are more impersonal and cosmopolitan in their social relationships. Persons in this category utilize a greater number of information sources than later adopters and display more opinion leadership (i.e. they are effective in influencing their co-workers and peers) than later adopters.

C. *Early Majority.* Individuals in this group are most apt to follow the lead of the early adopters. They also tend to be deliberate and thoughtful about a new idea before adopting it.

D. *Late Majority.* Adopters in this category tend to view a new idea or practice with some degree of suspicion or skepticism. This attitude often persists to some extent even after its adoption.

E. *Laggards.* This group is made up of those individuals who are last to adopt a new practice—if they adopt it at all. They are usually conservative and traditional both in life- and work-styles.

INSTITUTIONAL INNOVATION NORMS

Besides norms for individuals' innovativeness, there are also institutional innovation norms (Rogers 1962). An institutional norm is the most frequently occuring pattern of overt behavior displayed by the members of that particular institution. Two idealized types of norms can be identified for the purpose of comparisons in terms of the innovation-traditional spectrum. They are: (1) traditional, and (2) modern. Like other idealized norms, these are theoretical models only, since all educational institutions have elements of both the traditional and the modern within them.

The everyday educational operations of a two-year college that scores high on the modern norm would involve a considerable amount of advanced technological know-how. For example, it would tend to effectively utilize computerized instruction to some extent, modern highly-efficient laboratories, and various types of new media in its teaching endeavors. Its faculty would be more cosmopolitan, literate, rational, and highly empathetic to the leaning process and the students. Also, the teachers would tend to be more innovative in their instructional practices, frequently trying new approaches and applying newer findings within their subject matter fields. On the other hand, a two year college that scores high on the traditional norm would tend to utilize the laboratory designs that are not unlike those used twenty years previously, and the same could be said of the faculty's teaching practices and subject matter content. They would be among the last to accept, and then only passively, the changes in subject matter made necessary by technological changes.

There are three methods for measuring the placement of an institution on the traditional-modern dimension (Rogers 1962). First, the average innovativeness of the members of the educational institution can be ascertained in an appropriate manner by way of interviews and questionnaires. The second approach utilizes interviews and/or questionnaires to determine the attitude of the institution's members toward persons who are considered to be innovators (they are most warmly received by members of a school located close to the modern end of the spectrum). Thirdly, the overall institution can be placed at a point on the traditional-modern continuum using pre-established criteria.

Determining the norm of a given institution (in terms of the traditional-modern dimension) would be a useful, if not vital, piece of information prior to strategizing for introducing a new idea or practice. The office of institutional research (if the school has one) would be the best mechanism to conduct such an investigation.The importance of knowing where the institution stands in the traditional-modern dimension is further emphasized by the fact that innovativeness of the individuals within that college would likely be positively correlated with the norm of the institution (Rogers 1962). The strategies to be utilized in the diffusion of an innovation should be tailored to fit the traditional-modern norm of the college. The spread of new ideas is always a difficult process, and an innovation may be rejected at any of the five stages in the adoption process. Furthermore, it can be rejected after it has been adopted, and would then be called a discontinuance. Discontinuance is a common phenomenon in occupational education for a number of reasons, including failure to win lasting consumer support, evaluation after adoption which determines that it is considered to be undesirable, and displacement of the innovation by a still newer practice. The discontinued innovation may later be readopted, although this is not a common occurrence. The innovation-use tree shown in Figure 11-2 illustrates the possibilities through which an innovation passes over a period of time (Gillie 1970).

Opinion Leaders and their Role

An opinion leader, as mentioned in Chapter 9, is one whom persons within the system frequently turn to for advice and information. One of the chief influence mechanisms utilized by opinion leaders is the direct face-to-face exchange with their peers. This personal influence is most effective in the following situations: (1) at the evaluation stage of the adoption process; (2) for relatively late adopters—they are more influenced by opinion leaders than are early adopters; (3) where there is an atmosphere of uncertainty—opinion

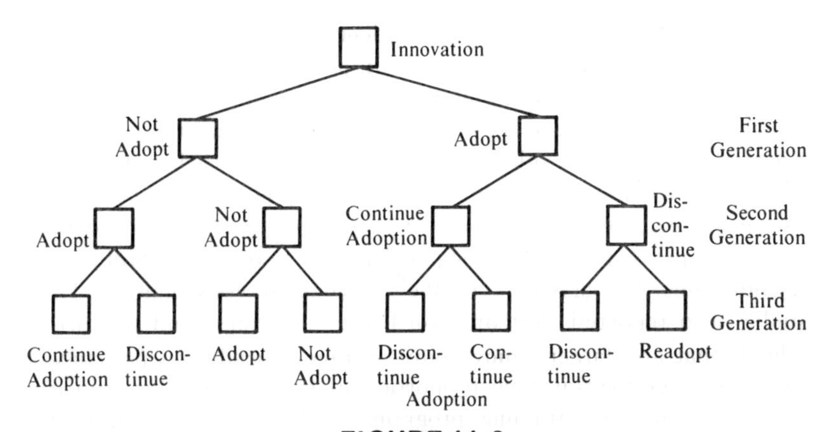

FIGURE 11-2

THE INNOVATION USE TREE
(WITH THREE GENERATIONS OF DECISIONS)

leaders wield a maximum influence in the type of situation where the "personal touch" may be the deciding factor as to whether the innovation will be adopted or rejected.

Personal influence tends to be more effective in overcoming human resistance to change because it can be more successful in overcoming the tendency for people to (1) hear only those things with which they agree; (2) interpret new ideas in terms of preconceived opinions and past experiences; and (3) remember best those ideas that are most consonant with their existing opinions. A good opinion leader can sometimes overcome this type of resistance long enough to provide the chance for the innovation to be at least examined.

IDENTIFYING OPINION LEADERS

Having described the opinion leader and his role in general terms, we should consider how such individuals can be identified. Three approaches come to mind. They are the use of sociometric tests, careful interviews of key informants, and the use of designating scales by workers within the institution (Hensel and Johnson, 1969). Opinion leaders apparently conform more closely to the norms of their social system than do typical members of the institution, i. e. they are very likely to be the least deviant members of the faculty and administration of their college.

When trying to identify opinion leaders among educators, the personal and social characteristics of the faculty members and the characteristics of the college must be taken into consideration. Several studies have reported that supervisors at the district and state level can reliably identify opinion leaders in certain secondary school situations (Hensel and Johnson, 1969; Parker 1969). These studies reported that state and district level supervisors can readily identify opinion leaders among a group of teachers by considering certain personal and social characteristics. They report that the opinion leaders: (1) are older than their peers (usually in the 35-45 year age group); (2) have been faculty members for longer than most of the other teachers; (3) have been teaching for a longer time in their present positions than most teachers in that college; (4) have participated in a greater number of past inservice training programs than their peers; (5) have participated in many social and professional organizations and activities in their residential communities. These studies also reported that opinion leader teachers tend to work in schools that are: larger, enjoy above average expenditures per student, have a greater than average proportion of faculty members who participate in inservice training programs, and have an annual faculty turnover in the ten to fifteen percent range. A common misconception about opinion leaders relates to their placement on the innovativeness scale. Opinion leaders have been identified in all of the adopter categories described in an earlier section (Hensel and Johnson, 1969). An earlier study found that the most innovative teachers were younger and had fewer years of teaching experience than the average faculty member (Christiansen and Taylor, 1966), which indicates that they have different characteristics than opinion leaders. Therefore the most innovative teachers in occupational programs are likely to be younger and less experienced than the typical opinion leaders in occupational education.

INFLUENCING AND ASSISTING OPINION LEADERS

One study reports that opinion leaders can be swayed by exposing them to demonstrations and pilots of innovative programs in question (Brown and Hartman, 1968). Based upon findings in other fields, the following generalizations can be made: (1) opinion leaders tend to draw upon more technically accurate sources of information; (2) their most common sources of information require only a small amount of their time to be utilized; and (3) they are more likely to be cosmopolites than localites in their orientation.

Considering these generalizations, we can develop some suggestions for influencing opinion leaders in two-year college occupational programs. The major one is that opinion leaders can sometimes be influenced by involvement in short workshops or conferences in which the innovation proposed is thoroughly examined and described. (The feedback conference discussed in Chapter 9 is an example of this approach.) Workshops or conferences of this type should be limited to not more than one or two days in length, and should be conducted in pleasant surroundings during weekdays (thereby avoiding the "extra work" aspect of weekend-type conferences). Resource persons used in these workshops should be capable of providing data and information in a dispassionate and easily comprehensible manner. A selected change agent (possibly an administrator at the dean's level) is needed to support the opinion leader in his efforts. The administration can help by convening feedback conferences, thus providing the means for appropriate faculty members to become involved, and by introducing secondary changes that would facilitate the incorporation of the adoption.

A General Strategy for Initiating Change

The initiation of a change in a two-year college can be most effectively facilitated by the incorporation of a well thought-out strategy. The following five paragraphs examine the major points to be considered when preparing the introduction of an innovation.

First the innovation should be sufficiently modified so that it blends in with the cultural values and past experiences of the potential adopters. This is a frequent point of failure in the introduction of new ideas or practices, particularly when the innovation is introduced within the context of a research or investigative endeavor in some other institution. This obstacle tends to be not as great when the innovation is developed within that same institution (such as under the auspices of that school's office of institutional research).

Then the opinion leaders must be accurately identified and must be convinced of the importance of the innovation to the institution and its members. They are the most important persons in the initial part of the adoption process. Schools could assign this most critical task to the office of institutional research (i. e. one which develops and disperses new ideas and practices which improve the institution) is one which includes the opinion leaders within the vanguard of its application efforts.

Thirdly, the intended users of the innovation must understand its nature and the need for its incorporation. This can be a very difficult stage since it is sometimes unclear as to whether an innovation is accepted by members because they really see the need for it or because they feel it would be easier to passively accept it rather than to resist its adoption. Acquiescence in the absence of commitment to the innovation is essentially a form of passive resistance and can prevent the successful incorporation of a new idea or practice on a long term basis. The opinion leader can be an effective catalyst in overcoming this hurdle in many instances.

Ideally, the intended consumers should understand how the innovation will enhance their teaching and/or administrative competence. A sure death knell to a new idea or practice is to have the potential users develop the feeling that the promotion of the innovation itself is the most important part of the project.

Finally, the social consequences associated with the adoption of the innovation should be carefully anticipated. Those social consequences that might be undesirable should be prevented or minimized by thoughtful planning.

A. Seminar-Workshop Level: For opinion leaders from all subunits.

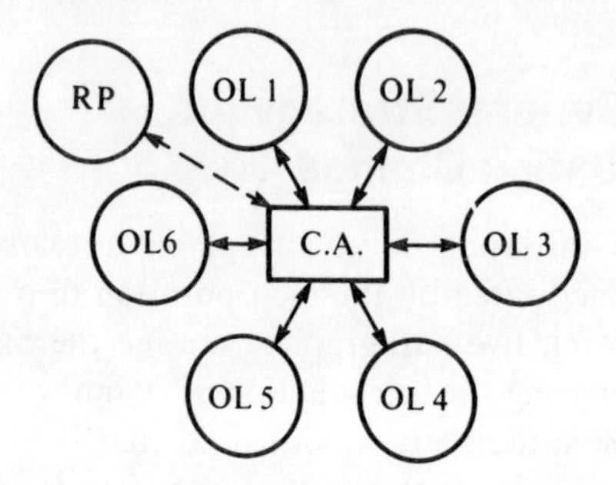

RP - Resource Person (university research, etc.

OL 1 - Opinion Leader College 1, etc.

C.A. - State Level Change Agent

B. Seminar-Workshop Level II: For appropriate faculty and administrators in individual subunits (colleges or college departments).

Seminars: Level II

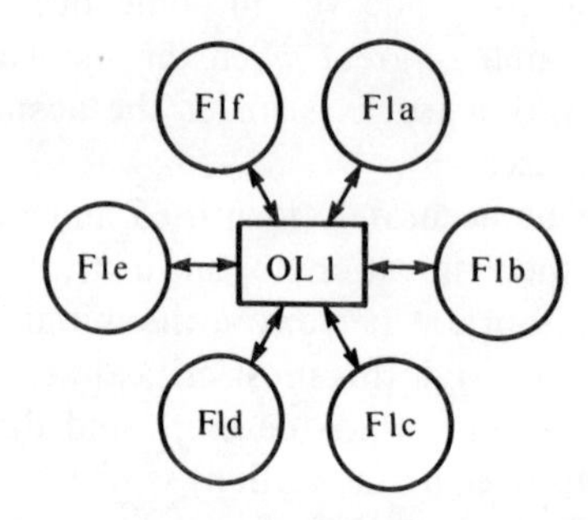

F1a - Faculty member a in College 1, etc.

OL 1 - Opinion Leader in College 1

C. Inservice Training Level III: Technical assistance, training-preparation of involved faculty-administrators.

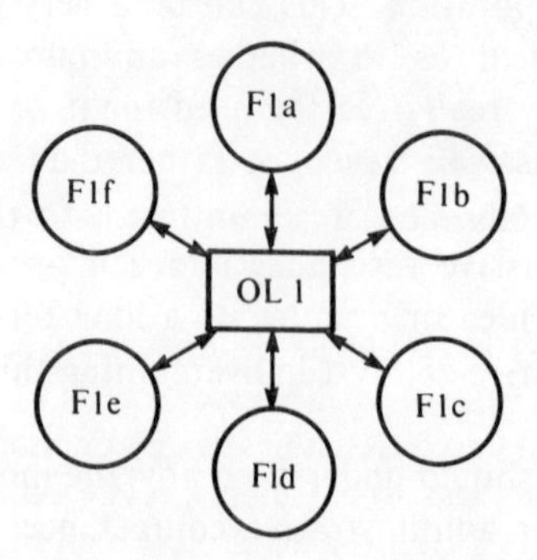

FIGURE 11-3

Adoption of Innovations, Knowledge, and Research Findings at the State or Regional Level

The discussion has thus far indicated that adoption of an innovation into the rubric of an institution will not come about by accident and must be carefully planned and executed. Since many innovations originate outside the institution in which they are to be adopted, ways in which faculty resistance can be overcome should be considered. A strategy to reduce this difficulty in occupational programs is as follows:

A. The subsystems and teacher-administrative groups that are to be reached should be carefully identified. This may vary from place to place, depending upon the administrative structure of the state or regional system. In highly centralized systems such identification is usually easier than where there is a relatively high degree of autonomy in the institutions.

B. The individual who influences these subgroups (i.e. the opinion leaders) should be identified. In many cases, particularly in the more centralized systems, the regional or state administrative leader probably can point to the influential members of the subunits. In those instances where the institutions have greater autonomy, it may be necessary to rely heavily upon key informants within these institutions for identification of opinion leaders.

C. After accurate identification of the opinion leaders, techniques and methods for winning their support should be prepared. It is suggested that this be done in several stages. Figure 11-3 depicts the organizational relationships.

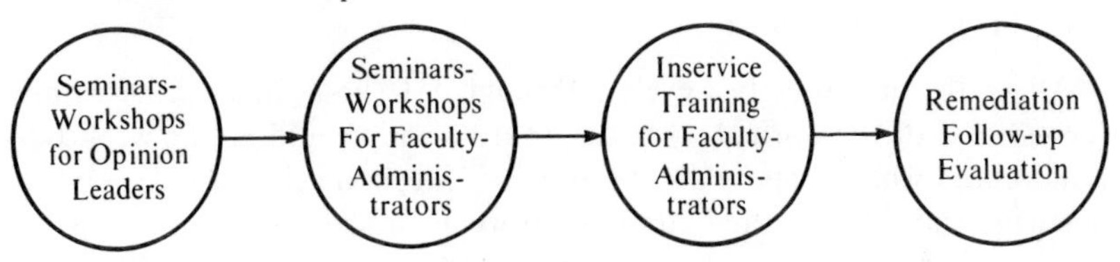

FIGURE 11-4

FACILITATING ADOPTIONS OF INNOVATIONS OR RESEARCH FINDINGS FROM THE STATE OR REGIONAL LEVEL

A. *Seminar-workshop level I.* This would be for the identified opinion leaders from each of the subunits (colleges or college departments). The meeting would be called and directed by the appropriate state or regional level change agent, who would draw heavily on resource persons (university researchers, etc.) for the presentation of the new idea or innovation to this select group of opinion leaders who would need to be won over to viewing the innovation or research finding as desirable for their respective colleges.

B. *Seminar-workshop level II.* Participants at this level would be the appropriate faculty and administrators in the individual subunits (colleges or college departments). The opinion leader, previously identified as a participant in the Level I seminar, would now serve as the seminar-workshop director as well as the opinion leader for his own institution. The participants in the seminar would be those faculty and administrators within the college who would be directly involved in incorporating the new idea or innovation. As in the Level I seminar workshop, it might be useful to utilize an outside resource person to better present some of the technicalities associated with the research finding or innovation. There should be a seminar-workshop of this type in any institution in which an adoption is being sought.

C. *Inservice training level III.* Technical assistance and in-service training for the involved faculty and administrators in each of the institutions should be provided here. This would assure that the faculty and administrators involved in the process receive the necessary additional developmental skills and knowledge that are required for adopting the new innovation into the institution. This inservice training is where the innovation whould be adjusted to suit the characteristics of the institution.

D. The process of adoption doesn't end at this point. After training sessions are over, there should be continuous encouragement and rewarding of faculty-administrators for making the new ideas workable within the college. The innovation should not be allowed to be forgotten upon completion of the intraining project. Frequent *follow-up* and *remediation* would be a strong inducement to fully incorporate the new idea into actual use by the faculty and administration. Figure 11-4 displays the flow of the state-regional level adoption processes described here.

All of the activities in Levels I through III should take place within the context of the normal work day routine and should not be weekend-type affairs which impose an added work load upon the participants. In most instances faculty and administrators must leave their normal work routine to take part in the seminars and workshops. The college administration should provide the time and facilities for this to occur.

Summary

Educational institutions generally resist the introduction of new ideas and concepts. The process by which an innovation is finally adopted is a multiple step action. During the adoption process, the innovation being considered is scrutinized by the potential adopters in terms of its advantages over the old practice, its compatibility, its complexity, its communicability, and the rate at which it can be adopted (slowness often results in a reduced number of adopters).

Some of the findings relating to the categorization of persons on the basis of their innovativeness are discussed. Individuals can be classified on the innovations continuum as innovators, early adopters, early majority, late majority, and laggards. The opinion leader is recognized as the chief influence mechanism for innovations in occupational education. He frequently uses his personal influence with his peers to win them over to considering the innovation or new idea.

A general strategy for initiating change is proposed, including the following major points: (1) The innovation should be made compatible with the cultural values and experiences of the potential adopters. (2) Accurate identification of the opinion leaders related to the innovation must be made. (3) The nature of the innovation should be clearly understood by its potential users. (4) The innovation must clearly lead to increased competence of its intended adopters. (5) The social consequences associated with its adoption should be carefully anticipated.

Using research findings as a basis, institutional innovation norms are discussed. The methods for measuring the placement of an institution on the traditional-modern norm are described, it is pointed out that determining the norm of a given institution in these terms would be of great assistance in strategizing for the introduction of a new idea or practice in that institution. Obviously, traditional institutions require approaches that are different from those that are appropriate for a more modern institution. The office of institutional research could be an excellent mechanism for conducting this determination.

The important matter of identifying opinion leaders receives special attention here. Research has shown that opinion leaders (generally considered) are older than their peers, have been faculty members for a longer time, have been teaching for a longer time in their present position, have taken part in more inservice training programs, and that they tend to participate more in social and professional organizations and activities in their residential communities.

An important question raised and answered was: How can opinion leaders be won over to accepting a new idea and innovation in occupaional education, and how can they then be helped in winning over peers? It was suggested that they be introduced to the new idea via a short workshop or conference which in turn would be the device utilized by them in winning over their peers. The final section of the chapter deals with a strategy for the adoption of new ideas or innovation at the state level, where heavy emphasis was again placed on the seminar workshop approaches mentioned above.

REFERENCES

Bice, G. R. *Working with Opinion Leaders to Accelerate Change in Vocational-Technical Education.* Columbus, Ohio: Center for Vocational and Technical Education, Ohio State University, 1970.

Brown, E.J. and Hartman, J. *Influence of an Educational Program on Dairymen's Adoption of Farm Practices.* Columbus, Ohio: ERIC for Vocational Education, 1968.

Christiansen, J. E. and Taylor, R.E. *The Adopton of Educational Innovations among Teachers of Vocational Agriculture.* A Digest of a Ph.D. Dissertation Research Series in Agriculture Education. Columbus, Ohio: Department of Agricultural Education, Ohio State University, 1966.

Gillie, A.C. *Essays: Occupational Education in the Two-Year College.* University Park, Pa: Department of Vocational Education, Pennsylvania State University, 1970.

Hensel, J.W. and Johnson, C.H., Jr. *The Identification of Opinion Leaders Among Teachers of Vocational Agriculture.* Final report, Research 40. Columbus, Ohio: Center for Vocational and Technical Education, Ohio State University, 1969.

Parker, F.Y. *The Vocational Homemaking Teacher Opinion Leaders as a Referent in the Communication of Change.* Columbus, Ohio: ERIC for Vocational Education, 1969.

Rogers, E.M. *Diffusion of Innovations.* New York: The Free Press, 1962.

Chapter 12 SELECTION OF FACULTY AND ADMINISTRATORS

The selection of faculty and administrators for two-year colleges has long been a matter of major concern for boards of trustees. A manifestation of this concern by state-level education authorities is the emergence of faculty-administrator certification. Although certification has been in effect in public schools for years, and all states now require that educators working in grades K-12 be certified (Ebel 1969), this practice has only recently spread into two-year colleges. This chapter will provide a brief review of the history of certification in education, followed by a discussion on a possible alternative to the traditional certification of teachers and administrators.

Another indication of the concern surrounding the selection of faculty and administrators for two-year colleges is the number of studies and publication efforts in this direction that were either sponsored or administered by the American Association of Junior Colleges (see Garrison 1967; Garrison 1968; Gleazer 1962; Johnson 1964; Brawer 1968; Cohen and Roueche, 1969; Kelly and Connolly, 1970; Brawer 1971; Park 1970). The selection of faculty and administrators poses a dichotomous problem. First, it is considered most desirable to obtain persons who have achieved some scholarly competence in their specialty area and have an educational philosophy that is in basic agreement with that espoused by two-year colleges. Examination of these two attributes show a basic contradiction, thereby resulting in considerable difficulty in finding faculty and administrators who qualify in terms of both these criteria. Two-year college faculty and administrators, like their counterparts in other areas in higher education, achieve their recognized level of scholarly competence via the formalized degree granting programs in senior colleges and universities. Such graduate programs dwell to some extent on the mastery of skills and knowledge in a specialized area. "Success" in such programs is seen as capturing the graduate degree. It seems reasonable to assume that those who acquire graduate degrees in this manner must subscribe, at least in part, to learning in this manner. When these persons appear in two-year colleges as faculty members or administrators, it would seem likely that some of the "graduate school philosophy" might remain with them in their new employment setting. Confronted with the radically different educational philosophy of the two-year colleges, they may encounter difficulty in "changing over". This very fundamental contradiction between the manner in which community college teachers are trained and the approaches they are expected to take when they teach can result in serious role-conflict problems among the faculty and administrators. It is suspected that quite often the egalitarian educational goal of the institution suffers, while the desire to "maintain standards" wins out.

This dilemma often extends to teachers of occupational programs as well. Here again the demand that the faculty be holders of some minimal degree (sometimes the bachelor's, often the master's) is the Trojan horse that tends to defeat the equalitarian educational goal in favor of the high standards syndrome. Academic requirements for occupational specialists are often supplemented by demands for evidence of competency in the occupational area, which in many instances constitutes a demand for related work experience. Therefore, the same kind of academic requirements demanded of the liberal arts and general education faculty is imposed upon the occupational faculty, *plus* a demand for actual work experiences. (In some cases, where a severe faculty shortage exists, the degree requirement may be lowered. These three requirements demanded of potential vocational-program faculty members—degree requirements, related work experiences, identification with the egalitarian educational philosophy—can make the problem of selecting faculty for occupational programs most difficult.)

Many of the individuals who make final the decisions regarding the selection of faculty and administrators, place considerable weight on the academic background of individual candidates. Examination of candidates' philosophic positions relative to the goals of two-year colleges is seldom conducted beyond a superficial level. Advertisements in professional journals seeking faculty and administrative specialists, often stress that the requirements include a master's degree and a desire to work in an open-door college. The final choice is often the applicant with the most impressive academic credentials. This trend extends to the selection of presidents as well, which tends to guarantee a continuation of this type of selection practice. Two-year colleges which take this approach can end up with a faculty which has a strong belief in competitiveness and the "standards must be maintained" type of attitude. Evidence that two-year college faculty of this philosophic disposition are common (and not particularly sympathetic to the egalitarian educational goals commonly espoused in the literature) has been found (Medsker 1960; Gillie, Leslie and Bloom, 1971).

The final section in this chapter proposes ways to prepare faculty and administrators for occupational programs so that they can be competent in their specialties, knowledgeable in their work areas, and at the same time, be strong advocates of the philosophy that makes two-year colleges unique among American institutions of higher education.

Finding Faculty and Administrators Who Support the Equalitarian Educational Philosophy

A good beginning to this discussion is to ask: Why do certain people elect to go into teaching in occupational education? Several studies have sought answers, some of which are reported in a research review (Moss 1967). One such effort found the most common reasons given were (Grinstead 1963): (1) the multiple job-related opportunities offered in teaching; (2) anticipated satisfaction to be found in working with youth in educational environments; and (3) the practical aspects of the subject matter. Another study found the two most important reasons for going into teaching (in business subjects) to be the dual career opportunities and satisfaction in working with young people (Thornton 1964). It is interesting that most of these respondents said they became interested in teaching before they entered college, and their interest was fostered by their office experiences or study of business subjects in high school. A third study sought to determine why former tradesmen decided to leave industry and enter the teaching profession. The respondents stated they wanted to satisfy their desire for self-realization in the social service area (Parks 1965).

Another study (Johnson 1965) found that the age at which the respondents decided to go into occupational teaching varied considerably and seemed to depend upon the nature of their prior experiences. These experiences apparently shape their need-value-interest systems, their views of the teaching role, and other practical conditions in operation at the time. This same investigation reports that most beginning teachers accept their first positions for several possible reasons. One of the most important reasons is the desire to teach a certain subject and the opportunity for professional growth. Interestingly, the opportunity for added income and being counseled into the position by college and commercial placement officers seemed to be among the least important reasons.

Interviews conducted with eighty-seven full-time junior college instructors, based around the problem of keeping up-to-date in their specialty area (Wallin 1966), found that faculty who worked under a merit-paced system tended to spend more time maintaining their teaching competencies than those teachers who operated under the standard kind of system that placed them on the basis of their academic preparation and teaching experiences. These findings have implications for in-service programs and recruitment.

Those individuals who end up in a teaching environment which coincides with their original job expectations are most apt to be happy at their work. And it's logical to assume that those who enjoy their teaching tasks and appreciate the surroundings in which they take place, are most likely to be effective teachers. While pronouncements about the educational equalitarianism of two-year colleges are frequently heard from various segments of the educational community, it is difficult to find valid and reliable indications of how the two-year college faculty members really feel about the proclaimed "community college philosophy." The question of faculty role conflict and the community college philosophy is an interesting one. Medsker (1960) investigated faculty viewpoints on some selected objectives of two-year college education and found almost unanimous agreement that the first two years of traditional college education (97%) and vocational programs (92%) were considered important goals of junior colleges. In other words, offering transfer program and vocational preparation were seen as their most vital objectives. A minority opposed other educational services, such as remedial high school courses (28%), supplementary study in English and mathematics (19%), occupational in-service class for adults (20%), general education classes for adults (10%), and college support of public forums, plays, or concerts (13%). Medsker found that transfer programs were rated as more important by teachers of academic subjects, and occupational programs were rated more highly by teachers of applied subjects. This reveals a tendency toward viewing one's own specialty as being most important, which appears to be a normal self-aggrandizement effect of organizations in general (Caplow 1964). Also important is that two-thirds of the faculty believed that two-year college faculties should have some agreement with the community college philosophy.

Clark (1960) reported that previous experiences and reference groups affect teacher attitude toward two-year college goals, and thus influence their role expectations. Former high school teachers and teachers who had no former experience adapted most readily to the student-centered atmosphere of the college. Former college teachers (15% of the Clark sample) were less sympathetic. It appears that regardless of one's convictions about the ways that two-year colleges should serve students, some conflict in role results when teachers within the institution have diverse goals. Former college teachers, and others oriented toward scholarship would find difficulties in adapting their roles to students rather than to their disciplines. Teachers of academic and occupational classes oriented toward the welfare of students would find the necessity of failing a substantial number of them for academic reasons a difficult part of their role. In other words, some role conflicts, no matter what one's philosophical orientation, appear to be inevitable in certain two-year colleges. Koile and Tatem (1966) found that occupational teachers scored highest in student-oriented interest, and teachers in the social sciences, humanities, and natural sciences all scored significantly lower. The concern for student-oriented teaching continues (Koile and Tatem, 1966). The authors found no significant relationship between student orientation, and age, marital status, academic rank, highest degree earned, years of teaching or size of institution. Therefore, like Medsker (1960) and Clark (1960), Koile and Tatem found a tendency for occupational faculty to be more sympathetic than academic teachers toward specific aspects of a community college philosophy.

A recent study sought to measure the extent of agreement with the community college philsophy among two-year college faculty in Pennsylvania (Gillie, Leslie, and Bloom, 1971). The faculties from three generic types of associate degree granting institutions were queried in this study: (1) public community colleges; (2) private junior colleges; (3) Commonwealth Campuses of The Pennsylvania State University. Three hundred faculty members from fourteen community colleges, thirteen private junior colleges, and eighteen Commonwealth Campuses of The Pennsylvania State University were selected for this study. The investigation sought answers to the following basic question: To what extent do faculty members in community colleges, private junior colleges, and The Pennsylvania State University's Commenwealth Compuses agree with the community college philosophy? The findings of this study showed a slightly positive reaction to the community college philosophy. As theorized, public community college faculty were somewhat more positive toward the community college philosophy than were private junior college and Commonwealth Campus faculty members. A total of three factors were extracted from this study that accounted for over ninety-two percent of the explainable variance. They can be described as follows. Factor 1: Quality (51%). This factor describes the two-year college faculty that is somewhat oriented toward the senior college-university mode of education. Factor 2: Goals (21%). This factor describes the faculty member who sees occupational program offerings and community service as important goals for the community college. Factor 3: Faculty role (21%). This factor indicates an opposition to research and publishing as requirements for faculty promotion.

The faculty members surveyed in this study shared the community college philosophy in regard to the quality factor and the faculty role factor (although agreement was with reservation) and were ambivilant with regard to the goal factor. It was found that the community college faculty felt that service to the community was an appropriate goal for the two-year colleges, and the faculty from the other two types of institutions disagreed. The faculty members who were thirty years old or less were significantly less concerned with policies related to admissions than was the "over thirty" group. Other differences found were that faculty holding the doctorate compared with all other degree categories were significantly more negative toward the goal factor; faculty identifying with occupational education were positive toward the goal factor, whereas those identifying with liberal arts were negative. Generally speaking, then, teaching in a public community college, *not* having a doctorate degree, and identifying with occupational education all contributed to a positive attitude toward community service goals. Being under thirty years of age contributed to an equalitarian attitude toward college standards. It is interesting to note that no significant differences occurred in any of the treatments in factor number 3: all agreed that degrees held and research published should not be requisite to promotion in a two-year college.

The general conclusion made by the investigators in the Gillie, Leslie, and Bloom study is that there is no overall consensus among the two-year college faculty queried relative to those aspects of the community college philosophy touched upon by the questionnaire. In those cases where the responses were supportive of the community college philosophy, they were only mildly so. What are the implications behind these findings? It is evident that the "community college philosophy" tends to be more in keeping with the beliefs of the community college faculty than with the faculty of the other associate degree granting institutions sampled. Therefore, the "community college philosophy" as inferred from the items in the survey instrument was found to be not totally in keeping with the *real* philosophy of the faculty. The first implication is, therefore, the *announced* community college philosophy is at variance with the *actual* community college philosophy. Secondly, diversity in the philosophy between the faculties of community colleges and the other two kinds of associate degree granting institutions should be expected. The community colleges attempt to assert their educational equalitarianism via their low cost to students and diversity in curricula offered at several academic levels. The private junior colleges tend to negate much of this by virtue of their high tuition, and the Commonwealth Campuses negate much of the equalitarianism by their equally high tuition and more demanding entrance requirements. Thirdly, certain types of faculty members within the community colleges (specifically among those holding doctorates, teachers of academic subjects, and those over thirty years of age) frequently tend to back off from strong endorsement of the community college philosophy. At the risk of building stereotypes, it seems logical to assume: (a) persons with earned doctorates have tendencies to subscribe to the senior college-university kinds of higher education; (b) teachers of academic subjects have tendencies to expect a certain degree of intellectual achievement from their students, whereas the occupational teacher is more apt to identify student success at the practical-performance level in the classroom and laboratory; (c) faculty beyond age thirty have tendencies to view their present position as a long-term or permanent one, which would tend to encourage them to uphold those more prestigious aspects of two-year college education; and (d) it is unlikely (and perhaps even undesirable) that new faculty for community colleges completely endorse the community college philosophy as stated in the literature. Although many of the faculty express deep interest in teaching, and alienation from the research-publication syndrome, closer inspection may find that they are really interested in teaching academic-type students and experience difficulty and disenchantment when teaching classes of occupational students.

Therefore, the results of this study point to some faculty problems. From the implications stated above, the following suggestions are in order: (1) A continuous, long-term in-service program for two-year college teachers should be inaugurated with a substantial portion of the effort aimed at dealing with the philosophical aspects of teaching in an equalitarian-oriented two-year college. This would provide well-planned efforts dealing with the real thorny issues of "quality" versus "open-door" education, faculty roles, and college goals (the three major factors uncovered in the Gillie, Leslie, and Bloom study). (2) If the announced two-year college philosophy is to become more like the actual philosophy of the two-year college faculty, then direct attempts at achieving support from the faculty must be made. Pre-service programs for potential two-year college teachers, designed to deal with the factors listed above, should be conducted as part of the graduate effort of the universities.

Certification and Licensure of Teachers

The attempt to establish and maintain good faculty and administrators has led to the certification movement. Currently widespread at the primary and secondary levels of public education, it has found its way into higher education in ten states via the two-year colleges. It is uniquely American in origin and present use (Kinney 1964). What is teacher certification? It can be broadly defined as *legal evidence that the faculty member is deemed competent in his teaching area,* and upon receipt of certification is eligible to receive public funds for the performance of teaching duties. What are the purposes of certification? There are three obvious ones. First, certification protects students from unqualified teachers. Secondly it insures the wise spending of public funds. Thirdly, it protects bona fide members of the teaching profession against unfair competition from unauthorized teachers. All of this is obviously based on the assumption that certification can and does identify the competent from the incompetent teachers and administrators.

Let us briefly consider the history of certification. One of the first teacher certification efforts was made in Ohio in 1825, and similar actions were taken in New York and Vermont within the following two decades. The movement gathered momentum and the certification of public school teachers was fairly widespread by 1860. Some felt the reasons for the spread of the certification movement were mixed, and included such motives as public demands for protection from unqualified teachers, a teacher profession movement to create monopolies that would result in increased salaries and decreased competition, and a desire for added prestige and psychological satisfaction by teachers (Carmen 1961). The Civil War seemed to be the dividing point between haphazard kinds of certification for the profession, and the initiation of more stringent certification control at the state level. In spite of this, only three states completely vested all certification authority at the state level by 1900. But the centralization of certification authority has steadily spread since that time. By 1967, all states had complete control over the issuance of public school teacher certificates via their state departments of education (Stennett 1967).

Two-year colleges became enmeshed in this movement in those states where they were considered to be an extension of the secondary school system. By 1967, ten states required the certification of teachers and administrators for their two-year colleges. There is some speculation as to whether this will spread to other states as they begin to view two-year colleges more as an extension of high school and less as a higher education institution. It is of some interest to note that certification goes beyond the determination of the applicant's ability to teach his specialized subject. In most states, there are additional general requirements. Thirty states require United States citizenship or declaration of intent, forty-three require a recommendation from the institution where they received their academic preparation, thirty-four states set the minimum age at eighteen years, twenty-one states demand a general health certificate, and twenty-five states demand a loyalty oath. The loyalty oath and general health certificate are also required by many two-year colleges that don't demand certification. In those states where loyalty oath requirements were challenged by the courts, the loyalty oath was usually modified to fit constitutional requirements and remained demanded in those states.

One of the greatest possibilities that could come out of requiring certification would be increased teacher mobility by the inauguration of regional and national reciprocity compacts. But efforts in this direction, which were common in the 1930s, have not produced anything approaching a workable plan on the national level. Authorities on teacher certification point to four steps that could be taken in the interest of enabling a teacher to move from state to state more easily. These include (Armstrong 1961): (1) a reduction in the number of certificates required by each of the states; (2) a statement of certification requirements by each state in terms other than credits and courses; (3) a combination of legal (state) and extralegal (professional groups) action for regulating the assignment of teachers to their specialized fields; (4) establishment of a national accreditation agency for certification which could be used upon their request by teachers who elected to move from one state to another.

There appears to be a modest drift in the direction of using examinations for awarding teaching certificates in the specialized fields. These are attempts, in many instances, to establish competency examinations. The following section considers the difficulty and merits of this approach.

Although certification has found its way into the two-year college to some extent, there are also indications that certification processes are becoming decentralized in some places. This may be in response to the demand from some quarters that the profession itself and the teacher preparation institutions be given the ultimate responsibility in this regard. There are now places where graduation from the teacher preparation program in certain institutions is tantamount to becoming certified. Some suggested changes in certification that appear to have gained support in recent years, are as follows (Stennett 1969): (1) the establishment of a national certification procedure for the benefit of teachers and administrators who desire to move across state lines for professional advancement; (2) a significant reduction in the kinds of certification licensures to as few as possible—there is considerable proliferation of certificate types at this time; (3) the processes and standards utilized in certification should be refined so that they are more clearly in line with the objectives of certification; (4) the standards and procedures used as guidelines leading to the approval of teacher-administrator preparatory institutions should be refined and made more objective; (5) certification should be based on the completion of programs in approved teacher-administrator preparatory colleges and universities; (6) the use of proficiency and qualifying examinations as a basis for certification should be increased, particularly for those who come into two-year college teaching or administrating in a manner other than the usual college preparatory route. This would be particularly valuable for occupational faculty members who often come from the business and industrial fields.

An Alternative to State Certification

There is no national group or association which deals in a comprehensive manner with the certification of faculty and administrators in occupational programs, although much could be derived from one—particularly for vocational educators who desire to cross state lines for new positions. A number of national professional associations in the health-related (Pennell 1972; Pennell, Proffitt, and Hatch, 1971) and engineering-related (ASEE, 1962) areas have established criteria for accreditation of programs. The Southern Association of Colleges and Schools has instituted a special committee for the establishment of standards for occupational programs in their region (SACS 1970a; SACS 1970b). They are the first regional accreditation agency to do so.

Several professional groups in the health related and engineering related areas have national committees which deal with the licensing of certain specialized program graduates (Pennell 1972). The criteria established by these groups for considering a program reflects upon the kinds of individuals the particular professional association considers to be most acceptable as teaching faculty for them. Therefore, accreditation of programs by the profession organizations and accreditation of institutions by the regional associations influence the colleges in selection of faculty and administrators in a manner that can, for all practical purposes, be considered a subtle form of certification. The kinds of demands made upon the two-year colleges by the regional accreditation agencies (with the exception of the one noted above) tend to pressure them into undue concern for such things as faculty with advanced degrees and other aspects of academia that don't necessarily insure good teaching and administration of occupational programs. An additional difficulty is that in all too many cases, occupational programs are treated as an interstitial component of education—they are not truly functioning within the rubric of secondary nor higher education, but somewhere in between. This interstitial positioning of occupational programs in the hierarchy of secondary and higher education can create an element of ambiguity for everyone involved (students, faculty, and administrators).

There appears to be a wide diversity of requirements for certification of occupational teachers and administrators on a state by state basis. There is considerable debate on the matter of educational background and work experiences desirable for occupational faculty and administrators (Cheney 1970; Stoddard 1970; Bohn 1969; Venuto 1972; Birnbaum 1966; Maul 1966; Sherman and Pratt, 1971). The accumulation of a predetermined number of years of work experience or attainment of a certain degree does not insure competency in the teaching of an occupational subject or in the administration of an occupational program or college. Yet these elements (academic background and work experience) have become the heart of certification, probably because of the ease with which they can be identified and catalogued.

There are strong feelings about certification of faculty and administrators in two-year colleges. The proponents, who are in the minority, claim the reasons for certificating educators in the primary-secondary levels of education are also applicable at the two-year college level, since two-year colleges are rapidly becoming an extension of the secondary school system anyway. Most two-year college educators oppose certification on the grounds that it fails to meet its own objectives and tends to restrict flexibility in hiring faculty and administrators who are competent but fall outside the traditional mold imposed by the certification requirements. But the fact remains that certification of occupational teachers is already established in many states (*Preparing Two-Year College Teachers For the 70s,* AAJC, 1969). In these places, it is probably easier to find ways to improve certification than to mount a campaign for its elimination. Taking this approach, and assuming the major purpose of certification is to facilitate the process of obtaining qualified teachers for the occupational subjects and able administrators for programs and institutional leadership, then we should seek to find valid and reliable criteria to meet these objectives. Ideally, a number of concerted efforts should be made to determine those things that would better identify good teaching and effective administration. After identification of these elements, studies to determine the approaches to assessing teachers and administrators as to the extent they have achieved these qualities should be made. Studies of this type are difficult to design and conduct, and should be done over an extended period of time.

The establishment of a national licensing bureau for licensing teachers and administrators of occupational programs and institutions is worthy of consideration. Such a board could serve in several very important capacities. First of all, it could be the funding agency for studies dealing with identification of quality teaching and leadership in administration of occupational programs and colleges. Where would this bureau obtain its funds? Federal sources like the National Science Foundation idea would be one possibility. Another source could be from assessments made upon the professional associations related to the occupational areas (such as the various health-related and engineering-related associations). A third source of funds could be in the form of fees charged each applicant seeking national licensing.

An important feature of the proposed national bureau would be its voluntary nature. Application for national certification would be initiated by the individual teacher or administrator. For a predetermined fee, he would be examined to determine whether he met the minimum qualifications for teaching in a certain occupational area, or administrating occupational programs. His credentials would be evaluated by a nationally selected group of his peers. National certification could be a success only if it was recognized by all states. The pattern of controls already established for the dispersement of federal monies to vocational education may decide which direction this will take.

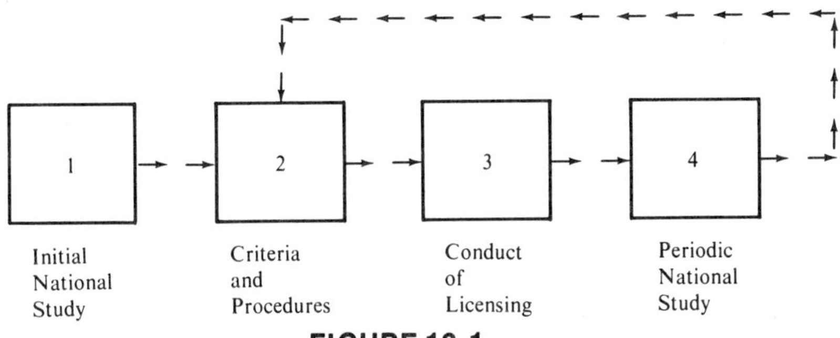

FIGURE 12-1

FLOW DIAGRAM: NATIONAL LICENSE BUREAU

Figure 12-1 is a flow diagram of how the national licensing bureau could function. The first order of business (Step 1) would be to initiate and support studies that establish the measurable qualities of good teaching and administration and to identify a mechanism for measuring them. Conducted on a national scale, such studies would include all the occupational areas that fall within the rubric of post-secondary occupational education. The identification of the measurable qualities of good teachers and administrators, based on the outcomes of these studies, would be Step 2. The established criteria should be sufficiently broad and flexible so as not to fall into the traps that many states' certification procedures have done in the past. The development of a broad-based criteria for national licensing of occupational teachers and faculty has a number of advantages. First, it provides an increased opportunity for faculty mobility (geographically and institutionally). In the past, a number of traditional certification requirements discouraged this type of mobility because of the individual state requirements that tended to favor residents of their own states and to contradict some of the requirements from their neighboring states. Second, a uniformity of reasonable and valid requirements for establishing threshold entry into teaching in an occupational area, would have an indirect but strong effect on curriculum improvement by virtue of having better teachers and administrators available. Thirdly, a direction from a national source could vastly increase the flexibility of certification requirements in general. After the licensing criteria and procedures have been established, the board would examine those individuals desiring national certification in their specialties; licenses would be issued to those who qualified. The board procedures should also include a built-in mechanism to assist in maintaining up-to-date criteria, including an updating national study in each occupational area every five years (Step 4). Although the proposed national licensing bureau may be considered "far out", it would be a reasonable alternative in those states where post-secondary occupational faculty are presently required to be certified.

Training Faculty and Administrators of Occupational Programs in Two-Year Colleges

Increased efforts toward preparing both faculty and administrators of vocational programs in two-year colleges need to be made. Pre-service training programs are needed to impress potential faculty with the equalitarian educational philosophy that serves as one of the cornerstones of the community college rationale. This is such a vital aspect of two-year college teaching that it should be a criterion for selecting potential faculty, although this may be disputed by those who would prefer to select teachers on the basis of academic standards—hoping they can be made to "fit in" with the two-year college environment. This has been the manner of hiring faculty in the past, and we have some evidence that shows it isn't providing two-year colleges with the most desirable teachers (in terms of meeting their pronounced objectives).

The fact that a potential faculty member says he wants to teach, is far from a sufficient reason to hire him. Only individuals who enjoy teaching students of middle and low academic ability should be considered for employment, because the major mission of these institutions lies with these students. The task that lies ahead for teacher educators is to prepare teachers who are both sufficiently competent in their specialized subject, and sympathetic with the equalitarian educational philosophy of the two-year college. This requires special pre-service programs for future teachers and a variety of in-service efforts for present two-year college teachers. Such programs would be a marked departure from the traditional academic efforts of the universities and would assuredly meet with considerable opposition from their faculties. A possible approach would be to generate a new graduate level program restricted to the preparation of two-year college teachers. This would be the most likely way to produce teachers of academic subjects who would be in substantial agreement with the institutional philosophies.

While the above problem is very important, the major concern in this book is the preparation of occupational faculty. As indicated by Gillie, Leslie, and Bloom (1971), there is greater agreement with the equalitarian philosophy on the part of occupational teachers. Therefore, the philosophic problem is not as severe with this group. However, it does exist to some extent and should still be dealt with by pre-service programs for existing faculty.

Occupational teachers for two-year colleges are recruited from a variety of sources (Maul 1966; Moss 1967; Medsker 1960), such as industries and businesses, other educational institutions, and in some cases, right out of teacher-training programs. Selection of occupational teachers is a haphazard business at best, particularly in those occupational areas where there are chronic shortages of instructors. The process would be much more successful if well established teacher-training programs for the occupational areas were more readily available.

A number of efforts have been made toward developing teacher training programs for occupational faculty, some with federal support (Venuto 1972). The most promising approach seems to be the combination of academic preparation, internships and selected work environments, practice teaching, and a selection of professional education courses. A well-prepared and conducted work internship would provide potential teachers with an excellent overview of what goes on in the occupational area. It could be waived for those with appropriate work experiences. The academic subjects would bring students to the level of academic competence needed to teach subjects in that occupational area at the associate degree level. The practice teaching would consist of carefully supervised and evaluative experiences which would provide candidates with their first teaching encounters. The selected professional education courses would deal extensively with the equalitarian educational philosophy and its relationship with two-year colleges. A teacher-training program of this type would probably require three years, starting with the junior undergraduate year and terminating with a master's degree in teaching in one of the occupational areas.

In-service programs should be continuous and would be required of all faculty periodically. The major purposes of in-service activities would be to help faculty members maintain a sound orientation toward the equalitarian educational philosophy and to keep certain faculty up-to-date in their specialty areas.

Although very little of the kinds of teacher preparation and in-service training described above is actually going on at this time, perhaps it will become more commonplace in the years ahead, as the need for it becomes more clearly perceived.

Summary

Two-year colleges have recognized the problems associated with the selection of faculty and administrators for a number of years. Some states have responded to this concern by extending their certification mechanisms into their two-year colleges. Concern about the selection of two-year college faculty and administrators is evidenced by the number of studies and publications devoted to the problem. Selecting faculty and administrators poses a dual-edged problem: most colleges want professional staff members who are considered to have scholarly competence in their specialty area and who are in agreement with the community college philosophy. The basic contradiction that exists between these two attributes has created considerable difficulty in obtaining faculty and administrators who are compatible in both respects.

Teacher and faculty certification is presently wide-spread at the primary and secondary levels of public education, and has found its way into two-year colleges in ten states. The three basic reasons for initiating certification are: (1) to protect students from unqualified teachers; (2) to better insure wise spending of public funds; and (3) to protect authorized members of the teaching profession against unfair competition from unauthorized teachers. These purposes, although basically good, may not in fact be attainable by the present certification approaches. Those two-year colleges in which certification is required for faculty and administrators are mainly those which were originally initiated as extensions of secondary education. As the number of two-year colleges increases, there is some speculation as to whether this trend will continue to the point that other states may begin to view them more as extensions of high school, and less as a higher education institutions. There can be some assets to certification, if it becomes more effective and rational.

An alternative to certification is the idea of a national licensing bureau. Such a board could be the funding agency for studies and could try to discover what really is required for good teaching and administration. The establishment of broad-based criteria for national licensing of occupational teachers and administrators has a number of advantages, which are listed in the chapter.

One study that dealt with the question of why certain people elected to go into teaching of occupational programs arrived at the disturbing conclusion that the actual philosophy of two-year college faculties did not really reinforce the community college philosophy as it is put forth in the literature. The implications this has for future teacher and leadership training were stressed. In the final section of this chapter suggestions for the training of teachers and administrators are made.

REFERENCES

Armstrong, W. E. "A Basis for Reciprocity in Teacher Certification." *The Education of Teachers: Certification.* Washington, D.C.: NCTEPS, National Education Association, 1961.

Birnbaum, R. "Background and Evaluation of Faculty in New York." *Junior College Journal,* Volume 27, No. 3. November 1966. Washington, D.C.: American Association of Junior Colleges, 1972.

Bohn, R. C. "Vehicle for Change in Industrial Arts." *American Vocational Journal,* Volume 44, No. 6. September 1969. Washington, D.C.: American Vocational Association, 1970.

Brawer, F. B. *Personality Characteristics of College and University Faculty: Implications for the Community College.* Washington, D.C.: American Association of Junior Colleges, 1968.

______. *Values and the Generation Gap: Junior College Freshmen and Faculty.* Washington, D.C.: American Association of Junior Colleges, 1971.

Caplow, T. *Principles of Organization.* New York: Harcourt, Brace and World, 1964.

Carmen, H. J. "The Historical Development of Licensing for the Professional." *The Education of Teachers: Certification.* Washington, D.C.: NCTEPS, National Education Association, 1961.

Characteristics of Excellence in Engineering Technology Education. Washington, D.C.: American Society for Engineering Education, 1962.

Cheney, J. M. "Teacher Education for Post-Secondary Programs." *American Vocational Journal,* Volume 45, No. 3. March 1970. Washington, D.C.: American Vocational Association, 1970.

Clark, B. R. *The Open-Door College: A Case Study.* New York: McGraw-Hill, 1960.

Cohen, A. M. and Roueche, J. E. *Institutional Administrator or Educational Leader? The Junior College President.* Washington, D.C.: American Association of Junior Colleges, 1969.

Garrison, R. J. *Junior College Faculty: Issues and Problems.* Washington, D.C.: American Association of Junior Colleges, 1967.

Garrison, R. H. *Teaching in a Junior College: A Brief Professional Orientation.* Washington, D.C.: American Association of Junior Colleges, 1968.

Gillie, A. C.; Leslie, L. L.; Bloom, K. L. *Goals and Ambivalence: Faculty Values and The Community College Philosophy.* University Park, Pa.: Center for the Study of Higher Education, Pennsylvania State University, 1971.

Gleazer, E. M., Jr. *A New Social Invention: The Community College, What It Is.* Washington, D. C.: American Association of Junior Colleges, 1962.

Grinstead, E. T. "A Study of the Relationship Between Stated Motives of Students and Graduates of Iowa State Teacher's College for Selecting Business Education as a Major to Superior Intellectual Ability and Reported Success On-The-Job." *National Business Quarterly,* 31, Spring. Washington, D. C.: National Business Education Association, 1963.

Johnson, B. L. *Starting A Community Junior College.* Washington, D.C.: American Association of Junior Colleges, 1964.

Johnson, W. F. "Reasons for the Choice of Initial Employment by Teachers in Relation to Selected Categories." Doctor's thesis. Knoxville, Tenn.: University of Tennessee, 1965.

Kelley, M. F. and Connolly, J. *Orientation for Faculty in Junior Colleges.* Washington, D.C.: American Association of Junior Colleges, 1970.

Kinney, L. B. *Certification in Education.* Englewood Cliffs, N.J.: Prentice-Hall, 1964.

Koile, E. A. and Tatem, D. W. "The Student Oriented Teacher." *Junior College Journal,* 1966, Volume 36 (5). Washington, D.C.: American Association of Junior Colleges, 1966.

Leighbody, G. B. *Organization and Operation of a Local Program of Vocational Education.* Columbus, Ohio: Ohio State University, 1968.

Maul, R. C. "The Biggest Problem: Finding Good Teachers." *Junior College Journal.* Volume 36, No. 4. Washington, D.C.: American Association of Junior Colleges, 1966.

Medsker, L. L. *The Junior College: Progress and Prospect.* New York: McGraw-Hill, 1960.

Moss. J. *Review of Research in Vocational-Technical Teacher Education.* Minneapolis, Minn.: Minnesota Research Coordination Unit in Occupational Education, University of Minnesota, 1967.

Operational Policies of the Committee on Occupational Education. Atlanta, Ga.: The Southern Association of Colleges and Schools, 1970.

Park, Y. *Junior College Faculty: Their Values and Perceptions.* Washington, D.C.: American Association of Junior Colleges, 1971.

Parks, G. A. "Circumstances Surrounding Situs Moves of Certain Tradesmen into Industrial-Vocational Teaching." *Journal of Industrial Teacher Education,* 3. Lafayette, Ind.: National Association of Industrial and Technical Teacher Educators, 1965.

Pennell, M.Y.; Proffitt, J.R.; and Hatch, T.D. *Accreditation and Certification in Relation to Allied Health Manpower.* Washington, D.C.: U.S. Government Printing Office, 1971.

Pennell, M. Y. "Licensing and Certification of Health Service Personnel." A paper in *Planning and Conducting Social and Health Related Service Programs.* A. C. Gillie, ed. University Park, Pa.: Center for the Study of Higher Education, Pennsylvania State University, 1972.

Preparing Two-Year College Teachers for the 70's. Washington, D.C.: American Association of Junior Colleges, 1969.

Redefer, F. L. "Recruiting and Selecting Teachers." *American School Board Journal,* Volume 145. Evanston, Ill.: National School Board Association, 1962.

Reed, J. L. "The Recruitment and Training of Vocational Teachers." A paper in *Guidelines for the Seventies.* 1967 Yearbook Trade and Industrial Division, American Vocational Association. V. H. Robertson, ed. Chicago, Ill.: American Technical Society, 1967.

Sherman, G. A. and Pratt, A. L. *Agriculture and Natural Resources Post-Secondary Programs.* Washington, D.C.: American Association of Junior Colleges, 1971.

Stinnett, T. M. *A Manual on Certification Requirements for School Personnel in the United States.* Washington, D.C.: NCTEPS, National Education Association, 1967.

______."Teacher Certification." *Encyclopedia on Educational Research.* Fourth edition. R.L. Ebel, ed. Toronto: Macmillan, 1969.

Stoddard, J. E. "Oregon's Short-Term Teacher Education Programs for Health Occupations Personnel." *American Vocational Journal,* Volume 45, No. 2. February 1970. Washington, D.C.: American Vocational Association, 1970.

Tentative Standards of the Committee on Occupational Education. Atlanta, Ga.: The Southern Association of Colleges and Schools, 1970.

Thornton, P. W. "Factors that Influence the Selection of Business Teaching as a Career Among Students from Selected Colleges in the United States." Masters thesis. Grand Forks, N.Dak.: University of North Dakota, 1964.

To Work in a Junior College. Washington, D.C.: American Association of Junior Colleges, 1966.

Venuto, L. J. "New Promise for Teacher Preparation." *Junior College Journal,* Volume 42, No. 5. February 1972. Washington, D.C.: American Association of Junior Colleges, 1972.

Wallin, H.A. *Incentive Systems in Educational Organizations.* ERIC, NO. ED-010-227. Eugene, Oreg.: University of Oregon, 1966.

Chapter 13 PRIVATE VOCATIONAL SCHOOLS

Private vocational schools have been making significant contributions to the area of occupational education in a quiet and almost invisible manner during the past several generations. This chapter will show how their present role relates in an important way to the overall efforts needed in future occupational education. The concluding section offers a series of suggestions for the enhancement of cooperative efforts between the public and private sectors of occupational education.

The Present Status of Private Vocational Schools

Table 13-1 indicates the manner in which private schools and their students were distributed in the United States in the year 1966. The programs offered by these schools can be classified in four categories. The schools of trade and technology, business, cosmetology, and barbering merit special attention. First, the employment prospects in these three occupational areas are found to be good in most years (Belitsky 1969). Secondly, these programs are generally short in length and lead to lucrative employment, which makes them at-

TABLE 13-1

DISTRIBUTION OF PRIVATE VOCATIONAL SCHOOLS AND STUDENTS BY OCCUPATIONAL CATEGORY (BELITSKY 1969)

Occupational Category	No. of Schools	% of Schools	No. of Students	% of Students
Trade and Tech.	3,000	42.4	835,710	53.4
Business	1,300	18.4	439,500	28.1
Cosmetology	2,477	35.0	272,470	17.4
Barber	294	4.2	15,876	1.0
Totals	7,071	100.0	1,563,556	99.9

tractive to many "disadvantaged" persons. The average enrollment per institutional type are: trade and technical, 279 students; business, 338 students; cosmetology, 110 students; and barbering, 53 students. The average number of students per institution for all of the 7,071 schools examined in a recent survey, is 207 (Belitsky 1969), which is considerably below the 2,100 student average reported for 1,028 two-year colleges (Harper 1970).

NATTS Schools

An examination of schools accredited by the National Association of Trade and Technical Schools illustrates the breadth and diversity of the programs offered by private vocational schools. Comparatively few trade and technical schools are accredited by this association however. NATTS is a voluntary organization of accredited private residence schools offering job-oriented specialty training in trade and technical occupations (NATTS Directory 1972). The curricula listed in Table 13-2 are those found in the slightly more than three hundred member schools of the NATTS.

TABLE 13-2

DISTRIBUTION OF CURRICULA BY STATES FOR NATTS SCHOOLS

Curriculum Title	Number of Programs[1]	Number of States[1]
Advertising Design	3	3
Air Conditioning	17	12
Airline Personnel Training	30	6
Appliance Repair	10	8
Architectural Engineering Tech.	6	5
Art	7	6
Automotive Mechanic	27	22
Blueprint Reading	9	6
Broadcasting	26	17

TABLE 13-2—Continued

Curriculum Title	Number of Programs[1]	Number of States[1]
Camera Repair	1	1
Chemical Lab Techniques	1	1
Clock Repair	1	1
Culinary Arts	2	2
Data Processing	71	26
Dental Assistant	49	20
Dental Lab Technology	16	11
Diesel Mechanic (see Auto. Mech)	12	11
Drafting	55	18
Dry Cleaning	1	1
Electricity	5	3
Electronics	81	27
Engraving	1	1
Estimating, Building	1	1
Fashion Merchandising	9	7
Food Service Management	2	2
Heating	7	6
Heavy Equipment Operation	2	2
Hotel-Motel Training	4	4
Illustration, Fashion	2	2
Illustration, Technical (see Drafting)	4	4
Instrumentation	2	2
Investment Operations	2	2
Jewelry Designing	1	1
Jewelry-Diamond Setting	1	1
Jewelry Store Management	1	1
Machine Shop	8	8
Mathematics	12	9
Mechanical Engineering Tech.	3	2
Medical Assistant	51	20
Medical Secretary	10	7
Medical Technician	11	9
Nurses Aide	5	4
Orderly (see Nurses Aide)	4	2
Personnel Administrator	1	1
Photography	5	3
Pilot, Commercial Airplane	2	1
Refrigeration (see air conditioning)	13	10
Time Study	1	1
Tool and Die	10	7
Transportation Management	3	2
Truck Driving	2	2
Watch Making and Repair	1	1
Welding	10	8
X-Ray	2	2

1 Compiled by the author from data in the *Directory of Accredited Private Trade and Technical Schools: 1971-72.* Washington, D. C.: National Association of Trade and Technical Schools, 1972.

ENTRANCE REQUIREMENTS

One of the unique characteristics of private institutions is the entrance philosophy they embrace, which is reflected in the following data (Belitsky). Forty-three percent of the slightly less than twelve hundred reporting private vocational schools had one or more courses that required *less* than a high school education for entry. In addition to this, almost one-fourth of them had courses that had admission requirements of nine years of schooling or less. Most of the barber schools (eighty-two percent) indicated that their entrance requirements did not require a high school diploma, and ten percent of them said their major entrance requirement was limited to the ability to read and write. Cosmetology schools appear to have the same entrance requirements. Over ninety percent of them indicated that they had at least one program in which a secondary school diploma was *not* part of the admission requirements. Furthermore, forty percent of them indicated that they required no more than nine years of formal education of their students prior to entering a cosmetology curriculum. The education requirements for admission to trade and technical schools, including both those that are and are not members of the NATTS, are distributed in a similar pattern (Belitsky): twelve percent indicated no minimum years of education required for entrance; two percent indicated a one to six year formal education requirement; thirteen percent required seven to nine years of prior schooling; nine percent indicated education requirements of ten to eleven years; fifty-six percent required a high school diploma or its equivalent; and other requirements were demanded by just over seven percent of these schools. The availability of various kinds of private vocational schools with low educational entrance requirements is of crucial importance to those communities that wish to provide an alternative type of education and training for persons with nonacademic type backgrounds.

Many private vocational schools require the applicant to take an achievement or aptitude test, the outcome of which is considered more important than the amount and kinds of previous schooling, since it is used for the purpose of learning more about the capabilities of an applicant. They feel this is necessary because student capabilities are very diversified, even among those who have had similar prior schooling, and such differences are best identified by use of special examinations. In some cases, depending upon the nature of the occupation, there are certain age and physical requirements.

Because of their educational requirements for entry, many private vocational schools admit people who have been "overeducated", that is, their actual educational background exceeds the entry prerequisites deemed necessary for achieving successful completion of their vocational programs. A comparison of the educational requirements for admission into 112 NATTS schools and the students' actual qualifications were found to be (Belitsky): undereducated, ten percent; requirements equal to the education they have, sixteen percent; overeducated, sixty-six percent; flexible (meaning both over and undereducated students), eight percent. The implication is that many individuals could have started on a work career earlier than they did—which has considerable import for the potential secondary school dropout.

OPERATION AND ORGANIZATION

Another major difference between private and public vocational schools is found in their operation and organization. As a whole, private vocational institutions seem to have the most flexible operating procedures, as seen (Table 13-3) by characteristics such as class starting intervals. Most of them have three or more starting times per year.

TABLE 13-3

CLASS STARTING INTERVALS FOR EIGHTY-THREE NATTS SCHOOLS (NATTS 1969)

Frequency of Class Starts	Number of Schools
Weekly	14
Monthly	7
Every 5 weeks	9
Every 6 weeks	5
Six times annually	8
Four times annually	17
Three times annually	14
Twice annually	7
Once annually	2
Total Schools	83

RETENTION RATES

Another characteristic of private vocational schools is the higher student retention rate. The two major reasons for failure of day and evening students to complete courses in NATTS schools (Belitsky) were problems concerned with (a) finances, and (b) personal and family difficulties, both of which are not unlike the reasons given by junior college dropouts (Cross 1968). Students in private vocational schools, where they pay their own tuition and provide their own support as well, are in need of financial assistance as much as, if not more than, students who enroll in public two-year colleges. The retention rates of these institutions are generally higher than many other post-secondary schools and some range up to seventy to eighty-five percent (Belitsky). At the time students enroll in private vocational school programs, most have selected their immediate occupational objectives, thereby providing them with greater motivation for successful completion of their program. This, coupled with the practicality of vocational curricula, may lead to reduced dropout rates. In response to questions relating to satisfaction with their first jobs, about two-thirds of the respondents replied affirmatively. It is reasonable to assume, if these findings are truly indicative of how vocational school graduates feel, that many of these institutions are achieving their major objective of obtaining suitable employment for their graduates (Belitsky). Another contributing factor may be that students who enroll in and complete vocational programs in private schools have more realistic job goals in the first place, thereby increasing the likelihood that their first job will be in keeping with their occupational goals.

Suggestions for Improving Relationships Between Private and Vocational Schools

Private vocational schools have been shunned by the public in many places. This probably has to do with the general suspicion of private schools, due to the fact that there have been "fly by night" private schools in and out of operation for years. However, the great majority of private vocational schools have been doing a good job preparing their students for work (Belitsky), and this fact is further assured by increased required state licensing. Considering the great increase in the need for occupational education, private schools should be utilized more effectively. (Many are presently operating below their maximum student capacity.) The following suggestions are aimed at establishing constructive relationships between the private and public sectors of occupational education:

1. There should be serious attempts to design, conduct, and evaluate joint ventures between private and public vocational schools at all academic levels. Example: broad vocational subjects could be best taught in the two-year colleges, while in some cases the skill center could be conducted in private schools and under contract to the school district.
2. Occupational and vocational guidance should become a more serious endeavor in the late elementary and secondary years for all students, thereby assessing them more accurately as to the modes and varieties of education that would be most consistent with their interests, abilities, and needs. Some students would succeed most easily by entering an occupational program of narrow orientation (which would be commonly found in the private sector).
3. In the interest of maximizing the educational attainments and occupational potentials of all our youth, there needs to be an enlightened program to provide financial assistance to those students who elect to go to private vocational schools. Much of this could come about in the form of contract learning, where the school district would provide a sum equivalent to what would be paid if the student was to enroll in a public two-year college.

4. If part of the job of occupational preparation was allocated to the private vocational schools, then perhaps the public two-year colleges could concentrate primarily on the general education and the broad aspects of occupational education. Specific specialties and skill developments could be taught in skill centers after the individuals had been committed to a particular job (as discussed in Chapter 7). As mentioned before, this is where private vocational schools could probably be at their most value—in the specific skill development areas.
5. In order to make themselves more attractive to the public in general and to educators in particular, private vocational schools should seek to raise the levels of sophistication in their programs.
6. In an attempt to increase the accessibility of private vocational schools to the public, and to increase their attractiveness to students and their parents, the private vocational schools should submit to some kind of a voluntary accreditation plan or association. Accreditation should be based on their ability to motivate students and to successfully prepare these individuals for the suitable occupations. Accreditation should be performance-oriented and should not depend upon a criteria used by the present regional accreditation agencies.
7. Because of its job-oriented instruction, and a pervading sense of achievement commonly present in private vocational school programs, it is suggested that these schools be made more available to many disadvantaged persons whose personalities and economic backgrounds severely minimize their chances of becoming successfully involved in the traditional kind of education. But students with this kind of background can be attracted to such programs only if the jobs waiting for them upon graduation are not of the "dead end" variety. Furthermore, the financial needs of the students, which in some cases even includes the support of their families, must be adequately met.
8. The private vocational schools throughout the country have the capacity to expand their enrollments considerably beyond the present 1.5 million. They could become the focal point in the skill center type of endeavor mentioned earlier, and could offer complete vocational programs in certain highly specialized subjects. They should be allowed to compete with two-year colleges for the offering of special programs and in skill development. A comparison of training costs in certain Pennsylvania private schools showed they were competitive with the cost of similar programs offered by public institutions. Their inability to compete lies in the fact that there is no public support for students in private schools. Contract arrangements could permit us to test the hypothesis that this type of training could be more economically performed by the private sector of occupational education.

9. Because of their very flexible operations and varying lengths of courses, it appears obvious that the private vocational schools can have more frequent starting dates and are capable of enrolling people on an almost individual basis (as would be required in a skill center).
10. The federal government or a consortium of national associations should make available a national directory of the private vocational schools and include such critical information as: minimum educational admission requirements for the courses offered, the accreditation held by each school, and the number of students enrolled in each. Such a publication could be of invaluable assistance to occupational and vocational guidance counselors in secondary schools and two-year colleges.

Unique Features of Private Vocational Schools

Private vocational schools have a number of features that set them apart from public two-year colleges. Besides being able to adjust the length of the courses in accordance with established objectives, they can readily change their objectives to suit the needs of newly emerging situations (Belitsky). Such flexibility toward types and lengths of courses is an invaluable and essential ingredient in the area of skill development. Public two-year colleges can not as a rule react as rapidly to a newly emerging job preparation demand.

Another unique characteristic of private vocational schools is that their objectives deal almost entirely with occupational development of students, leaving the general education aspects of the students' education with the public sector. Many of the private institutions will readily admit a student into a course or program if they feel his chances for completion are good, regardless of his academic background. Such admissions strategies are best described as flexibile and pragmatic. These unique features permit them to more quickly adapt to the changing needs of the industrial community, and lend themselves to the kinds of activities that should go on in skill centers and other varieties of "contract learning" situations.

Utilizing Private Vocational Schools in More Effective Ways

The idea of contract learning was attended to several times in the preceding paragraphs. Let us further consider the idea. Contract learning is based upon behavioral objectives, an approach that can be effectively utilized in all varieties of occupational education. In Chapter 8, it was pointed out that four steps were necessary in contract learning. They are: (1) establishing behavioral objectives; (2) establishing definite strategies for achieving them; (3) conducting the learning experiences; and (4) assessing the progress made, to see to what extent the objectives have been met.

Contract learning is applicable to virtually all aspects and types of education. Let us consider the mechanics of one type of contract learning. The contractor (i.e., a private vocational school or a learning corporation) stipulates that he will provide a certain number of hours of training to achieve certain agreed upon objectives for a specified cost. If he succeeds in achieving these objectives in more time than agreed upon in the original contract, then the price allocated to the contractor would be correspondingly reduced as a penalty, but a bonus would be provided if the objectives were achieved in fewer hours than originally stipulated. Achievement of the objectives in the stated time would be considered normal fulfillment of the contract for the agreed-upon amount of funding. Such arrangements have been tried on a limited basis in several places, particularly with a nonconventional (that is disadvantaged-poverty) type student. Some such arrangements have had mixed results. But there is reason to believe that contract learning would be suitable for more conventional occupational-type students and programs as well. The contention that contract learning can provide certain kinds of training in a less costly manner than has been traditionally given by the public sector of the educational system should be tested carefully.

The idea of a skill center ties in with the idea of effective utilization of private vocational schools. The philosophy behind the skill center blends with the underlying tenants of contract learning. Skill centers and contract learning both lay claim to flexibility and pragmatic approaches to occupational preparation. With the utilization of private vocational schools and learning corporations, there may be several skill centers, each specializing in some aspect of the occupational spectrum. For example, in certain urban areas there are a number of private schools that could be adapted to provide specific skill development in the business-related areas; skill centers for engineering-related para-professional programs could be performed by nearby area vocational schools, community colleges, or by special contracts with private learning corporations. In large urban areas, there may also be other private vocational schools or private learning corporations that could be contracted with to perform specific skill development in some of the other areas not mentioned, including basic education (communications, reading, social sciences) for the disadvantaged elements of the population. Similar kinds of efforts could be addressed to rural poverty areas as well. Movements in this direction could very well be the start of a trend to subcontract much of the specific skill training out to private vocational enterprises and to leave the more basic cognitive elements of occupational education to the public two-year colleges.

If private vocational schools and learning corporations are to be profitably and effectively utilized in the overall effort to provide excellence in occupational education, then improved articulation must be established between the public schools, private vocational schools, learning corporations, and the industrial-business community. It may even be necessary to smooth the way for the articulation channels by means of some legislation action (Figure 13-1 shows some of the more common articulation paths or channels that could come about through the suggestions made here, and Chapter 15 deals with the articulation problem in greater detail.) Although there is a channel between the public high schools and jobs, it is now apparent that graduation from high school is not considered to be sufficient for entry into the job market for many people. Added to this difficulty is the increased tendency of many employers to require some form of post-secondary occupational education. However, those youngsters who do not go on to a public post-secondary school may be guided to a private vocational school or to a contract learning project, or be placed in a job which would then release them to a skill center for the development of the skills required for that job. One of these possible avenues will likely be followed by as many as one-fourth or more of high school age youngsters. These possibilities could definitely take care of those youngsters who previously have been dropping out of school and going into the world of work (or to be more accurate, *trying* to get into the world of work) without any occupational skills.

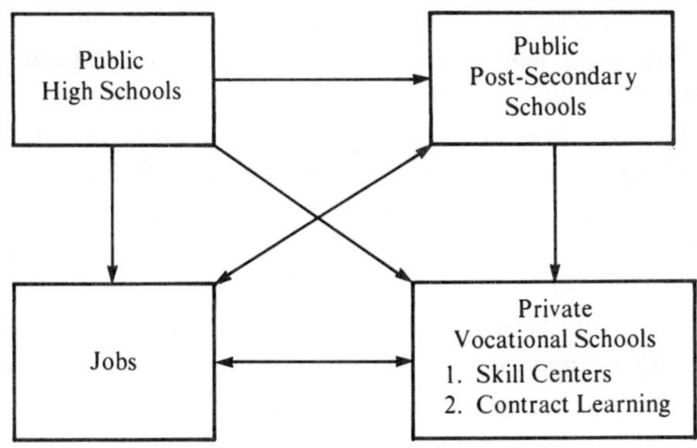

FIGURE 13-1

In addition, at least half of the students graduating from high school will be in need of occupational education. Vocationally oriented programs for these persons would be in the middle level occupations and would vary in length from less than a year to two or more years. A segment of this group could be served by private vocational schools, attending directly from high school or after receiving the general course work of an occupational area in a two-year college. This obviously requires some coordination between the public and private sectors (see Chapter 15).

Summary

Private learning corporations and vocational schools have facilities to provide a valuable extension of opportunities for occupational students. More than 1.5 million students are presently served by private vocational schools, and there is strong evidence that these institutions have the capacity to greatly enlarge that number. The unique features of private vocational schools include such things as their ability to conduct classes of varying lengths with and without academic credit; direct their objectives specifically toward occupational preparation, with little consideration for general education; have flexible entrance requirements; utilize behavioral objectives in their program planning; and institute new courses and programs within very short periods of time—and to discontinue them just as easily.

It has been suggested that private learning corporations and vocational schools be utilized to conduct at least some of the specific skill centers described in Chapter 7, perhaps centered around the relatively new concept of contract learning. Some means is needed by which articulation between private schools, public schools, and the industrial-business community would be insured by some type of legislation. Because of the greatly increased popularity of more years of education by the public in general, it is necessary that we utilize all available facilities and resources in enlarging educational opportunities for the American public.

REFERENCES

Belitsky, A. H. *Private Vocational Schools and Their Students: Limited Objectives Unlimited Opportunities.* Cambridge, Mass.: Schenkman, 1969.

Cross, K. P. *The Junior College Student: A Research Description.* Princeton, N. J.: Educational Testing Service, 1968.

Directory: American Association of Junior Colleges: 1970. William A. Harper, ed. Washington, D.C.: American Association of Junior Colleges, with assistance from the Research Division, National Education Association, 1970.

Directory: National Association of Trade and Technical Schools (1969-70). Washington, D.C.: NATTS, 1969.

Chapter 14 IMPROVING THE STATUS OF VOCATIONAL EDUCATION

The generally low status of occupational education is a three-segmented problem composed of programs, faculty, and students. The lack of acceptance of occupational education as being within the mainstream of American education relates to each segment in a common way, but there are unique features of each which lend themselves to remediation. The purpose of this chapter is to look at some of the possibilities for improvement and propose directions for action.

The status of vocational education is directly related to the position of the various occupations within the status hierarchy of American society. Several studies have pointed to the fact that people view occupations in terms of prestige (Blau and Duncan, 1967). Therefore, it is logical to assume that vocational programs which prepare persons for low status jobs will be considered low status curricula. The status problem is confounded by the fact that the amount of education an individual obtains is one of the major factors that determines the occupational level a person eventually attains (Blau and Duncan). It is foolhardy to think we can drastically change the status of a given occupation without actually changing its characteristics and the role it plays in our society. Raising the prestige level of middle level jobs to that presently enjoyed by the professions will not likely occur.

The lifetime income of persons with one to three years of college, which pretty much encompasses the middle level occupations, is only 20% higher than that of high school graduates (Adams and Jaffe, 1971). But the middle level occupations are more attractive to most young people than the blue collar variety, in spite of rapid increases in blue collar wages. And, of course, the middle level jobs are less desirable than the professional ones. Reportedly, the relationship between social status and a person's job in terms of its placement on the unskilled-cognitive spectrum has origins back into the pre-Christian, Egyptian, and Grecian societies (Power 1970); and like most deeply embedded traditions, it virtually defies our attempts to remove it. Finding the assets of middle level occupations, and utilizing them as status features, could blunt the more damaging effects of low prestige. This is a more realistic goal in the search for ways to gain increased acceptance of middle level occupations.

Programs

It is common knowledge that many students and their parents consider occupational-type programs as the least desirable offerings in two-year colleges. This is often reinforced by the manner in which such programs are organized and administered (Gleazer 1971). This is particularly true in the more affluent communities. The lower the cognitive level of performance called upon in an occupation, the less attractive that occupation is to students and their parents. This perhaps ties in with the American dream of open-ended social and occupational advancement, which is associated with a desire to have a job that is physically clean and mentally-oriented. For some, achieving such a position is considered the epitome of occupational success. This often takes precedence over salary considerations, as stated earlier. The physical-mental spectrum aspects of a job relate to the life style that the job holder expects to achieve by entering into that occupation. Unfortunately, the sterotype of the life style envisioned for the skilled and low-level cognitive-type jobs has not been an attractive one up to now. The holders of such positions have been pained in the literature and other media as being persons who besides working at an uninteresting job, also have equally uninteresting lives, and are trapped by American technology (Reich 1970; Whyte 1956; Townsend 1970; Galbraith 1967). We should develop new ways to utilize the communications media to create a new and improved middle level worker sterotype in the eyes of the public. This would require a well-planned, concerted effort. What can we do to minimize this negative attitude toward occupational education? Following are several suggestions.

Vocational education needs a general overhaul. New programs should be designed. Their development should evolve out of attempts to solve present day problems relating to urbanization, environmental control, cybernetics, poverty, minority group problems, and other pertinent issues with which we are being faced. The design of programs on such a basis would necessitate a completely new approach to curriculum development and evaluation.

Programs presently in existence that are to be retained should be redesigned in terms of people-oriented objectives. We should place much less emphasis upon serving the specific needs of industry. Such an approach, of course, requires a complete turnabout in the orientation of many present programs. We should view *our entire society as a mechanism for serving people, rather than consider people as devices for serving society.* This statement is the heart of the matter, and should be strongly and consistently reflected in the design of all curricula (see Chapters 7 and 8). Specific skill development, in this approach, would have no place in the basic curriculum, but would be a part of the job-orientation phase and would come about after the individual had been located in a specific job, not before, as is presently the tradition. This topping off process could be conducted in the type of skill development center described in Chapter 7.

The people-oriented objectives must be designed in behaviorial terms so as to provide the opportunity to continuously evaluate what is going on, both in terms of meeting the objectives for an entire program and for each course in that program. This would entail a tremendous effort, which should be considered a part of the work responsibilities of the professional staff, and provisions for doing so should be made at the very start.

Establishment of built-in evaluation strategies in the curriculum is a must from the start. No program should be started unless this aspect of it has been carefully thought-out and developed beforehand.

All occupational programs should be placed within a carefully designed plan that provides for both horizontal and vertical job mobility. Each occupational groups (such as group A in Figure 14-1), should have clear-cut avenues for vertical progression ranging from the semi skilled to the professional level. In Figure 14-1, this involves six steps, but in some occupational groups it may involve only two or three or as many as a dozen increments. Accessibility for the upward progression, without undue and painful repetition of course work, is an important aspect of this model. In some cases, progression from one vertical level to the one immediately above it will come about as a matter of acquiring a necessary amount of experience on the job, with no additional formal training. The reader may have surmised that the lattice or increment approach would be best implemented with utilization of skill centers. When

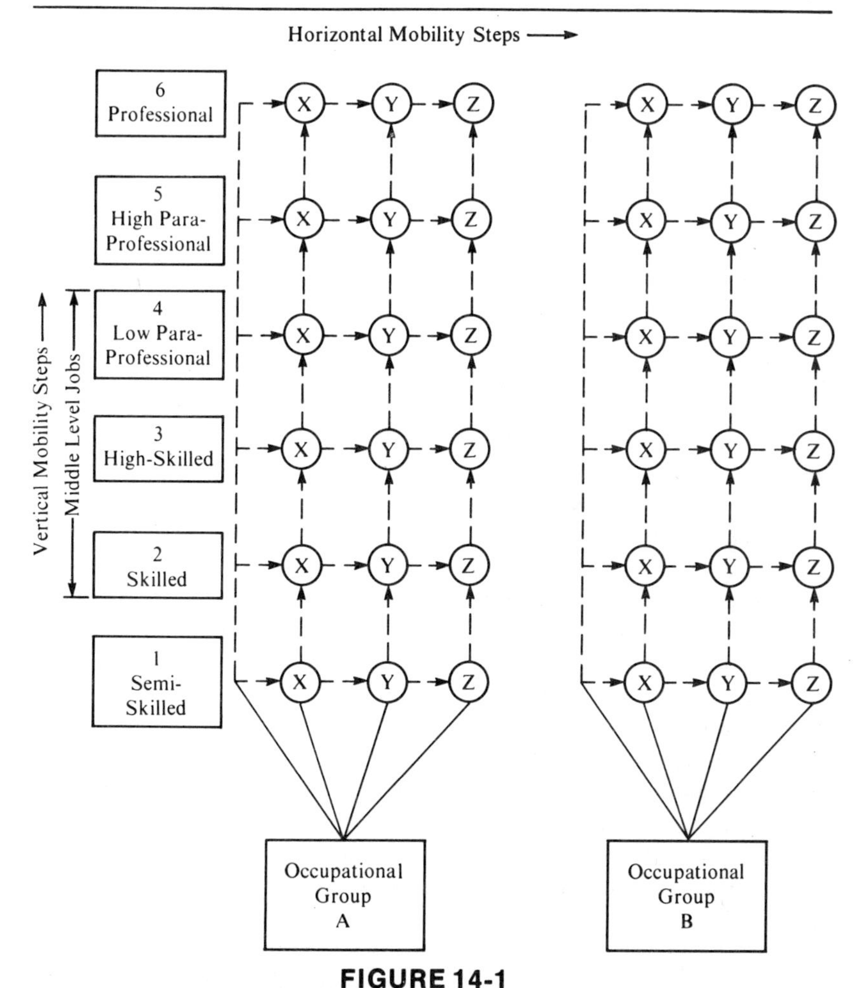

FIGURE 14-1

THE OCCUPATIONAL LATTICE

a person desires to move up to the next vertical job level, he would be able to return to the educational institution for the course work or laboratory activities needed for entry into that next level. Advancement of this type is most easily promoted by cooperative arrangements between the business-industrial and educational communities. An example is the situation where industries in a region permit and actively encourage workers to enter into vocational programs at local community colleges. This is an active expression of support for occupational education, and is quickly interpreted as such by the public. Some business-industrial firms permit such course work to be taken during "company time" with no loss in salary or other benefits. Such an approach is an effective way to elevate the status of occupational education. Furthermore, the "pay-off" for continued schooling is usually an improvement in the worker's present job situation, or a better job. The worker should be able to relate his present position to the next vertical step in the lattice. Repetition of previously taken course work should be undertaken only for necessary "refresher" purposes. Education for job advancement should be smooth and uncomplicated.

Most job changes are likely to be of the horizontal mobility variety. In Figure 14-1, three horizontal positions, labeled X, Y, and Z, are shown for each vertical level. In some occupational groups, such horizontal positions may number as many as a dozen or as few as one or two. Of paramount importance is that there be easy entrance and exit between each of these horizontal positions. Such easy two-directional movement between similar level positions is crucial, because many jobs disappear and new jobs emerge in short periods of time. In some cases, movement from one horizontal position to another may entail nothing more than a short period of specific skill training, either on the job or in a skill center. In other instances, the individual may be required to return to a two-year college in order to learn new concepts prior to entering the new position. Positions at the same horizontal level are at the same general cognitive level, and therefore require nothing new in the way of increased cognitive-type preparation. The development of horizontal positions is particularly critical since most individuals reach their ulitmate cognitive level sooner or later in their work years. Not everyone, obviously, will reach the professional level.

Provision of easy entrance and exit between jobs at one level (horizontal mobility) and from one level to the next (vertical mobility) for those with the required abilities, would do much to enhance the attractiveness of jobs within an occupational area. This would improve the status of occupational education because it refutes the charge that the jobs are "dead end." Achievement of such flexibility is presently difficult because of (a) institutional inflexibility; and (b) resistance encountered from the professionals. Some mechanism needs to be established to establish smooth job progression paths of this sort. This is happening in a few professions. Some states have a teacher aide career-ladder plan that provides for several steps of teacher aide categories, ultimately leading to the professional teacher rank.

The Faculty

Vocational faculty have traditionally suffered from lower status in two-year colleges where academic rank and other prestige factors depend heavily upon academic degrees held by the teachers. Furthermore, since occupational programs themselves occupy inferior positions in the overall school curriculum (for reasons stated in the preceding section), this will naturally be reflected in the prestige of vocational faculty. The tendency for this to happen in two-year colleges is a very real danger and a continuing problem (Cosand 1966). The administration must take strong measures to guard against its harmful effects to the structure and atmosphere of the college. Following are several proposals for maintaining equitable status for all faculty members.

First, criteria must be established for awarding faculty rank in terms of actual achievement and performance in one's specialty. The use of degrees should occupy a relatively minor role in the classification of teachers. Both academic and occupational teachers should be ranked according to their demonstrated abilities in their respective field. The advancement of all faculty (academic as well as vocational), should hinge on outcomes determined from the built-in evaluation of behavioral objectives. Such an approach would do much toward equalizing the status of faculty members in a comprehensive-type institution.

Secondly, a consistent equality in the position of curricula within the administrative hierarchy should be apparent. Vocational programs should be apparent. Vocational programs should not be subordinate to academic curricula in any way. The adminstrator of occupational programs should occupy a top position in the administrative hierarchy and should not be relegated to control by nonvocational individuals at levels below the president in larger institutions, or the academic dean in smaller colleges. Furthermore, occupational programs should not be "buried" by divisional schemes. A typical example of this is the placing of engineering-related middle occupational level programs in the same division or department as pre-engineering. Middle level occupational curricula cannot be in their most viable state when submerged in such a fashion. The positioning of occupational education belies the value given it by the administration, according to organizational theory (Etzioni 1964).

Third, faculty teaching loads and other responsibilities, and salaries, should be equated among all faculty members. Occupational faculty should be given a fair share of committee work and other institutional activities in which faculties are expected to serve. The faculty teaching load problem is a particularly thorny one, because much of the contact time of occupational faculty is spent in the laboratory where the number of hours are substantially greater than would be found in lecture type courses. An equitable method should be devised in which laboratory contact hours are equated with lecture hours, so that the instructor who spends most of his teaching time in the laboratory does not end up with an unduly heavy contact hour load. Techniques should be devised in which this can be accomplished without creating an undue financial burden upon the institution.

Upon graduation, occupational students should be awarded the same titles and benefits as the nonvocational students. The same associate degree, not a special certificate, should be given those who graduate from a two-year post-secondary curriculum, regardless of the academic rigor of the program. Until these equalization factors are incorporated in the institution, students will have a basis to feel that occupational programs are inferior to the traditional academic curricula.

Finally, because some teachers transmit their beliefs to their students in an almost unconscious manner, the occupational program faculty members must themselves believe in vocational education as a legitimate and extremely important aspect of American education. This can be best insured, particularly in comprehensive two-year colleges, by orientation sessions, and real in-depth discussions of occupational education with all faculty members and administrators (see Chapter 12 for further discussion on faculty orientation).

The Students

Students in occupational programs frequently consider themselves academically inferior (Cross 1968). This may be reinforced by the occupational teachers' rank on the faculty prestige scale. Vocational students score lower in academic ability than those in the academic programs (Cross 1968; Gillie 1969), and students themselves are aware of these differences. Also, feelings of inferiority may be engendered or heightened by the manner in which students are handled in the two-year college. Occupational program students should be given the same treatment as all other students in matters of curriculum, at least as much as possible. For example, some elective course possibilities within their curricula should be provided, and the lock-step arrangements common in older forms of vocational education should be minimized.

Setting occupational students apart from other students in terms of their overall curriculum loads should be avoided. Certain middle level vocational programs require as many as seventy semester hours for the associate degree (ASEE 1962), while typical academic programs demand around only sixty semester hours of credit for the same degree. This is obviously a highly undesirable situation.

Occupational students should be provided with access to all the opportunities available to other students—opportunities which are often denied them because of their longer laboratory classes. Since many occupational students would tend not to participate, actively encouraging them to take part in school activities should be strongly promoted. Vocational students should be given visible leadership positions in student government also.

Since occupational programs can change with community needs and job opportunities, they should be "sold" to the community on that basis. Therefore, vocational students should seize upon occasions to describe their curricula to other students, faculty, and the community at large.

Summary

This chapter takes the position that improvement of occupational education status is a threefold problem—it deals with programs, faculty, and students. Vocational education will not acquire the prestige it so richly deserves by accident.

It is important that education in general, and two-year colleges in particular, devote more of their efforts to improving the status of occupational education. Well over half of the youngsters in the nation need this kind of education in order to make their way into our society via the world of work. An education that prepares youngsters for occupations is our virtual replacement for the tribal ritual of initiation into adulthood. Furthermore, and although many two-year college educators would hotly dispute this (see O'Banion 1971, for example), the two-year college should become more vocational and less academic in its programs in the future. As entry into the four-year colleges and the universities becomes easier for the academically inclined, the need for taking the first two years of academic study in community abilities, ranging from those who are "doubtful" possibilities to those who are "sure" improbabilities (in terms of preparing for the professions), will be the spectrum of students in typical two-year colleges. Some educators feel that the major transfer effort of two-year colleges will be for the "doubtfuls," because those who score highest in academic aptitude type tests will likely be counseled into senior colleges and universities upon completion of secondary school. If this should come to pass, then the community colleges' major responsibility will be devising and conducting meaningful vocational programs.

REFERENCES

Adams, W. and Jaffe, A.J. "Does a College Diploma Still Pay Off?" *Change.* Volume 3, No. 7. Boulder, Colo.: Educational Change, 1971.

Blau, P.M. and Duncan, O.D. *The American Occupational Structure.* New York: John Wiley, 1967.

Characteristics of Excellence in Engineering Technology Education. Washington, D.C.: American Society for Engineering Education, 1962.

Cosand, J.P. "Implications of Urbanization for Community College Administration." *Administering the Community College in a Changing World.* S.V. Martorana and P.F. Hunter, eds. Buffalo, N.Y.: State Universtiy of New York at Buffalo, 1966.

Cross, K.P. *The Junior College Student: A Research Description.* Princeton, N.J.: Educational Testing Services, 1968.

Etzioni, A. *Modern Organizations.* Englewood Cliffs, N.J.: Prentice-Hall, 1964.

Galbraith, J.K. *The New Industrial State.* Boston: Houghton Mifflin, 1968.

Gillie, A.C. "Characteristics of Technician Students." *American Vocational Journal,* March. Washington, D.C.: American Vocational Association, 1970.

Gleazer, E. "Emphasis." *Junior College Journal,* September. Washington, D.C.: American Association of Junior Colleges, 1971.

O'Banion, T. "Humanizing Education in the Community College." *The Journal of Higher Education.* Volume 32, No. 8, November. Columbus, Ohio: The American Association of Higher Education and the Ohio State University Press, 1971.

Power, E.J. *Main Currents in the History of Education.* New York: McGraw-Hill, 1970.

Reich, C.A. *The Greening of America.* New York: Random House, 1970.

Townsend, R. *Up the Organization.* New York: Alfred A. Knopf, 1970.

Whyte, W.H., Jr. *The Organization Man.* New York: Simon and Schuster, 1956.

Chapter 15 NEW MASTER PLANS FOR POST-SECONDARY OCCUPATIONAL EDUCATION

Coordination in Higher Education

Coordination may be defined as "the act of regulating and combining so as to give harmonious results" (Glenny 1959). In higher education, three types of coordinating bodies fall within this overall view. They are: the single coordination board, which usually is a governing agency; the board that is authorized to coordinate and control certain selected activities of the schools but is restricted in general governance and administrative powers; and the board that is organized purely as a voluntary system, with representation from all of the involved institutions, which serve to coordinate activities that are of common concern to the participating schools.

There are five major means of coordination (Moos and Rourke, 1959): (1) direct legislative control; (2) voluntary cooperation among the various colleges; (3) consolidation of coordination for all institutions into one board; (4) the use of local boards for direct authority over the daily operation of the college; and (5) utilization of master boards which have supervisory power over the local governing boards. Considerable interest is being shown toward incorporating the coordinating agency approach, and leaving the matter of internal governance to the local boards of control (Berdahl 1971; Chambers 1965; Glenny 1959; Klein 1938).

The concept of coordination and unification in higher education is nearly two-hundred years old. Early unification attempts were made in New York, where the State Board of Regents was created in 1784, and in Georgia, with the chartering of the University of Georgia the following year. Progress in this direction was slow for a while, with only twelve states adopting some system of unified coordination in higher education by 1932. But interest in the development of higher education coordinating agencies continued. The increased complexity of higher education, largely the result of its enlarged accessibility, and the simultaneous increase in the size and complexity of state governments, demanded greater coordination of higher education at the state level (Glenny).

The categorization of various arrangements for control, coordination, and cooperation has been denoted in the literature (Chambers 1965; Glenny 1959). These include: (1) a single board for all higher education institutions in a given state; (2) several boards, with each responsible for a specific type of institution (example—a special board for community colleges, a second one for state colleges, and a third board for state universities); (3) individual boards of control for each type of institution, with one super coordinating board serving as an umbrella-type mechanism (such as a commission for higher education); (4) individual boards for each institution, with several coordinating units for universities, colleges, and community colleges; (5) individual boards for each college and a voluntary coordinative umbrella-type commission for the entire state or a region within the state; and (6) boards for each individual college and no overall coordination between them.

Although the tradition of institutional autonomy remains strong, there is a trend toward voluntary cooperation between post-secondary institutions. Several factors have encouraged efforts in this direction (Henry 1961), including considerations of educational adequacy, effectiveness, and economy, along with serious attempts to maximize the use of available educational resources. It is interesting that a number of research activities conducted in consortium-type configurations have proven to be fruitful in terms of efficiency and productivity, thereby serving to illustrate how voluntary kinds of cooperative coordination can serve the interest of participating institutions and their clientele. Arrangements for cooperation, coordination, and control of higher educational institutions are relatively far reaching in many states, and the areas of responsibility include finances, facilities, the establishment of new colleges, development of new academic programs for existing colleges, design of master plans, conduct of overall surveys, and coordination of overall services on a statewide basis (Berdahl 1971; Glenny 1959; Moos and Rourke, 1959; Hungate 1964).

ARTICULATION IN HIGHER EDUCATION

Difficulties in articulation have fostered demands for coordination. Considering the eclectic nature of American education, it is no surprise that articulation problems have developed. Examination of our educational system reveals that we have a German-type kindergarten, Prussian-type elementary school, American junior and senior high school, English-type four-year college, and a German-type graduate school (Russell and Judd, 1940). Recently added to this hodge-podge have been the area vocational schools, public two-year colleges, the public senior colleges, sundry proprietary schools, and the various public university complexes with their very large array of special curricula. Because of the diverse natures of post-secondary institutions, they tend to be a mere assemblege of schools and don't lend themselves to becoming a part of a coherent system of education unless special coordination attempts are made. When inadequate or improper articulation between units within this aggregate also exists, the inherent discontinuity is further aggravated by students encountering great difficulty in moving from one institution to another without undue loss of credit. It is ironic that we have a national commitment to universal education, and federal funds for higher education *are* available (PL 87-204; PL 89-752), but at the same time we have opposition to national planning for higher education in a centralized manner. Only recently has planning been given serious attention on a large scale, and this has been primarily at the state and not at the national level.

There are both horizontal and vertical inconsistencies in our higher education structure that adversely affect articulation. Vertical inconsistencies occur where there is difficulty in maintaining continuity in grade levels (not accepting students who graduate from certain lower level institutions, or only accepting a portion of their previous school work are typical examples of this). Horizontal articulation occurs between schools and from one school system to another. Because of the increased geographic mobility of our population, both types of articulation are of great importance. Vertical articulation is also of great urgency because of the socioeconomic mobility offered through increased education (Blau and Duncan, 1967). The great diversity in philosophic goals and functional purposes found in the various post-secondary institutions, which cover the spectrum from educational eliteness to equalitarianism, further confounds the articulation difficulties.

What are some of the consequences of poor articulation? Traditional articulation structures interfere with the continuity of learning experiences when the fundamental characteristics of students are not taken into proper consideration. We still need—after pronouncements to this effect more than a generation ago—to design a kind of school organization that would be congruent with the nature of the human mind and its way of growing and developing (Committee on Educational Research, 1937). The claims made by one group of schools toward another with regard to inadequate preparation of the student is a manifestation of articulation disfunction. Rather than attempting to remove the cause of inadequate preparation by improving articulation between schools, some colleges look to their own remedial programs to alleviate the problem. In many occupational programs, for example, it is common to provide initial upgrading courses in such subjects as mathematics so as to bring the incoming students up to a chosen proficiency level. In their attempts to compensate for inadequate preparation, many cases of duplication and course content result, also to the detriment of the student. It has been known for a long while that double exposure to course content does not produce significantly increased subject comprehension (Learned and Wood, 1938) and usually results in certain important subject matter being left out in the overall program. The quality of educational experience depends greatly on the extent to which learning is cumulative, which means occupational programs must begin at the entry level of the student. This demands clearer and more effective articulation of curricula and improved overall coordination of effort. Three levels of articulation between the secondary schools and colleges in common usage, include: (1) a level at which students with deficient preparation are admitted into the college and provided with necessary remedial work; (2) a level at which college work is made available to the gifted student while he is still in high school, thus permitting him to gain advanced standing in college at the time he formally enrolls; (3) a level at which little or no special help is provided for the average student, and his transition from secondary school to college goes on unnoticed (Meder 1956). Advanced standing examinations are widely utilized and have spread to the "open university" concept in New York and many other states. Improvements in college admissions procedures, and uniformity of records and transcripts have been under consideration for some time (Cook 1957). Recent research findings have led to the formulation of more advanced and improved procedure techniques for articulation, and have reinforced the realization that the experience of learners must be a continuous and cumulative process. The ideal situation is perhaps to provide each student with the opportunity to progress from his own educational experiences at his own social and intellectual pace. Some educators believe that with improved coordination of all post-secondary educational institutions, a continuous system of education can emerge as a unified entity in most states.

The Philosophy and Rationale for Master Plans

It is common knowledge that planning is often an afterthought which appears when a series of events have taken place that point to the need for some kind of coordination. This has been the case with higher education in many states—institutions of higher education that were on the scene long before there were any serious thoughts about coordination and planning at the state level. To some extent, this is also true of two-year colleges and post-secondary occupational education. Even as late as the 1950s, the use of state master plans for higher education was more often the exception than the rule (Glenny). A 1969 survey found only fifteen states operating systems of public two-year colleges under statewide master plans officially adopted by their legislative bodies (Hurlburt 1969). It was during the late 60s and early 70s when the idea of master planning for education became more popular, and gradually state-level master plans for higher education became commonplace. By 1971, forty-three states had developed some form of coordination and planning in higher education (Palola, Lehmann, and Blischke, 1971).

What are the pressures that resulted in state after state going the way of statewide planning and coordination in higher education? The three most obvious ones are: (1) an increased popular demand for higher education; (2) the realization that local and state funds are not sufficient to accommodate unbridled and unplanned expansion of higher education; (3) the sharply increased demand of legislators (and even some educators) to more clearly define the role of the various elements of higher education.

Master plans have several overall advantages. Most notable among them is the opportunity they provide for a state to engage in orderly immediate, intermediate, and long range planning. This encompasses the establishment of accepted goals, which is followed by an array of procedures by which they can be achieved within the means that state has at its disposal. Hurlburt (1969) listed fourteen major purposes for a state master plan for two-year colleges. The means by which such master plans are designed and implemented vary between the extremes of complete state control to almost complete local control. A sort of a middle-of-the-road position, combining local and state planning on a simultaneous basis, has been urged in some places (Erickson 1968). Morrissey (1966) advocated strong state control so as to insure effective state planning and coordination, and offered eight reasons to support his position on the issue. Still another viewpoint recommends coordination at the state level, while still retaining actual control at the local level (Clark 1964; Lombardi 1968). This latter position appears to be a popular one, based on the literature on this topic (Wattenbarger 1960; Martorana 1965; Pesci and Hart, 1968; Gillie 1967). Of course, there are also those who advocate no state control or coordination, using the rationale that each institution should be allowed to do what it elects to, in its own way. This position was most common several generations ago when the private sectors of higher education played a more dominant role. With the continued growth of public higher education, such a "hands-off" policy is indeed an unlikely possibility for the future. Regardless of the manner in which state master planning is superimposed or blended within the governance hierarchy of educational institutions, solid agreement on the reasons for its need has been reached in most quarters.

TWO-YEAR COLLEGES IN STATE MASTER PLANS

A special report on community colleges by the Carnegie Commission on Higher Education (1970) made twelve major recommendations that point to the place these colleges should have. These recommendations include the following (Kerr 1970): (1) They should be available within commuting distance of all citizens throughout their lives (with the possible exception of the most rural regions); (2) they should be comprehensive (i.e., provide a rich menu of academic, occupational, and general education programs); (3) they should remain two-year colleges and be discouraged from expanding into four-year institutions; (4) qualified graduates should be provided with complete transfer rights to senior colleges and universities; (5) complete support and status must be given to occupational programs; (6) the open-door concept ought to be a working philosophy of these institutions; (7) they should be tuition-free or nearly so; (8) occupational and personal guidance should receive major emphasis; (9) they should serve as the center of cultural enrichment activities for the communities they serve; (10) the optimum size should be from two thousand to five thousand students; (11) they should be governed or advised by a local board so as to better enable them to relate to their community; and (12) more liberal financing on an equitable basis by local, state, and federal sources should be provided.

These recommendations relate to what the community colleges ought to be to the regions they serve in the opinion of the Carnegie Commission on Higher Education. It is of interest to note that the commission membership is heavily weighted with private college educators, only one of its members is a nationally recognized authority on two-year colleges, and the commission has no individual with specific expertise in post-secondary occupational education included in its membership. It is ironic (although typical of what happens in many two-year colleges) that occupational education is, for all practical purposes, unrepresented in such a group when it is perhaps the most important contribution the two-year colleges will make in the overall higher educational effort. There are elements within the recommendations with which issue can be taken. The overall report states, and a number of two-year college authorities agree, that community colleges are the two-year post-secondary institutions to be emphasized in higher education, and should be given priority for financial support until they "catch-up" to the existing need for them. This appears to be unrealistic in some ways because area vocational schools have already grown in number to where they now exceed the number of community junior colleges. There are about nineteen hundred area vocational schools in the United States (*Directory AV Schools*, 1972) as compared to just over eleven hundred two-year colleges (Harper 1971). About fifty percent (931) of the area vocational schools are post-secondary occupational institutions and twenty-four percent of them (443) are also identified as two-year colleges by the American Association of Community Junior Colleges. Only forty percent of the two-year colleges meet the criteria (P.L. 90-576) to be defined as area vocational schools. Area vocational schools with post-secondary occupational programs are increasing in number. Some educators believe they will continue to grow at a faster rate than the community colleges. In view of this possibility, the place of community colleges in state master plans for higher education should be considered along with the post-secondary area vocational schools if all our educational resources are to be most wisely utilized.

Since twelve percent of area vocational schools are already concerned with occupational education at both the secondary and post-secondary levels (Directory of AV Schools, 1972), it is likely that a trend will develop in which the community colleges and secondary vocational schools will merge into one institution (not unlike the "universal college" mentioned earlier). In such cases, vocational programs would be available for students in grades eleven and twelve as well as for post-secondary students. Should such schools be considered within the state master plan of higher education? What about area vocational schools that have the facilities to serve in a post-secondary capacity but have not been authorized to do so? Planners must answer these questions in a realistic manner at the onset of determining the place of two-year colleges in the overall higher education efforts of their state. There is another question in many places: Is occupational education to be considered a part of higher education when offered in post-secondary occupational institutions? It isn't hard to find leaders in higher education who will say that is is *not* higher education. A wise planning body could solve this issue by straightforwardly declaring that included within the rubric of higher education are *all* those educational programs that take place in the post-secondary institutions. Such a decision quickly determines the place of two-year colleges and occupational education in the overall higher education scheme.

Many states have identified community colleges as local two-year colleges which are best suited for students who need to live at home while going to school. Many states either mandate or imply that two-year colleges should be available for any high school graduate or adult who can benefit from the offerings of the institution. At the same time, when making the two-year colleges more readily available to the public at large, many states have more clearly restricted admissions for the public senior colleges and universities. Such schemes usually restrict entrance to state universities to those who place in the top ten to fifteen percent of their high school graduation classes, and entrance to the senior colleges is usually restricted to the upper thirty percent, while all other students try higher education via a community college. Observation of trends throughout the country indicate this kind of approach is becoming commonplace, as pointed out by the California and New York experiences. In both these states, any high school graduate is eligible for admission to a community college, but entrance to the state colleges and universities is restricted to those with better academic achievement in high school. As this becomes the more common model of what two-year colleges are to be, they will become the capstone of education for a large segment of the population (replacing the old role of the high school in that regard). The two-year college will be the place where the student who is academically weaker will be provided the opportunity to demonstrate whether he should go on to the preparation for a profession or into occupational programs and the world of work.

Occupational Education: A Case of "Interstitialitis"

The popularization of college education has spilled over into post-secondary vocational education. Occupational programs are found in: (1) community-junior colleges; (2) area vocational schools; (3) secondary schools; (4) technical schools and colleges; (5) branch campuses of senior colleges and universities; and (6) other institutions including private and proprietary ones that fail to conveniently fit into neat categories.

The great majority of occupational programs are offered in secondary schools (USOE: DVTE, 1971), but each year an increasingly larger number of people are being prepared in occupational programs found in post-secondary institutions, both private and public (Hooper 1971; Wade 1971). Such diversity makes it difficult to place occupational education in one level of education. This difficulty is further confounded because similar programs offered in secondary schools in one region are available in post-secondary institutions in some other location. Some places have established their own criteria for defining an occupational program as secondary or post-secondary, but there is no large scale standardization in such matters. Therefore, occupational education has become an interstitial type of offering, and clearly does not fit within the rubric of either secondary or post-secondary education in terms of conventional definitions. The interstitial characteristics of occupational education are anomalies within the structure of American education, and create several unique governance difficulties. Specifically, if vocational education is controlled by the secondary schools, it becomes more difficult to develop and conduct post-secondary programs; whereas control by the post-secondary schools would minimize the efforts that could be made by secondary institutions; and if governance of vocational education emanates from a relatively autonomous agency, difficulty in simultaneously interrelating secondary and post-secondary educational efforts may be encountered. Added to this is the need to find the most effective ways to capitalize on the contributions made by the private vocational schools (see Chapter 13). Figure 15-1 illustrates the interstitial characteristics of occupational education found in many states (the shaded area depicts the overlap).

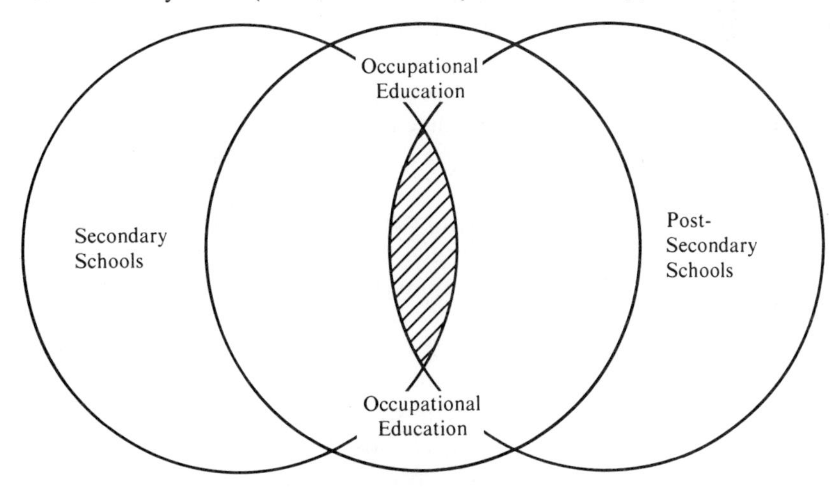

FIGURE 15-1

INTERSTITIAL CHARACTERISTICS OF OCCUPATIONAL EDUCATION

If we are to profit from this complex interstitial situation, we must move more affirmatively in the direction of improving communication between various elements within the overall rubric of occupational education. This can provide the bases for establishing a new kind of student articulation (both horizontally and vertically) by the development of a super-coordinating agency.

Provincialism and Interinstitutional Rivalries

Many students in occupational programs have experienced considerable difficulty in moving (horizontally) from one institution to another. Regardless of the rationale given for such difficulties, one cannot help but feel that a bit of provincialism and institutional rivalry is involved. Ironically, the individuals who suffer from this type of difficulty are those whom the institution is supposed to be serving—the students. Some vocational educators feel that truly smooth articulation between the various types of institutions and even between institutions of the same kind can come about only with the inauguration of a super-agency which has sufficient authority to insure complete fairness to every student in the matter of articulation.

INSTITUTIONAL INFLEXIBILITY AND CONSERVATISM

Inflexibility and conservatism at the institutional level is related to provincialism and rivalry. Criteria for admission into various programs and levels of instruction in some schools serve more as entrance barriers than as methods for the improvement of program quality. In some cases, the barriers are artificial, in that requirements demanded for entrance don't coincide with what is demanded for success in the occupational area. Careful assessment of entrance requirements should be made to minimize such errors.

In order to provide the means to admit more students into post-secondary programs from those who have come out of secondary occupational programs, a radical alteration of post-secondary programs would be required. This would include provisions to grant academic credit for earlier experiences and course work in vocational areas, and programs which intelligently match to the types of student in them. What many colleges are now doing, in their desires to be more educationally equalitarian (particularly in terms of the "disadvantaged students"), is to open their academic doors to all, provide some remedial types of academic assistance, and then force the person to conform to existing programs—or fail. Opening the institution's doors to a great range of student types while not seeking to accommodate them with special programs appropriate to their abilities and backgrounds, is an elitist approach to the problem. This approach has resulted and will continue to result in very high academic mortality rates, increased student alienation. It fails to address itself to articulation problems for the less academic-type person, particularly those who have taken a noncollegiate program in high school. Sorely needed are newly designed programs in post-secondary schools that are less demanding intellectually and more realistic occupationally. They will come about only if leadership in occupational education presses for their inauguration, since they would tend not to emerge the way higher education programs evolve in most places.

A Super-Coordinating Agency: An Ombudsman for Articulation

Equitable articulation (horizontally and vertically) among the several types of institutions presently offering programs in occupational education will most likely come about only through coordination by a state super-board with legislative powers. Such an agency admittedly poses a threat to institutional autonomy, and would therefore be mightily resisted by many schools. However, one wonders if the time has not arrived for some of our institutions (and their governing boards) to be willing to give up a bit of their autonomy in the interest of good articulation in occupational education, so that students will receive the fairest treatment in terms of moving on in their socioeconomic and educational development. Educational autonomy is a condition that cannot be fully held by both the institution and the students. The creation of a super-board would reduce institutional autonomy and increase student autonomy. The emphasis such an agency could exert would be to bend institutions to meet student articulation needs, rather than the other way around. It would serve as the ombudsman for student articulation, provided it was given considerable powers, either by the Department of Education, Commission on Higher Education, or directly from the state legislature. Included in the legalization of such a board ought to be the following: (1) a mandate that full transfer status between similar level institutions be an automatic process; (2) a mandate that post-secondary admission be granted to any eighteen year old, regardless of his previous high school status; (3) an affirmation that any citizen be entitled to a minimum of two years of post-secondary education; (4) the power to mediate special articulation disputes

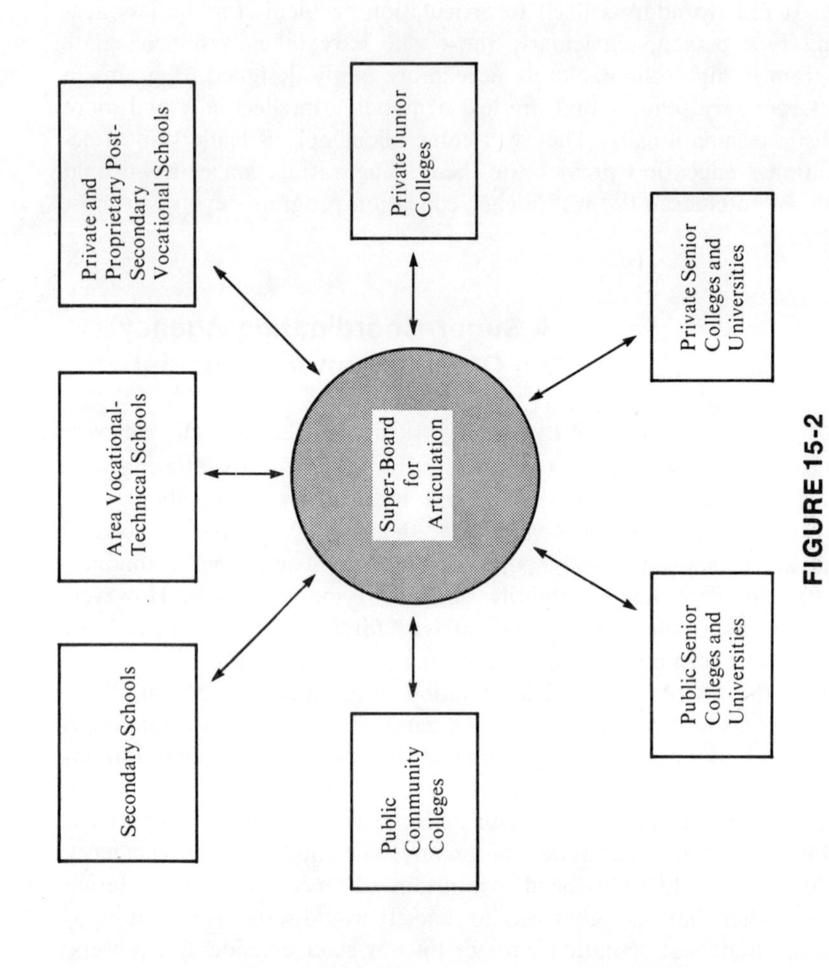

FIGURE 15-2

STATE-WIDE INTERINSTITUTIONAL ARTICULATION

with the authority to see that decisions are carried out; and (5) appointment of its board members and chairman in a manner that would assure representation of each type of institution that provides occupational education in that state.

The formation of such a group could result in an amalgam of people who hold contradictory views on vocational education matters. So the first task of this board would be to learn how to live with these contradictions and to discover ways to constructively coexist. In order to provide continuous leadership and viability, the board should have a full-time salaried executive secretary, and its members and chairman should be recognized leaders in their special segment of occupational education. Both faculty and administrators should be represented on the board. Meetings would be frequent, perhaps a dozen or more times each year, and would be held in various regions of the state. Figure 15-2 indicates the complexity associated with complete interinstitutional articulation in terms of the multiple interactions between people and institutions.

Summary

Because of the constraints listed and discussed in this chapter, the development of workable paths for articulation between the diverse types of institutions and programs that exist will not come about to the maximum advantage of the students unless there is some statewide authority to mandate such an occurrence. We cannot afford to allow students to suffer because of our inability to articulate them from one institution to another, or from institution to job, or from job to institution in an accurate and equitable manner. If we are to permit occupational education to go on in the diverse kinds of institutions in which it is now offered, then we need such a super- coordinating agency. The final result, although it may bring about some reduction in institutional autonomy, will be an enhanced possibility for each student to find his way through the educational maze toward the fulfillment of his objectives. Society at large will be the chief benefactor in the long run.

REFERENCES

Blau, P. and Duncan, O. D. *The American Occupational Structure.* New York: John Wiley, 1967.

Berdahl, R. O. *Statewide Coordination of Higher Education.* Washington, D. C.: American Council on Education, 1971.

Chambers, M. M. *Voluntary Statewide Coordination in Public Higher Education.* Ann Arbor, Mich: University of Michigan Press, 1961.

Clark, B. "Boards of Control in California." *Selected Papers.* Washington, D.C.: American Association of Junior Colleges, 1964.

Cook, D.L. "High School and College: Some Problems in Articulation." *Clearinghouse 32: 167-8.* Rutherford, N.J.: Fairleigh Dickinson University, 1957.

Erickson, C.G. "Illinois Balances Statewise Planning and Local Autonomy." *Junior College Journal.* Volume 38. Washington, D.C.: American Association of Junior Colleges, 1968.

Directory Area Vocational Education Schools: Fiscal 1972. Washington, D.C.: Department of HEW, USOE. Bureau of Adult, Vocational and Technical Education, Division of Vocational and Technical Education, 1972.

Estimates of Secondary and Post-Secondary Vocational Education Enrollments 1971. Washington, D.C.: Division of Vocational-Technical Education, U.S. Office of Education, 1971.

Gillie, A.C. "New Jersey Community College: A Report and Prognosis." *Junior College Journal.* Volume 38. Washington, D.C.: American Association of Junior Colleges, 1967.

Glenny, L.A. *Autonomy of Public Colleges: The Challenge of Coordination* New York: McGraw-Hill, 1959.

Harper, W.A. *1971 Junior College Directory.* Washington, D.C.: American Association of Junior Colleges, 1971.

Henry, D.D. *What Priority for Education?* Urban, Il: University of Illinois Press, 1961.

Hooper, M.E. *Associate Degree and Other Formal Awards Below the Baccalaureate, 1969-70.* Washington, D.C.: U.S. Government Printing Office, 1971.

Hungate, T.L. *Management in Higher Education.* New York: Teacher's College, Columbia University, 1964.

Hurlburt, A.S. *State Master Plans for Community Colleges.* Washington, D.C.: American Association of Junior Colleges, 1969.

Klein, A.J. *Cooperation and Coordination in Higher Education.* Washington, D.C.: American Council on Education, 1938.

Learned, W.S. and Wood, B.D. *The Student and His Knowledge.* New York: Carnegie Foundation, 1938.

Lombardi, J. "California's New State Board." *Junior College Journal.* Volume 39. Washington, D.C.: American Association of Junior Colleges, 1968.

Martorana, S.V. "Progress and Plans in the Empire State." *Junior College Journal.* Volume 35. Washington, D.C.: American Association of Junior Colleges, 1965.

Meder, A. E., Jr. "Articulation of General Education Programs." *Journal of Education Sociology.* Volume 29: 208-9. Washington, D.C.: American Council on Education, 1956.

Medsker, L. L. "Cooperative Action Among Two-Year and Four-Year Colleges: Opportunities and Obstacles." *Educational Record,* Volume 39: 114-21. Washington, D.C.: American Council on Education, 1958.

Minnesota Studies in Articulation. Minneapolis, Minn.: Committee on Educational Research, University of Minnesota Press, 1937.

Moos, M. and Rourke, F. *The Campus and the State.* Baltimore, Md: Johns Hopkins, 1959.

Palola, E. G.; Lehmann, T.; and Blischke, W. R. "The Reluctant Planner: Faculty in Institutional Planning." *Journal of Higher Education.* Volume XLII, No. 7. Columbus, Ohio: The Ohio State University Press, 1971.

Presci, F. B.; and Hart, R. "The Question of Governance in Maryland." *Junior College Journal.* Volume 38. Washington, D.C.: American Association of Junior Colleges, 1968.

Public Law No. 204, 87th Congress (Higher Education Facilities Act of 1963).

Public Law No. 752, 89th Congress (Higher Education Amendments of 1966).

Public Law No. 576, 90th Congress (Vocational Education Amendments of 1968).

Russell, J. D. and Judd, C. H. *The American Educational System.* New York: Houghton-Mifflin, 1940.

Wade, G. H. *Fall Enrollments in Higher Education, 1970.* Washington, D.C.: U. S. Government Printing Office, 1971.

Wattenbarger, J. I. "Changing Patterns of Control: Local to State." *Junior College Journal.* Volume 38. Washington, D.C.: American Association of Junior Colleges, 1968.

The Open-Door Colleges: Policies for Community Colleges. A special report and recommendations by the Carnegie Commission on Higher Education. New York: McGraw-Hill, 1970.

Chapter 16 CONCLUSIONS

Using sixty percent as the minimum acceptable proportion of occupational students in the two-year colleges, most states have a long way to go. Table 16-1 lists by state the percentage of full-time enrollments in occupational programs. (Gillie 1972). Based on this percentage and the full-time two-year college enrollment of each state (Harper 1971), the actual number of vocational students has been estimated. Some states have increased the proportion of full-time students found in vocational programs over the past five years, as shown in Table 16-1. As a whole, however, based on the returns from forty-five states, the overall gain was found to be disappointingly slow. Some vocational educators feel one reason for the slow increase is the lack of strong agreement of two-year college faculty members with the community college philosophy as it is propounded in the literature (Medsker 1960; Gillie, Bloom, and Leslie, 1971). Furthermore, one wonders if there would have been any gain at all but for the availability of federal funds for vocational programs and training (P. L. 87-415; P. L. 89-751; P. L. 90-576; P. L. 91-516). The figures in Table 16-1 illustrate the state of vocational education in the two-year colleges; but the whole story behind post-secondary occupational education includes the offerings of other kinds of institutions as well. Estimated 1971 occupational program enrollments, based on a federal compilation of the fifty state plans for vocational education (USOE: BAVTE-DVTE, 1972) show that two-year college enrollment is just over 1,000,000; senior college enrollment is 116,000; post-secondary vocational technical school enrollment is 417,000 vocational students; and 117,000 students are enrolled in institutions that are both secondary and post-secondary. Not included in this data are the efforts of the private and proprietary vocational schools. But it is known that in 1970 there were about 7,100 private vocational schools serving 1.56 million students (Belitsky 1970). Growth in this area continues, as indicated by the increase in schools accredited by the National Association of Trade and Technical Schools from just over 150 in 1969 (NATTS 1970) to 320 in 1972 (NATTS 1972). A conservative estimate of total post-secondary occupational education enrollment in 1972, based on data from several sources (Belitsky 1970; NATTS 1972; USOE: BAVTE-DVTE 1972; Gillie 1972; Harper 1971) is 2.8 million students. This exludes many vocational education efforts which are not easily categorized within the secondary post secondary classification.

TABLE 16-1

State	Total Students [1]	Total Vocational Students [3]	Percent of Vocational Students [2]	Percentage of Vocational Students in 1967 [2]
Alabama				
Alaska	697	NA	NA	NA
Arizona	14,327	4,255	29.7*	30*
Arkansas	2,046	818	40	**
California				
Colorado	14,330	7,452	52	**
Connecticut	10,778	3,487	32.35	28.49
Delaware	2,459	1,107	45*	**
District of Columbia				
Florida	63,339	15,184	23.95*	22.41*
Georgia	12,901	NA	NA	NA
Hawaii	5,900	2,360	40*	56* - 1968
Idaho	NA	NA	NA	NA
Illinois	64,626	16,350	25.3*	**
Indiana	3,939	NA	NA	NA
Iowa	4,425	1,991	45*	**
Kansas	12,418	NA	NA	NA
Kentucky	6,956	1,808	26+	**
Louisiana	4,286	NA	NA	NA
Maine	2,073	2,073	100	**
Maryland	19,087	4,772	25	**
Massachusetts	17,424	7,647	43.89*	41.49 - 1968
Michigan	48,298	12,075	25	**
Minnesota	15,995	4,158	26	**
Mississippi	18,083	5,967	33	25*
Missouri	15,993	3,940	24.63*	**
Montana	1,114	390	35	**
Nebraska				
Nevada	101	50	49	**

TABLE 16-1—Continued

State	Total Students[1]	Total Vocational Students[3]	Percent of Vocational Students[2]	Percentage of Vocational Students in 1967[2]
New Hampshire	354	354	100	**
New Jersey	18,968	7,587	40+	**
New Mexico	3,194	767	24	21*
New York	89,876	53,899	59.97*	65.47*
North Carolina	24,678	15,300	75	75*
North Dakota	5,143	1,800	35	**
Ohio	30,409	10,035	33+	**
Oklahoma	7,626	2,288	25	25*
Oregon	26,808	17,425	65	**
Pennsylvania	34,921	17,285	40	40*
Rhode Island	3,096	1,449	46.8*	40
South Carolina	7,567	7,567	100	**
South Dakota	NA	NA	NA	NA
Tennessee	4,425	1,991	45	**
Texas	57,865	25,455	43.99*	41.96
Utah	5,241	NA	NA	NA
Vermont	442	221	50+	50+
Virginia				
Washington	38,594	12,968	38.6*	26.7*
West Virginia				
Wisconsin	19,572	19,572	100	**
Wyoming	3,775	1,397	37	**
American Samoa				
Canal Zone				
Puerto Rico	2,246	744	33	33
Total	746,455	293,988		

Total Students in Institutions with Vocational Programs	706,973
Total Vocational Students in Institutions	293,988
Percentage of Vocational Students in Institutions with Vocational Programs	41.58%

NA - Not Available   + - Approximate
* - Confirmed   ** - Not Given

1 Extracted from Harper, W. *Directory of American Association of Junior Colleges.* Washington, D. C.: AAJC, 1971.

2 Extracted from A National Survey of State Directors of Two-Year Colleges. By Angelo C. Gillie in 1972.

3 Computed from 1 and 2.

Preservice and Inservice Training of Teachers and Administrators

The absence of strong endorsement of the community college equalitarian philosophy does not mean it should be abandoned. On the contrary, this lack indicates the need for special efforts in preparing teachers and administrators for two-year colleges. Many universities have established such programs (Reese 1970), some with considerable financial support from outside agencies. In the 1960s, the Kellogg Foundation funded such programs in several universities and continued to do so on a more limited basis in the early 1970s, but these programs did not focus exclusively on occupational program faculty and administrators. Some assistance has been obtained from other sources for this effort in the vocational area, beginning in the late 60s and early 70s (Venuto 1972).

Many two-year college theorists and practitioners believe that a new kind of vocational teacher-administrator training effort is needed. The preparation of vocational faculty and administrators for two-year colleges requires a different kind of effort than the preparation designed for academic faculty. The basic orientation of academic and occupational teachers should be different. In terms of subject matter, the former would have a more intellectual centrality while the latter would focus on practical learning. The two-year colleges cannot succeed in achieving any of their goals unless they are manned by teachers and administrators who heartily endorse an equalitarian educational philosophy. The conventional source of teachers for two-year colleges does not always provide teachers who serve these institutions well: Vocational education cannot become the major focus of two-year colleges as long as most of the faculty and administrators are prepared in the more traditional academic graduate programs. Teachers who complete a traditional elitist-type graduate program in an academic area must undergo a philosophic revolution on their way from commencement to the community classroom, if they are to walk into the situation with awareness of and empathy for educational equalitarianism. This awareness can best be developed if it is stressed in the training of teachers and administrators for the two-year colleges, beginning with a clear identification of the workable two-year college philosophy after which teaching candidates would be trained to practice its implementation in their roles as teachers and administrators. A strong element of orientation and indoctrination which demands overall acceptance of the community college philosophy should be a fundamental requirement for successful completion of the training program. It is agreed that pluralism and diversity are necessary ingredients in all segments of American education, but they must be restricted so that they will not create continuous head-on collisions with the basic tenets of the two-year college philosophy.

The Fundamental Philosophic Tenets of the Future Two-Year College

What should be the philosophic tenets of the future two-year college? First, students who are identified as academically able by high school performance and academic types of testing should be strongly encouraged to enroll in senior colleges or universities at the start of their collegiate career. The sources of encouragement should include parents and the senior institutions themselves. There may be a few occasions when such students should be sought by the two-year colleges, but this would be more the exception than the rule. Some educators believe it would be wise to encourage "border-line" academic students to try themselves in two-year colleges, where they could receive more personalized instruction and careful counseling, and to discourage students in the upper thirty percent of their graduating classes from enrolling in the two-year colleges by helping them gain entry to a suitable senior college or university. Student financial support, although far from adequate in many places, continues to become more readily available to academically capable youngsters. Using the two-year college as the starting place for "poor smart kids" is becoming increasingly less necessary because senior colleges and universities (both private and public) are now actively seeking out such youngsters for their institutions (Peterson 1972). A third basic tenet is that two year colleges should strive to become the major institution for offering post-secondary occupational education for over half of all high school graduates, a large segment of high school dropouts, and a large portion of the adult population. As proposed in several chapters of this book, about half the youngsters who graduate from high school each year should receive some vocational education in a two-year college, preferably within the type of model described in Chapter 7. The same overall approach could be used for high school dropouts, with the amount and level of academic support work carefully harmonized with individual interests and abilities. The most challenging possibility, an area which has only been superficially touched so far, deals with the adults who need to be occupationally updated, upgraded, or completely retrained. Assuming that about two percent of our working population will be in need of such assistance each year, and using a work force of over eighty million as a basis (Lerner 1970), this would involve at least 1.6 million adults. If the two-year colleges are to respond to the special vocational needs of the adult group, then new curriculum approaches are needed. Again, the model proposed in Chapter 7, in which specific skill development occurs after the person is hired for a definite job, is tuned to accommodate such a group. If the two-year colleges assume the role of serving as occupational education centers (as in the ways described in Chapter 7), they will in fact move far along the path to meeting the philosophic tenets listed here. Hopefully the leaders in two-year colleges will consider these their most cherished goals and relinquish the idea of trying to serve as the first two years of senior college-university academic programs.

Will this happen? The likelihood of it taking place is definitely related to how and where two-year college funding is allocated in the future. If the bulk of funding for two-year colleges is specifically earmarked for occupational programs for the three basic types of clientele described above, these institutions will indeed move in progressive directions. The more specific categorization of funding in the Vocational Amendments of 1968 (P. L. 90-576), as compared to that of the Vocation Act of 1963 (P. L. 88-210) points to the likelihood of more specific allocation of funds in the future. The concern with preparing people for the world of work, so that they can live the life styles they desire, is a national one and is expressed in legislation (see P. L. 90-576 for example). Most of the almost nineteen hundred area vocational schools receive substantial funding from federal sources (first P. L. 88-210 and later 90-576). Forty percent (443) of the institutions classified as two-year colleges by the American Association of Community Junior Colleges (Harper 1971) also serve as area vocational schools (see Table 1). A national survey found that thirty-nine percent of the students in forty-five states are in vocational programs (Gillie 1972). Although this is far from good enough, there are indications that it will increase.

In several chapters it is pointed out that post-secondary occupational education is not the unique property of the community colleges. Of particular importance, in spite of statements made in the Carnegie Report (Kerr 1970), are the area vocational schools (see Chapter 7). Their number exceeds those of the community colleges (about nineteen hundred AVS to eleven hundred two-year colleges, of which 443 are also AVS's). Many of the area vocational schools suffer from low enrollments, overspecialized curricula, and a lack of academic respectability. In the next two sections of this chapter, we consider ways to deal with the dilemma of two-year colleges and area vocational schools and ways to capitalize on their characteristics.

The Universal College

Although it was logical at one time to separate the stream of education into secondary and post-secondary elements at the end of the twelfth year, it no longer is so. The substantial increase in the number of associate degrees awarded recently (Hooper 1971) clearly indicates that fourteen years of universal education is gaining increasing acceptance as an educational goal in the United States. The associate degree awards do not reveal the true magnitude of this trend, as a substantial number of two-year post-secondary programs award certificates and diplomas other than the associate degree (Hooper 1971; Belitsky 1970; NATTS 1972; AVS Directory 1972). Regardless of the names given to the thirteenth and fourteenth years of education, they will become the capstones in vertical education progression for over half of our population. In view of this, it seems illogical to truncate the educational sequence at the end of the twelfth year and to place the thirteenth and fourteenth years in separate educational institutions. Such separation made sense when two-year colleges were first proposed by early leaders in the movement (see Tappan 1851; Folwell 1909; Butler 1904; and Spindt 1957), to provide an arena for sorting out those who should go on to a senior college or university (see Thornton 1966). However, two-year colleges have expanded their objectives since that time to include many other functions (Medsker 1960; Martorana 1966), particularly the education and training of middle level workers. They serve as the educational capstone for the large number of students who don't go on to a senior college or university. They could be even more effective if they became four year institutions, encompassing grades eleven through fourteen. This would require changing the traditional secondary school into a new kind of middle school that would include grades seven through ten. The elementary school structure could remain essentially the same (Preprimary to sixth grade). Therefore, the proposed new school system would be a 6-4-4 grade model (which has been suggested in many other places. See Butler 1904). A possible name for this institution could be the "universal college," and would blend the two-year community college, the area vocational school, and the last two years of traditional secondary school into one institution.

The universal college would be a regional-type institution, serving a number of traditional school districts. Enrollment should be composed of at least two thousand full-time students. In this way it would be most likely to offer diverse occupational programs, and to provide sufficient challenge for every type of student. The more academically inclined youngsters would be counseled into academic experiences that would encourage them to ponder those professional level occupations which would be most conducive to their interests, and in keeping with their potential. Universal colleges could provide youngsters with realistic appraisals of the relationships between their interests and abilities, and the occupations they ought to prepare for. Those students with distinct potential for senior college or university studies would be identified and intellectually prepared for appropriate experiences. They could enter a senior college or university after their second year (twelfth grade). Another group of students, whose academic acumen is deemed to be in need of further development and testing, would be provided the opportunity to do so in the third and fourth years in the universal college. These two groups of students (those who go directly into senior colleges and those who need more time to bring out their academic abilities) should comprise forty percent or less of the entire student body. The third and largest group of students would be counseled into occupational type programs.

The vocational program aspect of the universal college would be the most difficult to inaugurate. There are presently many forces working counter to the purposes of occupational education, some of which emanate from: (1) counselors who still think one of their main tasks is to find senior colleges for as many students as possible; (2) parents who still believe the American dream includes acquiring a bachelor's degree and becoming a professional; and (3) teachers, administrators, and education board members who feel that occupational education is outside the mainstream of American education. These forces have been the major impediment to the full development of occupational education. Fortunately, there have been a number of counter forces at work (such as P. L. 87-415; P. L. 89-751; P. L. 90-576; P. L. 91-516; P. L. 88-210) which have been successful (Gillie 1972).

The grade level where occupational programs are introduced in the universal college and their lengths would be varied. Some programs would begin in grade eleven, particularly for those youngsters who are likely to drop out of school, and these would be very short in duration. Others would begin at grade ten and last two years. And so forth. (The form of the overall effort is suggested and described in Chapter 7.) Good occupational programs would require well-planned cooperation and coordination between the business-industrial community and the college, and would need to be supported by appropriate incentives. Some suggested incentives would be: (1) special tax concessions to business and industries who participate in job placement followed by skill development approach; (2) partial salary subsidies for certain beginning workers, particularly teenagers and disadvantaged people whose initial labor market earning capacities are at a marginal level; (3) legislative backing relating to hiring practices, which would demand that certain percentages of specific labor groups be comprised of teenagers; (4) a truly open door skill center where necessary reentry would require a mere request for admission.

The universal college would also be a center for vocational recycling (upgrading, updating, and retraining) for adults in need of preparing for entirely new jobs during their work lives. The universal college would have a rich array of occupational program facilities and skill centers, and would be an excellent place to serve these people. Some provisions for assistance in this endeavor have already been made (Manpower Report of the President, 1971; P. L. 87-415; P. L. 89-751; P. L. 90-576; P. L. 91-516). Considering that the labor force exceeds eighty million (Lerner 1970), the number of adults in need of such assistance is larger than the number of younger people preparing for their first jobs. The mixing of such diverse age groups on a large campus would likely be of mutual benefit to all concerned.

If the universal college is to become a capstone educational institution for the bulk of our population, several small "miracles" need to happen. First of all, the universal college must be as autonomous in the educational spectrum as the secondary and higher education elements are today. If it were to be tacked on to either the secondary or the higher education segment, it would probably be diluted beyond recognition. Such a proposal might be opposed by secondary educators (since they would lose control of grades eleven and twelve), and by higher educators, including community college educators (since they would lose control of most of the present thirteenth and fourteenth grades), and by many traditional vocational educators (since they would lose control of vocational education as a separate entity). This presents serious problems. As pointed out in Chapter 11, an innovative idea stands the best chance of being adopted from within a system or organization when it fits into the overall sociocultural value system of its potential adopters. The proposed universal college idea obviously fails on this count, since it deviates sharply from the present educational structure. It would not likely be adopted on a large scale unless established by legislative mandate. Perhaps after the educators have reexamined their respective state master plans, the universal college proposal will be shown in its true light, and legislation for its inauguration will follow. Universal educational opportunities can only happen when occupational education is permitted to fully flower, and the universal college is the best vehicle to accomplish this. It remains to be seen whether state legislators will eventually revamp the public school system to include the universal college, or whether we will have to wait for the educators to do it.

Unification of Community Colleges and Area Vocational Schools: An Alternative

In Table 7-1 we find that 227 area vocational schools already operate at the secondary and post-secondary level, 931 of the schools are considered post-secondary institutions, and 443 are classified as two-year colleges. Therefore we see that in some places, community colleges and area vocational schools have consolidated their efforts (sometimes even on one campus). Although such endeavors have not been entirely free of problems, they do hold great promise. One of the greatest problems with such mergers deals with interstitiality (discussed in the last chapter). A maze of certification requirements for secondary vocational teachers and administrators exists, and these spill over to the post-secondary level in at least ten states (see Chapter 12). Further complicating the problem, most states have two offices or boards of control involved at the state level (one for secondary vocational programs and personnel, and the other for two-year colleges). The differences in financing formulas further confound the organizational difficulties, as secondary education often has one funding formula while post-secondary programs fall under a second financial scheme. Under the present circumstances in most states, it would take a very skillful person to get all these often antagonistic elements to congeal into an institution that could serve both secondary and post-secondary occupational education. State-level legislation in which two-year colleges and area vocational schools are merged into common centers for occupational education for specific regions is the most realistic way to bring about such an improvement. These centers could operate from several campuses in those districts that have these two kinds of schools presently operating in separate facilities. By careful planning and coordination, all the campuses could be efficiently utilized. Although the universal college is the most desirable model for achievement of universal opportunity for fourteen years of education, the unification of the area vocational schools and the two-year colleges into regional occupational centers would be a practical and viable alternative.

Abandoning the Impossible Dream

While many two-year colleges claim to have a wide variety of goals, an examination of them leads one to suspect that such declarations are largely for cosmetic effects. Typically, these announced goals include offering courses and programs in the academic and occupational areas, conducting special courses and other activities for adults in a community, giving guidance and counseling services to all post-secondary age persons in a community, organizing a cultural activity center, and providing remedial education for special groups (see Medsker 1960). Because of their great desire to simultaneously gain acceptance as a "collegiate" educational institution and to obtain financial support from their patrons, they have taken on such an amalgam of goals. Although their intentions are worthy, the overall goal of attempting to be all things to everyone can lead to disastrous results.

A wisely planned organization, whether it is educational or industrial, accepts as its goals those objectives toward which it can readily make a significant contribution (Caplow 1964; Blau and Scott, 1962; Etzioni

1964). Repeated failures to progress will in time create disenchantment with the organization among its supporters, and can ultimately bring about its dissolution. There are indications that present day two-year colleges may be heading toward this kind of difficulty. Let us consider reasons why. First, the goal of serving as the first two years of senior college for baccalaureate-bound students is becoming less feasible in many places. Many states, while expanding their two-year college systems, are also expanding their senior colleges and universities. In more and more states, it is becoming possible for the colleges and universities to enroll students in the top thirty percent of each high school graduation class (see Peterson 1972 for example). There has been considerable research whose reports include the revelation that senior institutions are more attractive than the two-year colleges to many youngsters and their parents (see Medsker 1960 for example). The economic factor is not as critical an issue as was the case a generation ago, since the senior institutions in many states have tuition not appreciably higher than the two-year colleges. Furthermore, with increased availability of various scholarship programs, many youngsters from the upper-lower and middle socioeconomic groups can now afford to attend a senior college or university if they can gain admission, as there appears to be a national trend to ease the financial burdens of students who can qualify for admission into a senior college or university. Also, special arrangements are frequently being made for disadvantaged youngsters to enroll in senior colleges and universities. If this trend continues, and it appears likely that it will, then the so-called "cooling out" function of two-year colleges will have automatically been performed by state master planning. This would come as considerable relief to many two-year college educators, since denying admission to certain programs on the basis of state master planning makes much of the cooling out process more impersonal, and hence more comfortable for community college educators. Providing the first two years of academic study for baccalaureate-bound students in the two-year college or the universal college should be limited to the academically "chancy" students, and even they ought to be carefully selected on the basis of having a statistically good chance of eventually moving to a profession. The academic failure rate for this group should not exceed ten percent of those entering. Other students, regardless of desires to prepare for senior college or a profession, would be guided into occupational programs that are most in agreement with their interests and abilities. Educators owe their students protection from guaranteed academic failure, which is best accomplished by allowing students into only those programs in which their chances of success (personally and academically) are best.

To abandon the impossible dream means to accept the fact that two-year colleges are institutions for educating and preparing people for the middle level occupations. This includes the realization that they are to share this responsibility with the area vocational schools, either by uniting their efforts with them or by entering into consolidations such as the development of universal colleges. Will this really happen?

REFERENCES

Belitsky, H. A. *Private Vocational Schools: Their Emerging Role in Post-Secondary Education.* Kalamazoo, Mich. The W. E. Upjohn Institute for Employment Research, 1970.

Blau, P. M. and Scott, W. R. *Formal Organizations: A Comparative Approach.* San Francisco, Calif.: Chandler, 1962.

Butler, N. "The Six-Year High School." *School Review,* Volume 12. Chicago, Ill.: University of Chicago Press, 1904.

Caplow, T. *Principles of Organization.* New York: Harcourt, Brace, and World, 1964.

Directory Area Vocational Schools: Fiscal Year 1972. Washington, D.C.: Division of Vocational and Technical Education, Bureau of Adult, Vocational, and Technical Education, USOE, 1972.

Directory of Accredited Private Trade and Technical Schools: 1969-70. Washington, D. C.: National Association of Trade and Technical Schools, 1970.

1971-71 Directory of Accredited Private Trade and Technical Schools. Washington, D. C.: National Association of Trade and Technical Schools, 1972.

Etzioni, A. *Modern Organizations.* Englewood Cliffs, N.J.: Prentice-Hall, 1964.

Folwel, W. W. *University Addresses.* New York: H. W. Wilson, 1909.

Gillie, A. C.; Bloom, K. L.; and Leslie, L. L. *Goals and Ambivalence: Faculty Values and the Community College Philosophy.* University Park, Pa.: Center for the Study of Higher Education, Pennsylvania State University, 1971.

Gillie, A. C. A National Survey of State Directors of Community Colleges. Conducted in 1972.

Harper, W. A. *1971 Junior College Directory.* Washington, D. C.: American Association of Junior Colleges, 1971.

Hooper, M. E. *Associate Degree and Other Formal Awards Below the Baccalaureate 1969-70.* Washington, D. C.: U. S. Government Printing Office, 1971.

Kerr, C. *The Open-Door Colleges: Policies for Community Colleges.* A Special report and recommendation by the Carnegie Commission on Higher Education. New York: McGraw-Hill, 1970.

Lerner, W. *Statistical Abstract of the United States: 1970.* Washington, D. C. U. S. Government Printing Office, 1970.

Manpower Report of the President: 1971. Washington, D.C.: U.S. Government Printing Office, 1971.

Martorana, S. V. "The Role of the Community College in the Future Education of American Youth." A paper in *Administering the Community College in a Changing World.* S. V. Martorana, and P. Hunter, eds. Buffalo, N. Y.: The School of Education, State University of New York at Buffalo, 1966.

Medsker, L. L. *The Junior College: Progress and Prospect.* New York: McGraw-Hill, 1960.

NATTS. Data obtained from W. A. Goddard, Executive Director of NATTS in mid-1972.

Peterson, I. "Applications Rise at Ivy League College, Drop at State Colleges." *New York Times,* April 20, 1972.

Public Law No. 415, 87th Congress (Manpower Development and Training Act of 1962).

Public Law No. 210, 88th Congress (Vocational Education Act of 1963).

Public Law No. 751, 89th Congress (Allied Health Professions Personnel Training Act of 1966).

Public Law No. 576, 90th Congress (Vocational Education Admendents of 1968).

Public Law No. 516, 91st Congress (Environmental Education Act).

Reese, J. E. "Structuring the Teaching Internship," *Junior College Journal.* Volume 42, No. 8. Washington, D.C.: American Association of Junior Colleges, 1972.

Spindt, H. A. "Establishment of the Junior College in California, 1907-21." *California Journal of Secondary Education,* Volume 32. Berkeley, Calif.: California Society for the Study of Secondary Education, 1957.

Tappan, H. P. *University Education.* New York: G. P. Putnam's Sons, 1851.

Thornton, J. W., Jr. *The Community College.* Second Edition. New York: John Wiley, 1966.

Venuto, L. J. "New Promise for Teacher Preparation." *Junior College Journal.* Volume 42, No. 5. Washington, D.C.: American Association of Junior Colleges, 1972

INDEX